THE WILDERNESS YEARS

Born in 1952 and the youngest of eight surviving children, T.C. Campbell was raised in Glasgow's slums and proceeded to carve out a reputation in its ganglands in his teens. A father and husband, he has been locked up unjustly for the past seventeen years.

A social worker in Glasgow for twenty years, Reg McKay has written for a living since 1998. A widely published journalist, he is also the author of *None So Pretty – The Sexing of Rebecca Pine* and co-author of the best-selling *The Ferris Conspiracy*.

THE WILDERNESS YEARS

T.C. Campbell & Reg McKay

CANONGATE

First published in the UK in 2002 by
Canongate Books Ltd, 14 High Street, Edinburgh EH1 1TE

10 9 8 7 6 5 4 3 2 1

British Library Cataloguing-in-Publication Data
A catalogue record for this book is available on
request from the British Library

ISBN 1 84195 331 8

Typeset by Palimpsest Book Production Limited,
Polmont, Stirlingshire
Printed and bound by
CPD, Ebbw Vale, Wales

www.canongate.net

DEDICATION

For those who wait and have waited for that day to dawn. God bless you. For my brother Lockie, shanghai'd in Shanghai for daring to be free. And for those unsung heroes who fought and died that he may presume to be. 'From the setting of the sun until the mornings dawn. We shall remember *REMEMBER* IF . . .'

If one night on a gently sloping hill of grass
You should lay dreaming
As the turmoil of the world
And time rolls past
To find you in the morning
With dew in your hair
And the scent of flowers in the air . . .

If you should be still and at peace
With yourself and all else
And time is without pressure
If you saw the moon fade
With the dawning of the sun
As they dance with heavenly leisure . . .

If in your thoughts of loving kindness
I should tumble through your mind
Even, as a shy nervous shadow
Perhaps you may care to follow
That fading track of memory
That's all that's left of me
For you're living now in the tomorrows
Of when you and I were free . . .

If you should see where I'm going
And once more live the part
Before it fades away
I will be honoured
What more can I say . . .

And if I should disturb you
From your slumber
As you recall the fate of me
Do not despair
But stop and ponder
For though I'm chained in solitary
My mind is free to wander . . .

Small consolation you may say
Yet small as it may well be
It's as good as wings to me
So smile and look yonder
And should you see me fade away
With the dawning of the sun
As your consciousness awakes
And the new day has begun . . .

Remember I was with you
And we danced across the heavens
With the wind in the wings of our minds
Fluttering softly back through time
Pray . . .
Please don't lock my memory . . . Away . . .

from the *Book of Passing Thoughts* by Tommy Campbell

Contents

Wilderness Years – Epilogue

Stand to Fight Again

Genesis

Upon the awakening of awareness
at the dawning of time
there arose from the chaos
a glorious shine.

Through all creation
relentlessly it shone
in rhythm and relation
until the sun did dawn.

With rays of hope, love & life
to mould from the chaos – water
from which depth came man and wife
and all mankind thereafter.

Thus by the laws of cause & effect,
light and water must reflect,
the image of the creator, unto the father,
and therefore eternally, all who come after.

Such is God's work in motion
we give it thanks and deep devotion
whilst the prophets and the poets say,
'God's child was born the natural way.'

So praise be to thy mother,
thy father too,
for creating a wonder
such as you.

And on that day the world rejoices
to lift their songs in cheerful voices
and on their tongues the lyrics say,
'God's child was born this wondrous day . . .

Upon its infinite anniversary
of life
Many happy returns.'

I became conscious in terrible pain, realising that I hadn't
been sleeping at all, merely drooling in a mindless daze.
Those moving shapes before me were people – No, they
were screws, giant mutant cockroaches, prison guards.
Fear gripped me cold like a body bag closing as my
mind zipped up a gear in awareness. I was taking in
the news from the TV high on the wall . . . Something
to do with the Scottish Council for Civil Liberties saying
that 'the prisoner, Thomas Campbell, had been brutally
assaulted . . .

'. . . A Scottish Office spokesman claimed that Campbell
had been moved to hospital two days ago suffering from
injuries sustained in a fall from a wall during an escape
attempt.'

I remembered the ambulance and I remembered awakening in hospital, my body convulsing back to life and
doctors all bustling around me. With that memory came
the shock recall of the sustained and brutal beating that
I had undergone at the hands feet and batons of these
creatures around me. The fear had been instinctive but
now it made sense, making sense was important. I tried

to move but the pain was intense, I groaned, my hand reaching for my stomach in reflex, my arm tugging at the IV tubes plugged into me. Turning my head to look, I tug at more tubes inserted into my mouth and nostrils. I was hooked up to life support. Raising my arms, looking at the plastic bracelets attached there, sure enough, I was in fact Thomas Campbell. Apparently born on 4/11/1952 but was dead on arrival on 4/11/1985. I was 33 then and had died on my birthday . . .

Yet, just who the fuck was this Thomas Campbell anyway? And, how come he makes the national news? Why the fuck so many polis and warders? Who am I? And how in God's name did I get here?

Mean Streets
(1952/56)

I was born in Milton Street, Cowcaddens in Glasgow. The youngest of eight survivors of ten kids, I was too young to remember those who didn't make it. We moved to Murana Street, then onto George Street near to George Square just across from the old Citizen office which became The Herald and the Times, when Murana Street burned down. We lived on the fifth floor of a four storey grey sandstone tenement. In a converted attic with sky light windows, this would have been the mid 1950s before it was the yuppie style. Gaslight and candles with a wood burning fire and cooker to keep the pots black. Outside cludgie was only a communal pan with flusher on the witch tower stairwell spiralling down to the dunnie at the back. Over our back on the Richmond Street hill to the original Rotten Row was our playground. Of course, it's all gone now, multi storey car parks, office blocks and colleges stand there now and probably just as well. It was overrun by longtails and polluted by scarlet fever water, which stank and contributed to the high infant mortality rate.

Da, Boaby Campbell, was in jail. I think he was then doing seven years PD (Preventive Detention) an early form of internment, now outlawed, but which was imposed under post war emergency measures during the hunger riots, to 'prevent' previous offenders from offending. I have no memory of him until I was about six and, by then, living in Carntyne.

In Geordie Street, I have no doubt we were poor, though that economic concept never dawned on me at the time. I just remember always being hungry and always scouring the streets for eats. The city centre, the toon, was on our doorstep and we had our daily routes for knocking from the shops. Each turn had its name, which described to the youngest, me, how it should be done in such a way so as not to spoil it for the next days run. Thus, the slide along would provide toffee. The duck doon would provide a loaf of bread from under the baker's counter. The lift snatch could provide cakes and I'm sure the proprietors were turning a blind eye on that one. It was a cake stand outside a posh bakers café. It had a glass domed lid atop a high stand and one of us, usually the oldest, Lockey, would lift the lid as myself and Robert would dart past snatching a cake and ducking between the pedestrians in our getaway. Lockey would replace the lid before scarpering himself with his choice delight. I doubt if we could have gotten away with this every day without some sort of nod and wink from the workers. People would gather in the doorway and watch us through the café window. Perhaps we were a novel attraction act for the affluent café set. I was four years old, Robert five and Lockey six or seven.

And so on to the old fruit market, now called the Candleriggs market. It looked like easy pickings but we knew better. Everybody there worked there and so there were too many eyes and too many boots aimed at your arse to get away with it. But it didn't matter cos that risk wasn't necessary. There were these huge cast iron grates built into the ground at street level. They had a handgrip designed so the lid could be lifted to allow the rotten and damaged fruit and veg to be swept into the subterranean bin. It could then be lifted directly out from the ground and tipped into the garbage carts at the end of the day. We would just get there first and pick out the best, cutting out any rotten or bruised parts with long thumbnails and feast on the exotic. Cracked coconuts were not saleable yet still edible and I was raised on that milk from within. The odd onion here, a potato there would find their way home for the family pot but at least we survived in the race against the rats for our supper.

My memories of those days are primarily that of hunger, scarlet fever and rats. Of waiting on Ma coming home so that we could eat. We had a wee song, someone would look out the skylight window and say, 'Here's my Ma' and as we all perked up the song would finish, 'a no comin doon the High Street wi a wumin'. I'm sure this song was created just to torment me. The first line, 'Here's my Ma' would put a halt to my hungry crying. The next line would have me howling all the louder for the disappointment. I'd have been about two then when I decided to climb out the skylight to have a look for myself. Sliding down the slates and dangling my legs over the edge at the gutter. Looking down onto Geordie Street fascinated by all these tiny wee people all gathering there below. I had no idea I was causing a fuss and was perfectly comfortable there. Seeing Ma drop her bags in the street and run up the stairs as I sung, 'Here's my Ma' and getting dragged back in the skylight by the hair of the head. My seat had been the roof gutter of a four storey tenement, Ma screaming at my sisters, 'You're supposed to be watchin that wean.' At the time, I couldn't see what all the fuss was about. I see her point now.

They say I was a bit of a child prodigy before I started school at Townhead Primary at four years old. However that seems to have been the start of the end of my academic career as it was all down hill from there. I recall that the teachers were always very frustrated with me for scoring exceptionally high in IQ tests and exceptionally low in exam grades. Probably the problem may have stemmed, at least in those early days, from the strict regimented regimes and terror tactic teachers who would knuckle us on the head, nig-nog style and demand that we, 'Get those wheels turning.' Fuck! I used to worry that I had no brain because I didn't have any wheels in my noggin. So I just gazed out the window day dreaming between nig-nogs. Thought so clear and coming so natural is taken for granted but school made me believe it was a mechanical process alien to me because I couldn't feel any wheels turning. I guess I may have tended to take things too literally and wouldn't have had a clue what a concept was, never mind an abstract one, and, of course, talking to one's self, thinking, is a sign of madness. So who knows what they would do if they found out about the pictures I could actually see in my head when there was really nothing there?

Oh wuh! They'll drag ye away tae the jail like yer Da, so they wull.

The High Jump

(1984)

Good morning, the worm your Honour,
The Crown will plainly show the prisoner,
Who now stands before you, was caught red handed
Showing feeling, showing feelings
Of an almost human nature . . .
This will not do . . .

PINK FLOYD – THE WALL.

The trial was a farce of Floydian proportions. Of the 300 witnesses cited by the Crown, 100 would be called upon to do their thing but only one . . . One William Love . . . would perform his song and dance to the tune of the prime puppeteer. 'Dooo't Doo't do-rue' ensnaring the accused, Campbell and Steele, in a web of deception and incarcerating them in walls of impenetrable prejudice through which they may never again see the light of reason, far less that of day.

The crime itself was horrendous . . . 'Now persons involved directly or indirectly in blasting off a shotgun at an ice cream van in a public street during the hours of darkness are villains of the first degree,' says the trial judge. 'And those who set fire to a top flat in a tenement at a time when the house is occupied and the occupants are liable to be asleep, where there are no visible means of escape except through the very place the fire was started, and who, as a result, cause the deaths of six persons, mostly young, are wicked and depraved persons, inhuman and evil, they merit no sympathy or consideration. No decent person could be other than appalled at such dastardly deeds . . .'

The very nature of the crime itself entailing that no one would walk out of that court with an acquittal. All it would take in the face of such a holocaust would be even the slightest of inferences . . .

'Now there is no evidence to say that these accused were near or at the scene of the fire at the time the fire was started,' says the trial judge. 'And so the evidence is that of inference from the evidence before you – which is that of the witness Love's evidence to an overheard conversation in a public house' . . . 'There is insufficiency of evidence in law to entitle you to convict without the evidence of Love . . . His evidence is crucial to the Crown case . . . the Crown case stands or falls upon his evidence, it is therefore crucial that you believe him.'

Love, an admitted serial perverter of justice, admits perjury in his evidence at the trial. 'It was all just one big fit up of a case. There never was any such conversation in that pub nor anywhere else, mate, it was all just put into my head by the polis as part of the deal,' he asserts, but not until after the trial jury returned a verdict of guilty and the appeal was dismissed.

Not until after I was incarcerated incommunicado under the terror administration of Peterhead prison's infamous Hell Block and was brutally beaten and tortured to within an inch of life . . .

There then ensued a long hard struggle for justice and freedom, of which this is the story . . .

All alone and in two's
The ones who really care,
Walk up and down outside the wall,
And when they've given you their all,
Some stagger and fall,
After all, it ain't easy,
Banging your head
Against some mad bugger's wall.
Doo, do-rue't do-rue . . .

PINK FLOYD – THE WALL.

The Word from the Well
(The Govan Arms, 1985)

'He's a right bastard that yin.'

'Whit yin?'

'That big yin – Campbell innit?'

'Who the fuck ye gibberin oan aboot noo?'

'Campbell, a fuckin said, TC fuckin Campbell, ye corn beef? How many eh'thum is there?'

'Aye'n so whit aboot'um?'

'A right bastard so'eh is.'

'Nah . . . ! Ah know'm frae the YO man . . .'

'Wiz jist thinkin . . . It's been ower a year since . . .'

'Whit the fux?'

'They Doyles died, they fire murders mind?'

'Aye! but a'm no sure . . . Dae ye believe that . . . ?'

'Torched the hoose in the middle eh the fuckin night man! Cunt he is. Six fuckin innisin people deid, it's a fuckin disgrace so it is. Like Glen fuckin Coe aw ower again . . .'

'Yer no sayin th'ye believe . . .'

'Aye! Ice Cream Wars ma arse. It's aw doon tae cally dosh man! A'm sayin thit only an evil cunt wid dae that right! . . . Oye! Whit's e'hink e'starin it?'

'Leave'm alane, it's jist a daft boy . . .'

'The wee cunt keeps clockin me – Hey! A'll rearrange yer dial, daftie!'

'Fuck sake! He's only a wean man, whit's wrang weh yeh? C'moan, leave it oot'n huv a swally, so ye were sayin?'

'Aye thone TC, wiz always a bad bastard wizn't eh? So whit makes ye think eh never done it?'

'Ah know the guy. Heid case right enough but . . .'

'Aye bit whit? Zat no enough? Fuckin maniac.'

'Aye but no that kinda heid case . . . Know whit ah mean. Ah know the fuckin guy right!'

'So whit? Panned big Malky's face in didn't eh?'

'Aye so, see whit ah mean? It wiznae fur nothin, nat'know!'

'Naw ah don't fuckin know, wiz nothin tae dae weh'um, Fuckin nutter . . .'

'Aye bit it wiz y'see, that's where yer aw wrang. He diznae bother tellin cunts, diznae think he needs tae justify'es sell tae naebidy. At's whit ah mean. It's no jist thit eh thinks e's in the right aw th'time, he fuckin – like knows eh is, know whit ah mean? Like eh disnae dae it fur fuckaw, an eh disnae dae it sleekit like either, know whit ah mean? Ah know the guy man. Big Malky never copped e's whack fur nothin.'

'Aye but they Doyles did, fuckin wakinin up tae the fuckin hoose'n fire an every cunt died. Whit did they ever dae eh? Whit did any cunt ever dae tae deserve that? Fuckin heid case man. Should've burned him at the fuckin stake, see how he likes it, at's whit ah say.'

'Ah bit . . . That's whit ah mean man. He widnae dae it, an iffy did, he'd've said so, so eh wid . . .'

'Aye so eh wid. Aye right! Fuck off.'

'Aye right, see! There noo, see there it's happin'd again up there in Peternapper . . .'

'Aye right, there ye go then, s'aw appin'd again in Peterheed, ye said it yersel. Fuckin tried tae kebab they screws aw ower again. Hey! ye remember Torchy? The fuckin battery boy? Fuckin battered him all right so they did. Nae messin weh they bastards eh! Mind they done you up there tae? Yer last stretch, that wiz a fuckin liberty so it wiz . . .'

'Aye bit that's whit ah'm sayin tae ye. Get it intae yer heid, It's aw happin'd aw ower again an eh never done that either . . .'

'It wiz aw ower the papers that eh did it man. Fuck sake, ICE CREAM KILLER STRIKES AGAIN Ah read it mah'sel, the guy's seriously dimentit.'

'Aye but aw the troops are still up there man. The word is that eh never hid fuck all tae dae weh it an e's gettin the blame aw ower again. It wiz yone fucker . . . Mind mad Andy McCann? Aye oor Joe Mac wiz there, stoaped'm. TC's fuck all tae dae weh it. It's just they fuckin papers . . .'

'Ah didnae know . . . Wiz oor Joe intae aaw that kerry oan up by there? How's eh gettin oan?'

'Fuckin centuries man in that digger, how the fuck dae ye think e's gettin oan?'

'Ah bit ah didnae know . . . Hey! that wee prick's still clockin me man! Ah'm gonny gee'm a dull yin oan th'weh oot . . .'

'Aye well, gie mah regards tae TC when ye get there then . . .'

'Fuck that.'

The History of PeterHell

It used to be even worse. Try telling that to the men locked in the digger, getting systematic beatings every day. But it's true.

In 1886 they passed an Act of Parliament to create Peterhead Prison. It was to be the first and only penal colony in Scotland. Up till then, Scottish residents sentenced to hard labour were sent to the south of England far away from their homes. Was this move far sighted, liberal humanitarianism on behalf of our politicians? Not a bit – the citizens of English towns complained that too many Scots were escaping on their long journey south although, in truth, the numbers were sparse. Besides, they needed convict labour to service the Harbour of Refuge breakwater near the town of Peterhead in the far north-easterly neuk of Scotland. The breakwater hosted ships which would carry away the granite torn by convict labour from the nearby Springhill Quarry. The decision to build Peterhead was determined by financial efficacy and issues of punishment and public safety fronted by politicians eager to sustain popularity. Nothing much seems to have changed.

By 1888, the first prisoners arrived in Peterhead brought in by a unique system – the first state owned railway in Britain which terminated inside the very walls of hell. Carted in cages stacked within barren, solid cast iron wagons with no facilities and barely enough water, the men were miserable, weak, often close to death by the time they staggered out into the grey light shimmering across the North Sea, blending into the rain-filled skies. They might as well have been dispatched to another planet. It was Hell, PeterHell and as far away from home as they could imagine.

The work in the quarry was exhausting, relentless and dangerous. The equipment allowed was basic – ropes, shovels, picks and the flesh of their hands – and had to be carried out with the men shackled to each other. Why waste good money on machinery when life was cheap? Injury was everyday, disease rampant, deaths commonplace. Minor breaches of discipline were punished violently and promptly. The practice of strapping men to a frame and lashing them with a cat of nine tails continued in PeterHell long after it had been banned in the Army and Navy. Freedom was always on the convicts' minds but escape was rare and attempted by few with good reason.

'All convicts confined in H.M. Prison, Peterhead, are hereby warned that should they at any time use violence towards an officer, or attempt to escape from custody, they are liable to have either swords or firearms used against them as may be found necessary.'

Thus ran the statement read to each and every man on arrival and there was no doubt of the veracity of the statement. The prison guards of PeterHell carried rifles and the wardens swords, brandishing and using them frequently. The rifles were only taken away in the 1950s after an inquiry into the shooting of an escaping prisoner. The swords were to last a decade longer.

Many of the wardens and guards were recruited from

the ranks of former service men. The prison needed men experienced in using arms who knew how to treat an enemy with harsh discipline and brutality. That was how the convicts were seen – as dangerous enemies, captured, worthless and in need of brutal punishment. The staff were paid well for the period and provided with houses nearby for their families. Not bad for a former soldier, say, in those pre-welfare state days. But it was Peterhead, miles from the nearest city of Aberdeen, and much further from the main population centres of Glasgow and Edinburgh. The combination of institutional brutality and geographic isolation led to a self-selection process that was to last for generations.

When the former soldiers moved into Peterhead, they often stayed on, creating a family career tradition as jailers much as fishing and farming was for others in that rural, coastal enclave. In the early 1900s when the British Government decided to crack down on Irish Republican rebels they sought men of a particularly sadistic nature, willing to carry out any order and happy to dispense terror serving in the ranks of what became known as the Black and Tans. PeterHell became a key recruitment location. Some prisoners serving sentences for vicious assaults were offered deals to serve in the Black and Tans. But so were the staff. Former inmates and wardens of PeterHell went on to serve together in Ireland in the name of the British Government raping, pillaging, slaughtering men, women and babies – innocents and combatants alike – in one of the most disgrace laden eras of the British Army in Ireland.

As the need for hard labour in the granite quarry reduced the governors of PeterHell found other ways to shackle the inmates. If it wasn't repairing the breakwater – a dangerous and miserable activity as the freezing North Sea lashed all in its way – they made up reasons. So, in the 1950s, a road was to be built within the walls of the jail. It served no greater purpose than to provide an improved surface running from the back gate to the sheds. And what a road. They dug twenty feet to create the base using convicts, of course, allowing the men only picks and shovels with one dumper at hand to shift some of the rubble. The warden in charge, a former soldier, named it the Burma Road since he had served active duty in that country in the Second World War. The name stuck but little did he know that the Burma Road became synonymous with misery, pain and violence in prison folklore. The Burma Road represented PeterHell's capacity to subjugate men within the rules of war – a war between the State and the individual. The ghosts of the inmates hacking at the hard, stone ground, their shackles rattling, their malnourished bodies aching with the labour, injuries suffered and untreated, the agony of beatings handed down to the exhausted – those ghosts haunted PeterHell though the 1960s into the 1990s. They probably haunt the place still.

Those special attitudes of PeterHell staff prevailed beyond the days of swords and rifles, past the reforming decade of the Swinging 60s, into the 1970s and 1980s. When a prisoner tried a rare escape, the alert mechanism at PeterHell seemed inadequate and inept compared to other jails. Put simply, they didn't need to panic. As the wardens paraded the walls, the locals guarded the bleak terrain of the surrounding countryside. The prisoners knew that if they succeeded in making it outside of the jail they had a gauntlet to run that was no less dangerous, dodging the locals with their shotguns and dogs.

Unsurprisingly, very few successful escapes were made from PeterHell. In its lifetime it became the repository for the men deemed to be the most lethal in Scotland – dangerous to the public or a threat to the state. The catalogue of murderers, big time gangsters and rebels goes on forever but there are a few former PeterHell's unfortunates who are worth special mention.

Oscar Slater, a German Jew convicted in 1909 of the killing of widow Marion Gilchrist in her Glasgow flat, after returning voluntarily from America to face investigation in Scotland. Slater's case dripped with anti-Semitism, anti-German sentiment and the need of officials to secure a conviction regardless of who is convicted. Slater was first sentenced to death which was commuted to a life of hard labour in PeterHell. By life they meant till the day he died. Serious doubts about the validity of his conviction were taken on board by Sherlock Holmes' author, Sir Arthur Conan Doyle, William Roughead, the leading Scottish criminologist, and others. It took them eighteen years and huge public pressure to get Slater free. Just one innocent dumped in PeterHell.

John McLean – Marxist revolutionary, workers' leader, great orator and the face of Red Clydeside. During the First World War they jailed McLean twice, seeing him as a risk to public security. Such was McLean's popularity they feared that workers would break him out of prison – where else to put him but in PeterHell. McLean went on hunger strike in peaceful protest. The regime of PeterHell was ordered to keep him alive to avoid his martyrdom and save the British State from the Marxist revolution which had happened in Russia and was threatening to break out all over Europe. No problem for PeterHell, they simply force-fed him, sticking a tube down his throat and pouring slops into his stomach. Eventually freed in December 1918, McLean was met by 200,000 workers. He and his family were to be dogged by government spies for the rest of his life – a life now plagued by illness. The man who scared Churchill so much he ordered tanks, troops and machine guns into the city's George

Square died in 1923 aged forty-four years. It is now known that McLean's force-feeding and deprivations in PeterHell contributed to his early and wasteful demise. There are those who believe the screws of PeterHell added a little poison to the slops forced into his stomach.

By the 1970s and 1980s official penal policy in Britain had changed. No longer were guns and swords every day gear for the wardens of PeterHell. Now the debate was about the prison regime as a change process, an opportunity to help the men leave crime behind and become good citizens. Human Rights was a phrase that was beginning to take hold. Up in PeterHell they went on as normal. Continued to hand out systematic beatings daily. Locked men up in solitary confinement for many, many months on end abusing the liberal laws with the connivance of successive governments. Threatened to hang rebels in their cells at night if they refused to conform – and rebels were found hanged. Spoke in their native Doric dialect, dense double Dutch as far as most of the inmates were concerned leaving them confused, bewildered, missing crucial information. Turned away weary wives and kids who had travelled the hundreds of miles from the Central Belt, Glasgow most likely. Told the women that the men didn't want to see them. Told the men that their wives hadn't turned up. They forgot to tell PeterHell that the world had changed.

PeterHell is where they sent the men deemed to be the most dangerous, the rebels, the ones too bright and spirited to accept a soul destroying regime. The modern list is endless. But to mention those who are well known would be to betray those who fought the hardest and never made the pages of the tabloids. The men who invented the dirty protests stripping themselves naked and smearing themselves in their shit. The men who wouldn't lie down to the boot but fought back. The men who took over the jails and protested from the rooftops. The men the system feared and wanted to bury. PeterHell – that's where they sent TC Campbell.

Eternals

. . . A Day in the Life (1986/87)

'Whit's that fuckin noise?' I thought, guessing that it could only be . . . but not daring to hope. 'Weggitweggiz eggatheggti egguckegginfeggi eggoizneggi?' (What was that fuckin noise?) I said it out loud in coded language without thinking about it. Clinging there to the bars, high on the window wall, I knew I wouldn't have much time to get an answer before I'd have to drop back down to the pits of my solitary silent cell.

These underground languages evolved literally from street culture – in the late '50s, early '60s, when the City of Glasgow imposed curfew under the 'City Powers Act' which meant that any teenager or known thief caught on the streets during the hours of darkness would automatically be sentenced to a minimum of thirty days imprisonment without trial. Four youths thus captured would be charged with breach of the public peace, but five youths constituted a mob in the legal sense and breach of the peace would become a charge of mobbing and rioting which carried a sentence of up to ten years imprisonment. Hence, when a fifth member of the local young team was rounded up to join his friends in the paddy wagon, coded conversation would break out as each agreed, for example, that they do not know and have never known the fifth and any further persons arrested. All the street gangs spoke thus. It was simply a case of basic survival by the street codes.

'Eggetzmegge, Teggesegge,' (It's me, TC) came the answer in semi-cypher. Identifying himself by voice, no name, a trooper, but not a full-blooded hell bound hound of the Eternals – those detained in solitary without limit of time.

'Weggitweggiz zeggiteggi?' (What was it?) I repeated, hopes lifted, grunting in pain and dropping to the floor. THOOMM. The bones of my feet echoed in the stone chamber as I landed. Four quick back steps to the cell door, four fast forward at a run, springing with one foot on the window wall, up and grasping the bars again. This time, swinging all the way up onto the sloping window ledge. Holding myself there in that more secure position. Feet and shoulders wedged to each alcove of the window, taking the weight from my hands and arms on the bars . . . We continued our conversation in this way.

I recognized the bold Ian Fisher's voice. He was remanded in custard to the digger again. He had this way of messing with the wires of his radio so that he could send Morse coded messages to anyone else in our Hell Block with a tranny. Even if you couldn't decypher Morse, like me, you'd know he was calling. You'd know he was back.

'Fuck sake, Ian,' I spoke in code, 'what the fuck y'done for noo?'

'Tanned the PO's office. Done the windae weh the telli,' he continued to answer in semi-cypher. 'Got some snout for yeh and . . .' his silence prolonged.

'And whit, ya fuckin heed case ye?'

'Obli.' (Blaw.)

'Eggexeggalleggenteggi.' (Excellent.)

'Yeeha!' the cellblock erupted into spontaneous applause.

'Y'got a line?' Ian enquired.

'I've got a fuckin jackhammer for you, m'friend.'

'Fire it doon.'

'Y'want it the noo?'

'Ah-haye! Like as if you don't eh!'

'Eggoneggireggi,' I shouted on Ronnie.

'Whit,' Ron answered in full cypher.

'Eggineleggi Teggesegge,' (Line for TC) the Fish fullah interjected.

The entire Block were at their windows now in expectation of witnessing the mastery and fine art of The Line. I flew a kite line to Ron, a poly bag on a thread through the wire mesh beyond the bars. He caught it with a spoon sling. Great shot. His weight on a thread lobbed over my kite line, pulling it in to make that first connection as the Fish fullah hooked in Ron's second line dropped down to him.

'Sorted,' said he.

'Cop yer whack, Ian,' I told him.

'Nae borra,' he confirms, taking his cut first.

'You too, Ron,' I say as the contraband reached that stage. 'Eggexeggallegganteggi,' Ron says, adding, 'Your blaw,' in the same code.

'Eggoteggit,' (Got it) I say as the lines dissolve into thin air. All night long, all through the night, the conversations went on this way. Window to window, line to line as the digger buzzed with this unexpected windfall. Not only a smoke, but blaw an a'? Brill. A tear and a cheer for the Fish fullah. This guy did twelve years out of twelve years without a day's remission just to get snout and such like down to me and the Eternals buried alive down there in Hell Block dungeons.

'Give us a poem big man,' he cries out, puffing on his eggointjeggi.

'Whit wan?'

'Y'know whit wan.' They always want the same old trip and so, here, under this same sky as your still starry night sky, I would render it to them. Always the same poem they wanted though never the same trip twice, but always with the same ending . . .

> . . . So come let me show you the way
> Out to the rim of the galaxy,
> You can get there faster than light,
> By instantaneous inner sight,
> All you have to do is say,
> 'Fuck it all,' and you're on your way,
> Beyond the bounds of boundary . . .

Stand to Fight Again

And so the beat goes on. While Liz and the kids struggled to cope with the trauma in the wider world, I dealt with my own horror in the isolation of Hell Block Peterhead, Sol Con.

They had tried to kill me. There was no doubt in my mind. They had done their damnedest to murder me and thus to bury the potential scandal and controversy with me. How could they explain away that a man, held innocent imprisoned in solitary confinement in their custody, was so brutally beaten and tortured as I was? Now here, transferred, almost paralysed in this prison hospital bed, isolated from the world, my mind screamed, in horror at the danger I was in. For an alleged hospital, it felt more like a condemned cell. More like captivity in the vampires larder awaiting selection as lunch.

Surrounded by the mutant cockroaches who had done this to me. Officially and under orders, they had carried out their task with lethal efficiency. Yet still I live here in this box on the dark side of the moon with only my torturers clunk-clicking in their armour beyond the double-barred caged gate and steel door of my vault. I could hear the furnaces of Hell Block in constant roar amid the clunk-clicking of the cockroaches. I could smell the decaying flesh of corpses. So powerful the stench that I could picture the teeming maggots, I could see the heaps of wretched dead right there in my head. Fodder for the furnace. Am I imagining this? No! The creepy crawlies are real, teeming over my battered body like the minions of hell arisen.

They had beaten and tortured me to death yet do I really live? Yes! They had come again. Gassed my chamber with poisonous insecticides, blasting billows of toxic fumes with their pump guns. Cockroaches' revenge. Backing out the chamber door, slamming it closed behind them leaving me there to die. Yet again I survive. I had broken off the aerial from the radio, extending it, and managed to smash the windows without moving from my prone position on the bed. They know I am paralysed. Spine broken in two places under their jack boots and zipped from dick to naval from ruptured gut. They know it's toxic gas. They wore masks as they filled the chamber with it as they backed out the door. So what next? What officially sanctioned murder scheme is now on the cards for me? Will I be found hanged like so many lost and forgotten souls before me? But who shall write my epitaph?

As Thatcherite armies of mutant cockroaches marched, over, under and into every crevice of the infested land, my mind screamed in isolation, 'No matter what you do to me ya bastards, I shall live and I shall stand to fight again.'

Charged now with riot, escape attempt, hostage taking, six attempted murders by fire bomb and assault, the police refused to take my complaint. Now being shipped up and down to court, hobbling like some ancient spectre . . . at least I was on my feet. Still in strict Sol Con isolation but at least I was alive, sane and on my feet. That was a start.

They wanted to keep me in isolation. So instead of taking me to the reception area to collect my civvy clothes for court, as would be standard practice, they would bring my clothes and property card to me in the flea pit strong cell at the prison hospital wing. From there, direct to court and back again. I would change and sign the clothing out into use and back again on return. This was done under the direction of Chief Cormack, Director of Torture, now a governor. He told the reception screws that they were just to leave me in charge of my own civilian T shirts. They could be kept 'in use' within the main prison population but not in Hell Block proper where I'd been detained since arrival. There were two T shirts, each distinctively personal. One with the legend 'Innocent Imprisoned, Free the Glasgow Two' and the other, 'Nelson Mandela? What about TC?' This was all well and dandy but am I supposed to be grateful? They had literally kicked me to death and charged me with assault for having the audacity to pull through and, I'm sure, the six attempted murders by fire bombing would look good on my rap sheet for my appeal against six murders by fire bombing. I was being fitted up again, put through the mincer again by these evil bastards and I'm supposed to be softened up by the allowance of two T shirts?

With a heart and soul fuelled by the storms of fury and fuming hate, within six weeks I was not only sitting up by myself, I was on my feet. Sit-ups 100 times each morning before breakfast. Pressing up 100 times before lunch. Building up and building up strength like a demented dynamo. The power of the storms within me, driving me on and on. Two hundred, three hundred, four, five . . . They would not have a cripple to deal with when next they came that's for sure.

My case to the Scots Secretary, Malcolm Rifkind MP QC, regarding my appeal under Section 263 for reference back to the appeal court was in progress. As was my case Campbell versus The United Kingdom at the European

Court of Human Rights in Strasbourg. Now that the case was TC – v – UK and, with all these new charges on top, it actually felt like taking on the entire country one at a time. Bring on the fucking world for all I care . . . 997, 998 . . . You can restrain this body ya bastards but you cannot chain my brain . . . 1000 and 5, 1000 and 6 . . . You can fit me up, lock me up, beat me up, but you will never shut me up, for my mind is free from the fear you feed me . . . 1000 and 28, 1000 and 29 . . .

Seems I was getting too fit too fast and it was worrying someone. They came back again. Same mob, fully clad in cockroach armour with baseball bats and chains.

'Cell search, anything here that shouldn't be?'

'Aye me! Youse are not touching my legal documents,' said I, adopting a crouched fighting stance protecting my legal papers.

'Get him,' and they pounced. The usual scrum ensued and I was stripped, chained up, stuffed into a sack and bundled naked and bruised back over to Hell Block. So much for my fighting fitness then.

Up before Governor Smith next morning still held in restraints was a revelation. The charge, apparently, was 'Possession of unauthorized articles'. Something fishy going on here I thought but this was Peterhead after all, so nothing unusual in that.

Smith was seen as a bastard by most, if not all of the prisoners there simply for the fact that he allowed all of this nasty to go on. But I had found that, beyond that, he was generally pretty fair.

'It's a wee bit more serious than that, TC,' he was saying. 'These T shirts may be sent to the procurator fiscal as production evidence on the pending riot trial as proof that you must have got them from reception and therefore that you must have been in the reception area is evidence of guilt in that disturbance. Do you have any other explanation?' Still held tightly in restraints and surrounded at close quarters by half a dozen mutant cockroaches, I looked at Cormack and growled.

'You are just a low life scum bag, mister.'

'What has he to do with any of this?' asked Big Alfy Smith looking back and forward between us.

'Not a lot,' I answered, 'just that he left those T shits in my cell over by there in the hospital when I was taken to court.'

'Is that right, Mr Cormack?'

'It is not, sir. He's nothing but a liar and . . .'

'Is that right?' Alfy raised his voice and glared at the senior reception screw. 'And never mind looking at the chief, look at me. I want the truth.'

'Yes sir, we were instructed to leave them there in his cell, in use.' Alfy was livid. Glaring at Cormack.

'So it's as simple as that eh. As simple as that.' Nodding his head slowly, surveying the crowded room. 'I will have none of it! Do you hear? None of that nonsense in my prison, do you understand? I will have nothing less than the truth, the whole truth and nothing but the truth from my staff on these matters. There will be no further hanky panky in this case. Do you understand,' he raged, rising to his feet, bright red in his anger.

Surprised and puzzled I was let away, charge dismissed but Cormack was ordered to stay. Looked like he was on the carpet now. Yet it was so close. Just so close. If not for Alfy I would have been well and truly fitted up all over again. As it was, that evidence at least was abandoned and that trial was yet to come. This had actually done me a favour. It had far reaching effects beyond the immediate. Alfy's speech to the screws would be passed on by word of mouth to the rest of the cockroaches and the effect of that was that they would stick to the truth so far as I was concerned and this took me out of the frame more than they could ever have realised at that time.

In the meantime however, it was back to those dank and dismal dungeons of dire despair of Hell Block to prepare my defence. First, for the assault trial . . .

Lost Souls

I was not the only innocent imprisoned there. Wee Ronnie Neeson was there too. Fitted up for a lifer by another supergrass. The Gimp's brother, Toe Elliot, had committed the murder. Toe had gone on the trot and Ronnie was arrested and identified 'Unsure' by his hair style. By the trial, Toe had been arrested during an armed bank raid and was there in the dock with Ronnie as a co-accused. The ID witness had pointed to Toe at his first sighting in court. 'It was HIM,' he'd said, but Toe was bald and when asked about his previous unsure ID of Ronnie at the earlier parade he had replied, 'Aye him (the baldy one) but with his (Ronnie's) hair.' It was common knowledge throughout the prison that Toe wore a wig. Had worn a wig on the night of the killing of a reformed drug dealer. 'A Ronnie wig' we would joke but it wasn't funny for Ronnie. Toe has never denied it. He just would not take the stand to take the rap when there was a chance that he might be acquitted. The trial judge had then instructed the jury that it was the witness's previous ID which counted over and above his evidence in court. This allowed sufficiency of evidence to convict Ronnie who was still there in the digger from B Hall segs, still refusing to conform and still fighting his case against conviction.

Tam Moffat, serving seventeen years for the robbery of an armoured truck, witnessed by an accountant in the car park. The witness had watched the entire dramatic event and had followed the robbers in his car. Had seen them switch cars and burn the first car and had telephoned the police from that scene. He had then handed over a partially burned money band to the police and given them a full statement right there on the scene. Sure he could identify them . . .

However, this only independent witness wasn't called to give evidence nor even to appear at the trial. Though the money band did. Alleged to have been found some time later in Tam's possession. It would be sufficient, together with polis verbal, to convict the Moffat brothers for the robbery.

However, having traced the witness for appeal, it was discovered that not only could he identify the band and not the accused but, being an accountant, he could also provide the full registration number on the band said by the police to have been found on the brothers. However, this didn't seem to hold out much significance to the Appeal Court who dismissed it as irrelevant and upheld the convictions, merely reducing the sentence by three years to fourteen years as a consolation prize. Tam was still there in Sol Con fighting his case.

Bally, Billy Ballantine's was one of the most sad and tragic cases of all. He was convicted of a murder he could not remember and, for a time, assumed he must have committed. It had started as a drunken brawl spilled out onto the street from a party. Bally and his three pals had struggled with four others until one man was stabbed in the buttocks and later bled to death. Bally's tragedy stemmed from the fact that he couldn't remember any part of any of it. His three pals, once co-accused, turned Crown evidence as witnesses for the prosecution with immunity in exchange for their evidence. Bally, on hearing part of the evidence changed his plea to guilty. This would also prevent his wife Marie from being charged with perjury for saying that the knife did not come from her house. He was sentenced to life imprisonment.

As a first offender, Bally was transferred to Edinburgh's Saughton prison where he'd had his nose broken by a prison officer. This triggered off a series of anti-social behaviour patterns which led to Bally being transferred again to the arsehole of the universe, Peterhead Prison. Hundreds of miles from home and where, for some reason unknown to anyone to this day, he was refused temporary transfer for visit facility to his home town of Glasgow. Isolation led to a breakdown of his relationship with his wife Marie. Finally, she left him, moving south with their son, and took up residence with another man. While in protest at the refusal of visit facilities, Bally took to the rooftops with his banner **TOO FAR TO VISIT** in one of PeterHell's many riots. He was sentenced to a further eight years. Meantime, however, Marie's new man was convicted of abusing their son and she moved back to Glasgow. Still visits transfer was refused. Again and again Bally joined the roof toppers in protest. Again and again he was sentenced to an eternity of years.

By the time his co-accused finally admitted that Bally's lack of any memory of the murder was due to the fact that he had been sparkled out cold, unconscious and drunk when they had in fact committed the dastardly deed, it was already too late to help Bally. They had put their heads together to blame him and had succeeded in ending two lives to save their own skins from the consequences of the first. With the heart of a hero, Wee Bally had fought the system with all that he had and in the only way left open to him. He fought to the death and died in prison after twelve years with twenty odd left still to do. The straightest and bravest wee guy I have ever known. May god have mercy on his weary soul.

Then of course there were the usual suspects. The like of the Paranoid Android, now a Crown rap against us in the riot trial. It had been he who had threatened the screws with a petrol bomb, 'Ye'r kebab ya bastards.' He served three out of three years in Hell Block and was gate arrested for assault, eventually released, then was sentenced to four years for tying up and torturing the judge who had sentenced him. This guy is the original Rab C. Nesbit, he was finally sentenced to life imprisonment for murder and is presently serving his time at the State mental hospital at Carstairs where he should have been from the start.

Then there was wee Spike who also claimed to be innocent imprisoned, though it seemed that his case turned on the fact that he didn't understand the principle of art and part complicity to murder. He, according to him, was innocent of murder because he had only struck the guy over the head with an axe during a teenage gang fight when, in fact, it had been the sword wound which had killed him.

The digger was full of malcontents. Besides those charged with me on the riot – Al Brown, Bill Varey, Gary Mac, Ace Campbell and Joe Mc – there were all of these and more. They all had their own grim story to tell. Mostly of planted evidence and verbal yet, even then, they would freely admit their guilt. The ratio of innocents imprisoned to guilty was about one in five. So our anthem from UB 40 'I am the One in Ten' was not exactly accurate but who cares?

> I am the one in ten.
> Nobody knows me
> but I'm always there.
> A statistical reminder
> of a world that doesn't care.

On to the assault trial then. The issue of innocence or guilt doesn't come into it. Saying as much to my lawyer John Carroll. Trying to point out that this was a railroad. This was an exclusive club for the wee frees of the masonic variety. They all wore the same school tie. How better could I put it? He would just smile and say, 'We all have our own little alliances, Mr Campbell.' I thought that he just didn't understand.

The Press were full of the sensation.

Fire Bombings
Hostages
Riots
Ice Cream War Killer Strikes Again.

Spouting out the propaganda of how I 'continue to run his evil empire of the Glasgow underworld from his cell in Peterhead'. Aye right! Canny even get a bloomin fag paper under the door. Gee's a break eh, Jimmy!

The trial started at Peterhead Sheriff Court around June 1986. Standing room only. Only a few of the family there, the rest was just a wall of Press jostling the wee judge on his way into court.

'All rise.' John Carroll turned to me in the dock and bowed. Out popped his own little club tie. The winged dagger with the motto 'Who Dares Wins'. Deary me! I'd known JC had been a police officer and a prosecutor but I hadn't known he had also been a paratrooper. The cavalry had arrived it seemed. He had also instructed Gordon Jackson QC for my defence. This guy was brilliant. Seems this simple assault trial was not going to be such a straightforward railroad after all.

Cormack gave his evidence. He and two other officers, he names them, entered my cell to inform me that my visit was called off due to the disturbance in the prison the night before. He said that I had leapt forward, reached over the shoulders of the two officers and punched him on the chin. The officers had pushed me backwards and they had stepped backward out of the cell and closed the door. End of story. On cross-examination he was forced to accept that no other visits were cancelled that day but otherwise stuck to the script, denying any knowledge of how I had come by my injuries.

The prosecutor called one of the screws named – he also stuck to the script but with the one exception in that he said that there were four of them in all including Cormack. He named the other who Cormack had omitted. We called the second screw who Cormack had mentioned and he too stuck to the script. Again with one exception. He named two further officers as being present. One of whom was named by the first screw but neither named by Cormack. This took us up to five. Another was called and he too stuck to the script but naming yet another two screws not previously mentioned by anyone. All pled ignorance to any knowledge of how I had come to suffer such multiple and traumatic injuries.

Now we were up to seven. Cormack was re-called to the witness stand. Still he swore to three screws present. His head slowly bowing as the other names were put to him together with the evidence of the last witnesses naming them.

'Are these witnesses liars? Tell us before we call each and every one of these named officers. Exactly how many were present during this incident?'

With head down Cormack muttered a sob.

'Pardon? Speak up that the court might hear you,' said Jackson.

'Fourteen. There were fourteen or so of us,' he groaned. He accepted that he had not in fact made a mistake but had lied on oath. Dismissed from the witness box in tatters, a broken and shattered man, he turned to exit by the door he had entered, the witness waiting room. But that is not allowed. The police officer on duty took hold of him by the arm, his other hand upon his shoulder to turn him around and redirect him the other way. Cormack, assuming he was being arrested for perjury, let out a yelp in panic. Crouching down almost to his knees, arms outstretched, pleading to the judge for clemency. The judge, I think it was Sheriff Murphy, embarrassed, motioned for him to be ejected from the court and he was ushered away amid the hubbub of activity from the Press. So ended round one.

I was called to give evidence. On swearing the oath, I was astounded to notice that the court was on ground level and, from the stand, I was looking right out the window across the room into the street. There were throngs of people and TV cameras out there looking right in at me there on the stand. Zoom lenses and high tech microphones had the perfect camera angles for the witness box. Christ! They had it all on tape. Cormack, the lot. I told my story.

The judge recessed to chambers.

He returned with his judgment, giving me his deepest sympathy for the terrible trauma I had undergone and giving the screws a blasting as liars attempting to cover up for their evil deeds in the meting out of corporal punishment. I was acquitted Not Guilty. One down then. Two to go. Now, besides the pending riot trial, I would be suing for attempted murder, assault and torture. Also, there was yet the infestation with lice. There was TC – v – UK in Strasbourg and the case for appeal against conviction for murder in the first place. Otherwise I would end up buried alive under an eternity of years like Bally and so many other wretched souls who'd passed this way before me.

It should be understood that those held in Hell Block digger were all, either officially or unofficially, Cat-A-List prisoners. Yet they cannot keep someone on permanent Sol Con just for being an A Cat and, the more especially, when they are not officially on the Cat A listings. Therefore, we were all held there under what was then called Rule 36 which, under the terms of the official rule book, simply referred to those prisoners 'excused' work detail. In other prisons, Barlinnie for instance, this simply meant what it said. However, in Peterhead standing orders, the unofficial rules, not working was an offence against GOD (Good Order & Discipline) and in practice Rule 36 entailed twenty-four hours per day Sol Con in the digger for indefinite periods often lasting years. Such Catch 22s were often used merely as an establishment loophole to get around the international rules that prisoners could not be held in solitary confinement for more than fourteen days on mental health reasons. A petition to the Scots Secretary enquiring as to why you are held in Sol Con will take an average of nine months for an answer. The answer you get back will say, 'You are not being held in solitary confinement, you are held under Rule 36.' Which simply tells you that your confinement is unofficially sanctioned and officially denied by the establishment. A particular trait of the Thatcherite era.

Of course, they had many ways around the rules. A prisoner held for a year in Sol Con under Rule 36 for instance may blow his top and throw the contents of his piss pot over one of the mutant cockroaches. He would then be subject to a civilian charge for assault. Thus the rule under which he was held changes from 36 to 39 – Convicted prisoner held awaiting police investigation. This meant that he could legitimately be held in isolation until the police charged him. In practice, however, it was reinterpreted to mean that the prisoner could be held in the digger until after the trial, which could be up to a year away. The rule on 'Not exceeding fourteen days' could be thus circumvented to allow for fourteen years if they wanted. In fact, serving nine years, seven years and five years was not unusual. I only served four years Sol Con before the riots blew the roof off completely and the SAS had to be called in.

Al Brown pled guilty to the digger riot and was sentenced to twelve years bringing him up to about fifty-four years. Big Bill Varey also pled guilty and he too was sentenced to twelve years bringing him up to around thirty-six years. Gary Mc pled and got seven years on top of his lifer. This left only myself, Joe Mc and Ace Campbell to go ahead with the trial and the Paranoid Android, Andy McCann, as the Crown rap with immunity from prosecution. So what else is new? It is always the ones who have sins to hide who turn against their brothers in arms to save their own worthless skins.

My lawyer was John Carroll. My QC was Ian Hamilton, the alleged blagger of the Stone of Destiny back to its rightful home in Scotland. His book, *A Touch of Treason* tells its own brilliant story. The man is a legend in his own time.

Ian Hamilton opened the trial with a point of law and principle that the handcuffs and manacles should be removed from the prisoners before the jury. I was very interested in this point for the fact that I had been impeded by handcuffs at my appeal. He argued that under Section 2 of the European Communities Act 1972 all articles, rules and protocols of the European Community were to be given immediate effect as legally enforceable within the United Kingdom and shall be henceforth referred to as Enforceable Community Rights. Blah! Blah! This would include Article 3 of the Convention for Human Rights that 'No person should be subjected to inhumane, degrading treatment nor torture'. From which Article stems 'The European minimum rules for the treatment of prisoners in custody as adopted by the United Nations in the Treaty of . . . Blah, Blah . . .' Under Rule 62A of which 'All chains and manacles must be removed before any appearance in court'. That 'on this basis, the handcuffs should be removed forthwith . . .'

The judge called for consultation in chambers where he advocated that if Ian Hamilton withdrew his point of law he would order the removal of the handcuffs anyway. This was refused on the grounds that there was a point of principle to establish here and a ruling in open court was insisted upon.

'Due to the point of law raised by learned counsel, Ian Hamilton, on behalf of the accused, Thomas Campbell, I have no other alternative than to order the removal of the handcuffs. Take them off.'

Principle established. The second move was yet to come. The Crown proceeded with its case totally oblivious as to what our next point would be and with apprehension of Ian Hamilton getting back on his feet again. They trod carefully in my case.

The drunken camera man, the only screw still on duty who was not a hostage that night, having committed suicide, this left the Paranoid Android as the main evidence. The only other evidence against me, besides the fact that I was there on the scene of the crime at the time it was committed, was that of the assistant governor, Inhumane McBain, aka Rupert the Bear for the fact that he always wore the same clothes as that character right down to the checked pants. He said that it was my voice on the telephone making demands. This, and the fact that I was there and out of my cell, may have been sufficient for it to have gone to a jury. There was always the point to be made that I was a prisoner in a cellblock and couldn't very well have been anywhere else. However, it wouldn't matter. This attack on me brought Ian Hamilton back to his feet on the second point of law.

The principle having been established in the handcuffs issue, rule such and such of the European minimum standard rules for prison in custody notes that solitary confinement is a recognised form of punishment. Rule such and such states that no prisoner shall be punished twice for the same offence and, as the accused has been held in solitary confinement for a year under Rule 39 of the prison rules as a direct consequence of these charges being alleged against him, in these circumstances, having already been so punished by a year in solitary confine-ment, it would thus be in violation of those European minimum standard rules, adopted by the United Nations and enforced under Article 3 of the Convention and enacted as enforceable under Section 2 of the European Communities Act 1972 . . . Blah, Blah, Blah . . . for this court to deal with or to punish this prisoner for a second time.

I was removed from the court. Charges dismissed. Checkmate in two moves. Leslie McBain, the governor who had first given the order that I be sent to the digger under Rule 36 to begin with, the man who had given the order to Cormack to do me in, witnessed by Ronnie and others through their cell doors, had again tried to do the nasty on me and it had backfired on him. Their sly reverting from Rule 36 to 39 on the charges had been their downfall. This should have applied to all the accused there but, for whatever reason, their counsel did not pursue the point on their behalf. Maybe it's because they get paid for their time spent in court and not for an acquittal.

The screws wrung it on Joe Mc, putting him in the place of the Android with the petrol bomb at the cell door trying to light it and threatening the screws. Remember,

Joe was the one who had committed himself to disarming the Android but, having prevented the six screws from becoming 'Kebab ya bastards' as the Android had threatened, here they were now trying to convict him for it and thus let their real tormentor off the hook. The Android didn't do any of the accused any damage in the box but he didn't do them any good either. He denied that it was him making the threats when in fact it was him and he could have admitted it with impunity as a Crown rap.

I was not called to give evidence and Joe Mc and Ace were found Guilty and sentenced to seven years each. Everyone on Rule 39 was immediately returned to normal circulation. As for us however, we just reverted to the old routine under Rule 36.

Under Siege

Still held in Hell Block Sol Con, I was under siege. Still pursuing my case against conviction for the fire murders. Still pursuing various human rights issues at Strasbourg. Still suing the Scots Secretary (Prison Division) for attempted murder and torture and, of course, there was the other little matter of infestation with lice.

I had simply stuck around sixty odd beasties onto a piece of tape. One strip from my body and had sent them to the Secretary of State. Eighty odd on another strip to the European Commission in case the Secretary denied he'd got them. Sixty odd to my lawyer, John Carroll, with the message, 'Whomsoever the flea bites, it bites for me.' I used to flick them onto the screws and the governors. They want to give them to me? They can have them back was my attitude. Anyway, they caved in on that one, awarding damages and expenses, thus depriving me of my day in court to tell the story. The cash settlement was donated to a children's charity

Throughout all these trials and cases yet pending censorship was strictly enforced. All outgoing mail had to be left open or else it was returned to you by the censor and would never be posted. All incoming mail, including those from lawyers, QCs, MPs and even the European Court of Human Rights and the Crown Office were all handed over opened and most often without the envelope at all. Mail took between five to seven days either way on delivery. Not that the pony express was lame, it was the censorship was slow and meticulous. Each of my letters was directed under standing orders to the governor for even more specific scrutiny pending approval.

Now how in god's name am I supposed to pursue the proper legal channels against the evils of a screwed up system while that system's administration controls all communications and information? Unimpeded confidential communications are an absolute necessity but they were non-existent. Communication lines down. The first principle of a siege.

More than that, held in a box for years with the knowledge of countless more years of the same ahead for the future – that box is all there is, ever has been and ever will be. It is your world and your only known universe. There is only up and down, right and left. There is no known north, south, east or west. Never mind time of the day or telephone. You are, for all intents and purposes, encased in a concrete cube orbiting on the dark side of the moon.

There is no way out of this box. Your head is encased in concrete. No communications in or out without first going through your captors. Control of information and communications are the key and they hold that key. Therefore, the only logical solution to the problem is to get out of that box as the first step towards anything.

I had succeeded in having PeterHell hospital closed down and condemned as infested. I had achieved that much at least. The only other prison hospital capable of facilitating an ill prisoner was, in fact, Barlinnie, way down south in my own hometown of Glasgow. So what options are there? Cut your wrists or do the fan dangle? Nae danger! I resorted then to hunger strike. Desperate situations require desperate measures.

Those early days, from 1986, these were in fact real

hunger strikes. I would starve for around thirty days or so before being shipped down to Barlinnie hospital. I would hold out for another ten days or so, gaining the time to get data over to my lawyer and family without censorship letting the authorities know what I was planning in my cases against them.

My dilemma was always the issue of self inflicted death. These bastards wanted me dead bad enough without any help from me. Sooner or later I would have to eat. I had to eat to live to pursue my case and clear my name. So round and round the magic roundabout from PeterHell to Barlinnie and back again. Hunger strike after hunger strike. They were all about access to unimpeded communications facilities. I seemed to be holding my own at the loss of five-and-a-half stone at nine stone average.

It got so that I would be leapt upon by Barlinnie's mutant cockroaches, bundled into a van and shanghai'd back to Hell Block as soon as I tasted the first nibble of anything. I had to hold out for longer and longer. Though holding out was killing me, nevertheless my body was adapting to starvation as the norm. Now holding my own around eight stone.

I have the dubious honour of being the first man held in the new segregation unit in Barlinnie. This became a pattern. Besides being recognised as Scotland's most Shanghai'd prisoner, I was always the first man in and the last man out of every sticky situation. The screws in this Wendy Hoose all wore white coats over their mufti gear this being part of the new enlightened policy of 'treatment' rather than punishment. In effect it meant that they now referred to punishment as treatment and if you got out of line you were given The Treatment by having the shit kicked out of you before knocking you out with the liquid cosh injections. Each night, or in the wee small hours of the morning, the sound of rumbles, thumps and bumps (the sound of bone on stone) could be heard amid the curses and squeals as some poor anonymous soul was given The Treatment. The sound of bodies being dragged past your door to god only knows where. Never to be seen or heard of ever again. I mean, we were already in the segregation unit, where else can they go? How deeper into the pits can they take you in the wee hours of the morn? This was Terror Hall. Psychological control by terror in the new enlightened regime's machine. They call it the Wendy Hoose, wonder why? This place became widely known and infamous for this kind of treatment when a prison doctor broke ranks and testified against the screws for meting out this brutal treatment under the guise of medical care. They simply sacked him and carried on as usual. The orders come from Olympus y'see.

As for time? No clocks allowed then. The only time you know in Sol Con is Breakfast time, Dinner time and Dark o'clock. But when you don't eat and cease to have any hunger cravings even those times are meaningless. You live in the constant moment like a rabbit held transfixed and entranced in the glare of a headlamp. You become transfixed in the glare of the cold harsh light of the living reality of your living nightmare. Without time nor any sense of time, you may lose your anchor to the earth, tumbling free in your cube, orbiting aimlessly . . .

Beyond the bounds of boundary, of time and shifting
    sand,
Deep in the heart of nowhereness one billion light years
    from land.
Through the uncharted reaches of limitlessness,
Beyond the bounds of man.

Beyond the barrier reef Regret, through the sphere of
   the fear
Around the new security net in the system of the Prime
   Puppeteer.
There! Lies yet another lost cosmos, deep in the
   darkness there
Lost forlorn to all, but found, beyond profound
   despair.

This is where the hunger strikes cease. This is where
the horns of dilemma cease to gore. You can guarantee
that a hunger strike will test you to the uttermost limits
of your motivations and moral fibre. Here is where you
surrender all illusions and revert to the core of the light
of the living reality. Here is where the power of the storm
will either destroy you or feed you with strength. Here is
where I solved the dilemma of life or death in my situation.
Reverted to the foundations of the facts.

There comes a point in time where the struggle for
justice evolves beyond the personal struggle for life and
freedom. It comes to mean more than ones personal cause
and will to survive. The patriotic love of one's country for
example, where, in that wider view, the affront of the
travesty of justice meted out feels like an insult upon
ones nation. That your country and its people deserve,
and are due, better than this abomination drummed up
in the name of justice. Yet still closer and more personally,
what hope then for ones children? And of their children?
They too deserve better than this. Drawing even closer,
what the fuck's my life matter in the face of such an
on-going travesty? The pain, the physical pain is intense
sure enough, constant and seeming to go on for all eternity
but the emotional pain of life in the acceptance of the
alternative is by far more the greater. I would rather
die a thousand deaths than live one single day without

protest. Suppression of the outrage I feel brings pain in equal measure. Constant exposure to such pain of such a life threatening quality brings its own kind of insanity to survive in an environment where one has to go half mad to stay half sane.

'There is no gain without pain,' they say. Tell me then what clarity of vision a severe kick in the balls might bring? And tell me then, just what would it take to hold that clarity in ones brain, in all of its bounty, and dare not wince? Why then do I keep going? Why then suffer so? I think therefore I am beyond these bars, beyond the limitations of my confines, beyond good and evil where there is only pure reason, a place in my soul where my mind takes me. Transported in the power of my pain, an insight to perception dawns upon the cold harsh light of the living reality. Beyond death, and the struggles of life, where death embraces like a mother's shroud, therein I find the clarity of reason required to retain that fragment of sanity in the face of my living nightmare.

Innocent until proven guilty by a fair trial. Innocent regardless of whatever the world might say or believe. I know the truth, I had not received a fair trial according to my rights before god. Thus, I would eat but I would only eat food as supplied by my family as per the rights of an untried prisoner. I was no longer on hunger strike. I was asking to be allowed to eat, to live, to clear my name as per my right before god. Now the horns of the dilemma were reversed. The onus as to who was killing who was reversed. I was not starving myself, I was being starved. Food was being delivered for me to the prison on a day-to-day basis but it was not allowed and not given to me on the order of the prison governor. The issue now became which law is greater? God's law in the commandments that thou shall not kill? The common law on the preservation of life? The statutory law empowering a governor? The rules which say I can eat my own food as an untried prisoner? Or the standing order that allows the governor the authority and discretion to refuse? Thus where it is in violation of the by-law to step on the grass at pain of fine or imprisonment, it is not therefore reasonable excuse not to step on the grass if one must do so to throw a drowning man a lifeline. For not to do so would be culpable homicide by omission. The person, in all conscience, is obliged by law to violate the lesser law for the sake of the greater, common law of God. The preservation of life.

The King's Threshold

Three days ago ...
I listened to the outcry of my courtiers,
bishops, soldiers and makers of the law
who long had thought it against their dignity
for a mere man of words to sit among them
at the great council of state and share
in their authority.
Although I felt they had the right of it,
but when Sechran bade to speak,
I granted such indulgence.
But when he pleaded for his poet's right,
established at the establishment of the world
and that all men had equal right before god ...
I said that I was king
and that all rights were bestowed
by one king or other and
that it was for those of noble stature only
to sit at the great council of state
and to deal with the affairs of the world and,
not for those who sing to it.
I bade him go.
My courtiers, bishops, soldiers and makers of the law
shouted approval.
And amid the noise, Sechran went out.
And from that day to this, he has eaten nothing.
Refusing to eat or drink

that he may bring disgrace upon me.
For there is a custom,
an ancient and foolish custom,
that if a man be wronged,
or think that he be wronged and starve
upon another's threshold, and die,
then the common people, for all time to come,
shall raise a heavy cry against that threshold,
even though it be
The King's.

W.B. Yeats 'The King's Threshold'

So do your damnedest then. Kill me if you can. But they could not say now that it was my own choice or action. For it was now by their choice that I would be left to starve for 120 days. Dropping from fourteen to seven stone before the roof came off at Peterhead and the system in chaos, before they would allow access to food from my family. They would have been accountable for their actions before a court of law had I died.

I was simply showing that, as it could not be reasonably expected that my family travel to Peterhead each day from Glasgow to feed me and sustain my health, neither could it be expected that my lawyer could so traverse those 200 odd miles to take confidential instruction on those cases pending and while all correspondence was strictly censored. Neither was there a phone.

Communications was the key. As essential to me as food to my belly, air to my lungs. Without it, I cannot defend myself and will remain buried alive in concrete for ever . . .

After that time, the Press would always talk about me breaking a hunger strike after so many days or whatever. They never could seem to understand that I was no longer on hunger strike. I was a hostage. Innocent Imprisoned, under siege, Hungering for Justice in a fast for freedom. I have always refused to eat prison food to this day. Not missing much, I can tell you.

The Furies and the Fairies

Shanghai'd back in the dungeons of PeterHell. It's still freezing. The misty condensation from my breath gathers as ice on the walls. In the morning, when the light finally dawns, spreading patterns of bars and barbed wire around the walls. It could then be seen that the fair frost fairies had called secretly in the night to sprinkle those snowflake designs all over the walls. Wow! Colours Man! See how they sparkle so? So beautifully . . . Sitting there wrapped in a blanket shivering, forgetting the cold, mesmerised for hours in awe. The places they can take you in your mind, beyond the bounds of boundary, beyond the dreary drudgery of the digger. Beyond the limitations of mere words to tell . . . They cast their spell . . .

Back to life, back to reality. The hours of light are so few and far between and I must shake out of this hypnotic trance. Work to do, notes to take, points to make on the legalities. Sneezing, fingers freezing, no time for flights of fancy in 'If only' dreaming. Scribbling down points on any old scraps of paper I can lay my hands on. The back of an envelope, more precious even than gold. I'm going to die here and I need to make some points, leave some trace, a silver thread through the labyrinths. Must let people know what they've done, what they do otherwise I may as well already be dead here, hungering for justice in a fast for freedom, under siege. Already buried alive here deep in the tombs of Hell Block. The cyclone roaring in its spiral rages, battering the bars, howling round the cell like the demons of the damned arisen. Only the warmth of the storms raging like the furies in my soul responds. Let the battle for life commence and in our struggle blend till, once again, I am the storm. At one with the rage of Angels . . .

The 100th Day

As the flower in my heart my love unfolds its petals blue
Each morning as the sun comes up to gather diamond dew
Sweet teardrops, of angels, sustain my love for you
Through the snowy winter's wasteland on the weary
    winding way
My love reach out her caring hand to keep the storms at bay
Each tear she shed she fed me; and gave life to each new day
From sunshine in the morning, colours gold and gay
To starlight in the evening, forever and a day
My love is everlasting dear! beyond eternity.

Unfinito, no desire

TC Campbell on the 100th day without food

John Carroll stood as the shield against an administration which would have buried us alive in the closed coal mine shafts if they could have gotten away with it. His many legal actions in my defence entailed, for example, the hiring of a firm of solicitors to mount a surprise invasion of Peterhead prison to seize all relevant documentation pertaining to my various cases before the criminal, civil and European Court of Human Rights. With a warrant to enter the front gate, one lawyer had remained on guard there to ensure that no tip-offs could be transmitted by the prison staff to their colleagues beyond the first doors and the first layers of security. On through the system like this, leaving one man behind at each stage, directly into the governor's office and the rifling of his files.

Ian Lang was the Thatcherite Tartan Tory Minister for prisons at the time. Thus it was, from such seized documentation, that we were to uncover his directives to the prison governor on how my case should be dealt with. It transpires that, as my death from starvation . . . (Hungering for justice in a fast for freedom) would be a source of embarrassment to the administration should I die (isolated in solitary confinement) in prison, I was therefore to be removed to hospital when that time came, that the hospital was to sign the death certificate and not the prison doctor. It was not to be seen that I died in prison.

So! here was I on the one hand, having gone down to around seven stone and, having 'escaped' by one half of my body weight (under siege, hungering for justice in a fast for freedom) simply trying to enforce unimpeded and confidential access to communications facilities to conduct those criminal, civil and, human rights issues through the courts, whilst the administration, on the other hand, were discussing how to dispose of my body rather than let me speak freely. It seems that I was having even less of an effect or impact upon their collective conscience than I had, at the time, imagined.

John Carroll had full power of attorney over my legal affairs so that he might carry on with these cases on my behalf should I slip back into a coma or die. Exhausted, immobilised but accustomed to the pain, swamped in a sea of negatives, pending death sentence. Death is not only perceived as the inevitable norm, but as a blessing. I'd grown weary of waking up again, plugged into life support systems, only to be shanghai'd back to those dull grey dusty dungeons of dire despair and sensory deprivation. Conceding ground was not an option. It would lead to being buried alive in a granite tomb on the dark side of the moon for all eternity. Better to die in resistance than to concede a single day without struggle and protest. Roll on sweet oblivion.

So it was then that John Carroll had my last instructions to carry on with those cases and not to allow them to plug me into life support systems should I slip, once again, into coma. Just let me go. Let me take this struggle to the death if that was what it was going to take to bring about an enquiry. So, just let me be, forever free, blissful in oblivion, for I can see no peace for me, here on god's creation . . .

Yet awaken again I did. Plugged into mad beep-beeping computers.

'Oh naw! back to Hell Block we go,' I thought. JC reminding me that, with the power of attorney, it was left to his decision and, not mine. That he would never make the decision to let me die. And so the seasons go by, winter into spring. The rain and the pain yet still no birds sing. Into yet another summer of sweat in that box. Don't know which is worse, the heat or the cold. Shanghai'd in and out of hospitals all over the country. Who is this mystery man whom they smuggled in, and smuggled out again. The man in the Iron Mask and always back to Hell Block again, seasons in the rain . . .

It was the usual freezing winter's day in the cold harsh light of the living reality within the confines of my dingy dungeon. Curled up in a foetal position, swathed in a rough dark horsehair blanket, shivering beyond fatigue in the pits of Hell Block, sixty days and sixty nights into this particular siege.

The jingle of cell keys and the clunk of mufti armour alerts me to movement outside my steel door just before it clatters open. The mutant cockroaches in their armour part ways to allow the entrance of this strange little dwarf like character. Not quite yet fully bald, but what sparse spattering of hair remaining on top of his head sprung outward like so many threads of wayward loose wire from a snapped cable. The remaining hair around his ears hung straight in strands to the rumpled collar of his scurfy sports jacket. His flannel trousers were equally as rumpled, as if he had just rolled off the couch from a drunken stupor. He had pieces of toilet paper stuck to his face forehead and ear, as if he had cut himself shaving and this was intended to stem the blood flow. Yet no razor had touched that face in the past week. He had no teeth whatever and his chin almost touched his nose as he spluttered in speech, walking up to me there curled on my stone bed, pointing a grubby finger . . .

'See you, you're nothing but a bloody nuisance you,' he spluttered gummily. 'Any more trouble from you and I'll be sending you to the bloody cages.' His crooked finger shook as if in outrage.

I'd never seen this guy in my life before, had no clue as to who in god's name it could be. He appeared to me like some old wino dosser tipped out of the skip where he'd kipped for the night . . .

'Who the fuck are you? Ya fuckin heed case ye, comin in here pointin fingers and threatening me?' I tried to rise but the chill of the cell and hunger fatigue made this a slow motion like movement.

'Oh! so you take me as a threat to you do you eh? Yer PARANOID!' He pronounced the last word with emphasis, like a magician pulling a rabbit out of the proverbial hat. DA-RA . . .

'What the fuck are you babbling about, ya fuckin heed case ye?' I'd managed to get to a semi sitting position, 'Who the fuck are you anyway?' I said bemused.

'I'm Doctor Innes, the resident psychiatrist, and I'm here to assess your mental health and it's my opinion that you're paranoid and . . .'

'Don't give me your crap, mister, you just walk in that door and threaten me and noo ye say I'm paranoid? Aye well it's my opinion that your aff yer fuckin heed not me . . .' I was interrupted as he thrust his hands into his low slung jacket pockets to rattle around in plastic bottles of pills, thrusting his head forward with wide eyes staring and a wide smile. It appeared that I was supposed to be impressed and bow down to conformity at the promise of drugs.

'I can do you a lot of good,' he said, rattling at his bulging pockets. 'I can help . . .'

'Just get tae fuck out off here, ya fuckin maniac ye,' I said, laying back down and pulling the blanket back over my head until the door slammed shut again behind them.

Next time I seen this guy a couple of days later, I was dragged from my bed by the riot screws in the digger and half carried down to the governor's orderly room. There sat Dr Innes in the big throne chair behind the governor's desk. Chief Cormack and the principal officer at either side of him and the six mufti screws in full riot gear to escort me made an even ten men present in the room . . .

'I've been assigned to write a psychiatric report on you,' nodded Innes threateningly, as if to warn me that my life and very credibility were in his hands and I'd be wise to be impressed and defer to his superior position. I must say though, I was impressed that he seemed to have had his clothes pressed, had his teeth in and had had a shave. What least impressed me was that there was no seat for me and he seemed quite content with a room full of screws to listen in as they held me up by the elbows . . .

'So now you're here to assess the state of my mental

health – now, after exposure to long term isolation in solitary confinement – shouldn't you have done that before?'

'What does that have to do with anything?' he argued back irately.

'Well I think that it's well established that long term isolation in solitary confinement is detrimental to mental health.'

'And where exactly is that established?' he paused to make a reference note.

'I'm sure you'll find something about it in some medical journal somewhere . . . but hold on, are you here to interview me?'

'Yes! I'm . . .'

'Well, would you mind asking these people to leave?'

'I certainly will not.'

'I'm entitled to privacy and confidentiality in a psychiatric interview am I not?'

'No! You're a dangerous paranoid psychopath.'

'Is that your report assessment?'

'Yes.'

'Not much point to this then is there?'

'That's YOUR assessment. No one is forcing you to see me.'

'Is that right? I've just been dragged from my sick bed and carried down here to see you.'

'No one is forcing you to stay.'

'I'll be reporting this to the Medical Council,' said I as I turned to leave.

'Suit yourself,' he replied.

My next encounter with this guy was back in my cell some weeks later. This time he was alone and seemed to have opened the door with his own keys. I got the impression that he was playacting out some obscure role only known to himself but his tone was serious enough. He had a deal for me . . .

'My report will say that you are intelligent and sane – IF you withdraw your complaint of incompetence against me.'

'Why should I?'

'Well, not many people have a bona fide certificate of sanity and if I'm not competent to say so, then neither are the conclusions of my report.'

'Fine then,' the deal was struck and the record shows that I was thus rendered back among the land of the sane and fit to plead.

Hell Arisen
1986/87

The fog smelled strange, it was after 5 p.m. of a winter's weekend. This entailed that the entire population of Peterhead Prison would be locked down for the night, not merely those of us held 24/7 in Hell Block digger all the time anyway. Something was odd though. Something was up. Something different and out of the ordinary. Even the fog shrouding the black northern sky smelled strange. Then it struck me. The silence. No foghorns nor the usual high pitched whine. I wrote, 'I could see the fog whisp through the bars, almost as smoke would.' Smoke! that was it. It WAS smoke. The lack of any foghorn now triggered a new alarm of its own. Something somewhere nearby was ablaze.

POW POW POW! RATTA TA TATTED like a TV war movie and soon had me unravelling from my blanket to get up and go have a look see. I took it for granted that no one would be watching TV in this establishment.

Struggling wearily up onto my cardboard chair and table, I could see immediately that there was some part of the prison nearby ablaze. Something somewhere near the Cook House or the old Armoury which now housed the prison riot gear, gas bombs and so on. Soon, the sound of choking and banging doors alerted the screws to the danger. Prison cells became gas chambers. There are few things more scary and dangerous than a chamber filled with toxic fumes when there is no way out. The ghosts of the Doyle Family would testify to that.

Rather than let the prisoners out, the screws wasted time reassuring and telling prisoners to lie on the floor. Then the nightshift tried to tackle the blaze themselves. It was the Cookhouse roof lighting up the sky right enough. Now well ablaze as three screws in full riot gear struggled up onto an adjoining roof with a fully inflated fire hose. However, the weight of the water was too much for them and their comical antics the cause of some hysteria among the prisoners. (Only half of whom were upwind of the smoke.) The screws had tumbled off ladders, tripped ladders and generally fallen over each other in an attempt to get the hose onto the adjoining roof and, amid the general hilarity and helpful commentary from the prisoners . . .

'Phone the fuckin fire brigade you fuckin halfwits' and 'It's yer ladder that's upside doon ya dafty,' Until finally, after tying a rope round the neck of the nozzle, all three ascended the ladder and managed to haul the rope up onto the roof beside them, itself, by now, well ablaze. Give them their due, if raw courage put fires out then these guys would've been heroes. They stood their ground bravely clad only in their plastic riot gear and visors, using their plastic shields as if to ward off an enemy. They had not been informed that their gear was not fire proof and would melt and burn as fuel for any open flame. In fact, I think it possible that this ignorance contributed to the reason as to why controlling this blaze was attempted by untrained prison staff at all.

Nevertheless, the three stooges made their gallant stand. One standing at each side of the hose bearer guarding him with their shields as he adopted a fireman's stance, aiming the hose in the general direction of the fire ... and aiming the hose in the general direction of the fire ... again and again repeatedly. This guy was stuck on rewind or something. Tucking his elbows in, knees akimbo, as if the stance itself was enough to instruct the hose to do its thing. Still nothing happened.

'Turn the fuckin nozzle,' I shouted, lives were at stake here. He did so and a gush sprayed from the power hose sending its bearer shooting backwards off his feet as if on a jet ski, finally landing on his backside tumbling backwards while the hose escaped his grasp and struck back with a vengeance. Wrestling with the remaining two wardens swaying and weaving all over the roof as if in mortal combat with some giant mutant cobra. By now, half the prison population were at their windows in hysterics. The other half were laying on the floor screaming blue murder in yet another form of hysteria.

That half was down wind of the blaze, I among them, but I wouldn't have missed this for the world. Once again, The Roof Comes Off. While one half of the prison populace shouted their cynical advice, 'Put the bastard on report' and '3 to 1 the snake', the other half of the jail shouted advice that they should 'Turn the fuckin nozzle back aff ya halfwit ye' and 'Phone the fuckin fire brigade.'

Which they did, giving us the finger as they did so, but only after re-enacting the same pantomime again and again to the general abuse and hilarity from the prisoners. The fire brigade arrived in time for the third roof to have collapsed under billows of sparks and toxic fumes. The fire was out in a jiff, but the Cookhouse, Stores and General Armoury were long gone.

Over 100 prisoners reported ill at the next morning's sick parade. The effects of toxic smoke inhalation were noted on separate loose leaf pages. My own complaint was discarded offhandedly as the result of a smoker's cough. We called it the Peterheed Chernoble, as it was around that time and, oddly enough, prisoners were thereafter fed with extra daily rations of mutton dressed as lamb. Some still retain an afterglow of the memory.

Throughout this escapade, I had been writing a petition to the Scots Secretary and replying to the European Court, recording the entire incident blow for blow as it happened. I volunteered myself as a witness in any forthcoming enquiry but there never was one. Soon, fires were breaking out in Glasgow's Barlinnie and in Perth prison, reported in the news with hundreds hospitalised from the effects of toxic smoke inhalation. There never was any inquiry.

Slasher Gallacher

Riot upon riot ripped the Scottish prison system apart. It was getting heavier and heavier as tactics and counter tactics evolved. For as the prisoners were being power-hosed off the rooftops, skited slate and hostages would soon put a stop to that malarkey. PeterHell was exploding into violence on a regular basis. Finally being burned to a shell and rebuilt. Saughton was next. Perth went up a few times, as did Glenochil, Low Moss and the YOs in Dumfries and Longriggend. A system on its knees and in chaos.

I was back in Barlinnie when that exploded. Held in Sol Con next door to the death cell. Hungering for justice in a fast for freedom, under siege. I was surprised then when my door was opened and a gaggle of mufti half carried me out into the hall. Being quite weak from starvation, even though still able to stand on my feet with some effort, the scores more mutant cockroaches out in the hall to escort me out onto the main route, once an old farm road called Lee Avenue, now the centre of the prison march route, seemed a wee bit over the top . . .

Sammo the Bear was discontented. Although he had always been a bit of a rogue, he and the bold Jaimba fullah had been fitted up with false evidence for this particular series of robberies. Now serving an eight stretch, Sammo was built like a bear and growled like one with a toothache seeing it as his god given duty to make his time in prison as difficult as possible for the screws.

'Justice for the innocent imprisoned,' I heard the rebel yell. Looking up towards the towering rooftops I saw Sammo, war lance clutched in raised clenched fist. 'Justice for all,' he yelled in triumph at the sighting of me. Small triumph. I was just about collapsing under the weight of my own ribs stabbing into my lungs like talons, crushing me sharply in its grip.

'Justice for the Bear,' I gasped in a feeble attempt to respond in solidarity, leaning forward with hands on my knees for my own support, head spinning. They led me away.

'Nothin better happen to him, ya shower o bastards, or yous'll be gettin it next. Nae justice, nae peace,' his voice faded into the distance as Gallagher simply sneered. He was the top man. The Governor. Never tired of telling everyone that he was the number one governor of the Scottish prison system and the most senior governor in the whole of Europe. Once known as Square Go Gallagher from his days as governor of the young offenders institutions, he would take the troublesome youngsters and challenge them to his own particular brand of Square Go to establish who was the real Donner, the top dog, in his prison. Four screws would then form a square around the young prisoner, gripping his arms and shoulders while Gallagher beat the living daylights out of them. Later he became more commonly and publicly known as Slasher Gallagher when rooftop banners displayed his crimes to the world . . .

While governor of Peterhead prison, after doling out one of his Square Gos to a prisoner on report, the prisoner, Boaby Broady, had attacked him with a razor blade melted onto a toothbrush but had been disarmed by the screws. While they held him in restraints, Gallagher had slowly zig-zagged the blade down Boaby's face.

'Try and slash me, ya fuckin' bam, eh! I'm the fuckin' governor here.'

This is the man then who stood outside the hall in Barlinnie trying to negotiate with Sammo. Having conceded to Sammo's demand to see me and that I was okay, the incident should have ended there peacefully. But this is also the man who would participate in Sammo's severe beating. And this is the man who would go on to participate in the beating of my old friend Davie, who, in his turn, had demanded to see that Sammo was okay. This then is the man who sparked one of Scotland's most brutal and destructive riots. One that would end his career with his prison as a heap of rubble at his feet. The Governor, Slasher Gallagher, he always was a wee bit no well in the heed that yin.

And so, once again the roof comes off in style. As usual, the screws just abandoned their posts and bolted from the hall. Blankets were draped over the gallery railings to prevent the negotiators from seeing what moves were afoot. Negotiations broke down when Gallagher refused to give assurances that no further brutality would ensue. It was apparent to all that he took this situation as a golden opportunity to show the world, once and for all, how best to deal with this scum, ordering in the elite of his riot squads to charge at the first barricade on the second flat. They met with no resistance until the vanguard had assembled atop the first floor. Then, from above and from behind the blankets, massive slate slabs from the gallery floor dropped behind them onto the stairwell, totally demolishing and collapsing it, trapping them there in the heart of the chaos as bricks, boulders, iron beds and lockers rained down on their reinforcements below – who wisely beat a hasty retreat, isolating their elite advance guard who, by now, found themselves the focus of scores of mad masked prisoners screaming down on them with iron bars and home made knives. They also, wisely, beat a hasty retreat into the empty cells, locking themselves in, only to be heard whimpering in terror as the prisoners proceeded to dismantle the two foot thick walls to get at them. Their elite vanguard mufti squad now held captive as hostages, the real negotiations could begin as the very structure and fibre of the building, walls, floors, roof and stairwells were systematically dismantled and demolished to make ammo for the oncoming waves of riot screws who fell for the same simple tactic, time and time again. They would be allowed to advance so far before bombardment prevented their retreat, finally raising their hands in surrender as hostages. Eventually they simply refused to obey orders and Slasher Gallagher was relieved of duty, dragged away by the medics screaming insane blue murder.

The Do-Lally Dine-Ins
of D Hall

They had me in D Hall Barlinnie at the time. I was still on Cat-A-List and once again housed next door to the death cell on the ground floor. The Thatcherite armies were on the march with their campaigns to bring back hanging going to a vote in parliament. The gallows mechanism tested and oiled each Wednesday, I could hear the sand bags as they hit my cell wall on the drop. Obviously then, they didn't have the balance quite right yet. Allowing executed corpses to strike the wall on the swing would have been considered inhumane.

Another of the Thatcherite masterstroke policies was the so-called Care in the Community scheme. This, in effect, meant that those poor inadequate and senile souls under mental health care units were to be evicted out into the streets to cope for themselves. As patients, they would be entitled to total care but out in the streets they were quickly swept up again on vagrant and incapable charges, then dumped back into institutions only now as prisoners no longer entitled to any government benefits nor pensions nor support. Thereby, in one foul stroke, wiping billions off the social security and health budgets. Such was the ethos of the Thatcherite era that none would raise a whimper of protest on behalf of these weary old souls as the prison population almost tripled overnight.

They were banged up like sardines in a tin. Three and

four to a cell not legally big enough to house a single ape. Animal rights were making waves but human rights were yet the stuff of mythology here in fortress Britain.

Each morning they would all be seen tripping out of their cells shuffling in single file with two piss pots each, full to overflowing, to the slop out bin and back to their cells for the rest of the day like mindless zombies, never a whimper of protest. This would be the only time anyone would ever see the Dine-Ins.

This morning they were out of their traps before I could get out of mine and I was stuck in the throng of Do-Lally Dine-Ins. Someone had plonked a day's waste of crap, wrapped in newssheet to contain the stink throughout the night, down the slop out bin and choked it. The other Do-Lallies by the score had shuffled along the line duly emptying their own crap into the mess like so many automatons unaware that the assembly line had malfunctioned. Shit and urine was overflowing in floods all over the floor. They waded through it like old jungle warriors confronted with yet another river crossing, obediently dunking their own twenty-four hours of piss and shit onto the flooded floor.

One old guy takes a wobbly, starts shaking and just topples over like a fallen tree. The sound of his head cracking the stone floor was like a gunshot but nobody raised an eyebrow. Just another fallen comrade on the Burma Road it seemed. They all carried on in their automaton malfunction as if nothing at all had just happened. This old sojer was drowning face down and up to his ears in urine and they simply stepped over him and carried on regardless.

I got down on one knee and rolled him over onto his back. Placing my folded towel under his head I could see the gash on his skull wide open and smeared in shit. I could also see from the contortions of his facial expression that he was epileptic. I shouted to the Cat-A-List screw there with me to get the doctor as I used my toothbrush to prize his tongue out from the back of his throat to stop him choking.

'It's only an epileptic fit,' says the screw, afraid of leaving me on my own. 'Just leave him and he'll come out of it himself. He nodded wisely to himself that he knew about such things.

'Get the fuckin doctor, ya halfwit ye, he's fuckin choking to death,' I screamed back at him and he beat a hasty retreat to do as I said rather than confront my anger.

The PO arrived with the MO and the latter took charge of the toothbrush while the former took charge of the chaos. Ignoring me kneeling there in the shit with this old guy bleeding to death with a toothbrush protruding from his gullet, he turned to the nearest Do-Lally and barked, 'You! Aye you. Unblock that slop out bin.' This old sojer had just been issued a direct order from a commanding officer. He jumped rigidly to attention then without hesitation plunged his hand and arm deep, deep into the bin of stinking raw sewage and came out with the offending shit bomb, once tightly wrapped, but now sodden, disintegrating under the pressure of his fingers puncturing through the package. Shit up to his bicep he addressed the PO, 'Sur!' The PO nodded and the Do-Lally dropped the dripping package back into the slurping bin with an air of a job well done as I vomited all over the PO's bulled up boots.

Next time I seen this Do-Lally Dine-In he had been promoted to pass man. Still with his sodden, shitty-sleeved jacket on, he was doling out the half-cup measures of tea from the tea urn. This was a long, tubular insulated bin into which he would extend his sodden and dripping arm to scoop out a half-cup measure of dirt water jail tea for the line of prisoners whilst the screws looked on in great mirth . . .

'G'oan, ya shower o dirty bastards,' I shouted as I kicked the tea urn over, spilling its contents onto the floor. Tray by tray the breakfast followed the way of the tea before I wandered back to my cell with the Cat-A-List screw ever at my elbow. It was none of my business, I had my own tea bags and didn't eat their crap, but these old guys were war veterans and I felt that they deserved better treatment.

Next it was the phone. They had allowed pay phones to be brought in to the prisons in response to some of the riot demands. Only one £2 phone card per week, but it was better than nothing. Not for me, however, I was the one prisoner in the Scottish prison system expressly refused access to this new communications facility. Not that I was likely to pay any heed to that order of course. Fair's fair. One of the troops acquired a phone card for me and I strolled casually over to the phone. The Cat-A-List screw pounced, punching the riot bell as he did so. Wrestling about with me, trying to grab the phone receiver out of my grasp.

'Get the fuck affah me, ya fuckin idiot ye,' I told him but he wasn't for listening. Grabbing me in a head lock and trying to twist. 'Fuck this,' I thought duly removing him from my person and, as he stumbled across the floor, the mufti cockroaches in full riot gear were weighing in. They had been tipped off with regard to the possibility of just such an event and were waiting in the wings on stand by. While they clung to me, I just stood there and smashed the Perspex phone bobble to shrapnel with my fists, cutting my hands in the process. As they dragged me away backwards from the phone I put up no resistance until I felt the baton bounce repeatedly off my head from behind. With arms held straight out to either side, I simply first pushed backwards, causing the throng to resist that momentum, then using their resistance force forward, I pushed forward and spun as I did so, freeing my arms and myself from their grip. I could have done this at any time but hadn't until the baton struck. They had upped the ante not me. Fine! Y'want to go to town then? Let's go! That's what I'm good at.

As I spun free facing them now, seeing the shock and alarm on their faces *How the fuck did he do that?* I seen John Gallacher take a flying header and plant it right on the screw who had used the baton, disarming him of it at the same time. They both went down under a scurrying bundle of mutant cockroaches. I decked the nearest screw and took his riot baton. If they want to use weapons they should be prepared to have them used against them. Live by the sword and all that. This was my life's training. A lifetime of street fights had prepared me for just such situations.

Wee Rab Leslie was bobbing and weaving with a brush pole, holding his own. I seen the commander and went for him as the primary target. Tripping him to the floor and taking his baton, pinning him down with my foot, looking up, with him as hostage at my mercy and shouted,

FREEEEEZE

Wee Rab was pinned in a doorway with a rat bastard battering his riot baton into his stomach, bayonet style. The prisoners were all vaulting the gallery and charging down the stairs to weigh-in to the fight.

'Fuckin FREEZE I said,' said I, and everybody froze. The commander under my foot was saying, 'Ok! Ok! that's enough, do as he says now.' The rat on wee Rab scurried away. Exit, stage left. I put out my hand and took the old commander's and pulled him to his feet.

Handing him back his baton, I told him, 'You're too old for this gemme. Take it easy now, you'll end up with a heart attack.'

'Ha! look at you,' he said smiling, as if in some proud camaraderie. 'You look fearsome.' Sure enough, my shirt was in shreds, my long hair and beard dishevelled and I was spattered in blood. Like some wild castaway driven insane with madness glaring out of my eyes. I threw down the other baton and the screws parted as I walked alone towards my cell. I was only trying to phone my lawyer for fuck sake.

Wee Rab was the only one charged. But with myself and John G as witnesses, he was acquitted Not Guilty.

Much Ado about the Buddha Tree

(1987)

By mid '87 after a few more Shanghais I'd ended up in the new Wendy II isolation and segregation unit in Barlinnie, overlooking the old gatehouse. I had been 110 days under siege by then and I'd lost half my body weight, down to around seven stone when the news of the dire situation at home got through to my brother Lockey in China. I received a letter from him saying that he had found that wood carved Buddha from the Buddha tree I'd wanted and he was on his way home with it. I was just to stay alive till he got there with it and all would be well again.

There then followed a series of hurriedly written cards and letters describing the most fantastic of adventures and tales of daring do as he had hopped overland from country to country without any money and only his wits to guide him through various war zones, natural disaster areas, tempests and revolutions along the way in his race to reach me before I died.

Somewhere along the way his epic odyssey and struggle to survive and reach home became one, synonymous with my own struggle for survival against the forces of darkness. Lockey, on his impossible mission to deliver the sacred carving from the Buddha tree, and me, living on air until he could get there. And he got there on the 120th day. It had taken him just ten days to travel overland from China to Glasgow only to be halted by the dark forces of prison bureaucracy at the prison gate.

I'd been told of his arrival there yet time passed and still he did not appear at my bedside. What could be wrong? I enquired of the prison assistant governor then in charge, Much Ado by name. This ex-social worker disputed that I was due a visit that evening and, bit-by-bit, I had to go over proof that Lockey was indeed my brother. Bit-by-bit in proof that he had come all the way from China to see me. Bit-by-bit in proof that a special request had been duly made, noted and granted to see him. Much Ado, as per the nature of the beast, then made much ado of establishing his authority by allowing that the visit should proceed.

Meanwhile, at the gatehouse, Much Ado had already planted the seeds of chaos by asserting his authority with the order that Lockey was not to be allowed in. There remained disputes that Lockey had come from China at all for the fact that he did not have a sun tan.

'Fuck sake! The snow is six foot deep in China right now,' says Lockey, producing his passport. However, Much Ado had already left word that he was not to be allowed in before coming over to dispute with me. This led to some altercation at the gatehouse when Lockey refused to leave without seeing me. The screws had made the mistake of trying to remove him bodily only to discover that they were dealing with a martial artist when Lockey had landed the PO on his arse with a Glesca kiss.

'Aye! Pleased tae meet yeh, hope y'guessed ma name.'

With the polis on their way, and visiting times over, Lockey left with the promise to be back tomorrow.

Meanwhile, Much Ado was conceding to me that the visit was in fact valid but as he turned to leave my cell the Cat-A-List screw in charge of me blocked his exit.

'TC he's already ordered your brother to be ejected from the gate,' he told me.

'Whit!' I yelled, stumbling shakily from the bed. 'Ya dirty rat BASTARD, y'are.' They say I looked like some kind of mad biblical prophet around these times, with wild long hair and beard. I must have looked a scary sight as I thrust my face up close to his, wild eyed and glaring. In panic, he raised his right hand above his head, either to strike or to defend from an anticipated blow. It didn't mater which to me. Reflex and instinct took over, with adrenalin as fuel for the rising storm, I parried his right with my left and, as he ducked down, he came straight into my right uppercut to the jaw, landing square on the chin and sending his head shooting back up, dunting it off the cell wall. As he slid sideways semi conscious down the wall, I landed a few more left right combinations to the chin before he hit the floor.

I should never have been able to have done this and the power, which had surged from nowhere like a blast of psychic storm, passed as quickly as it had come. I staggered back, dizzy and gasping for air, blacking out. My legs gave way and I flopped exhausted onto the hospital cell bed.

Much Ado got up off the floor and charged like a raging bull with his head down, arms flailing, his left hand clutching a bunch of keys. I parried this weakly with my right, and he slashed me across the back of the hand from knuckle to wrist with his pen knife open on the ring. I grabbed at his hair where his head had struck my stomach area, stopping his withdrawal. Lifting his head by the hair I bit into his ear growling and shaking my head like a hungry wolf trying to tear his flesh off as he screamed.

The staff didn't come to his rescue. They were themselves preoccupied coping with the other prisoners who had decided to take this opportunity to vent their own frustrations with brush poles and anything else they could lay their hands on. Finally, it was my old friend, Davie C, then charged with the Barlinnie riot, who came to Much Ado's rescue. Before passing out, I noticed that the slash wound on my hand, though wide, had yet failed to bleed. The white cell walls were spattered and speckled with blood. A welcome addition to the decor. More so that it wasn't mine.

The psychiatrist's report stated that the incident which had occurred was due to my emaciated state. It had been a malfunction of the parathyroid gland which entailed that I could not be held responsible for my action at the time. A starving man has the instinct to eat and, apparently, nature provides carnivorous creatures with a last dash burst of energy by which it may catch its prey or die. At seven stone under weight I should not have been able to do what I did and, in the circumstances, could not be held responsible and no charge ensued. Lockey arrived with the wood carved Buddha the following day and, as he'd promised, all would be well.

Before taking to the rooftops, Davie had said that my peaceful protests were futile in this environment, 'If you want these bastards to see reason, take an eye. If you want them to listen to you, take an ear. It's the only thing they understand.' And he was right. Their jail left as a heap of rubble at their feet and their top governor broken in mind, body and spirit. They could not do enough to accommodate. The siege was broken and I was allowed access to my own food supplied by my family as per the rights of an untried prisoner. This also allowed privacy at visits and thus for the occasion for my daughter Cheree Anne to be conceived. She was born on 8/8/88, the same day as Princess Beatrice. Which only goes to show that, even without the silver spoon, from the most dire pits of darkest doom, a flower blooms . . .

'Yes, these wars go on all around us in dimensions which you may, pray god, never come to know. Each flower, each leaf, each dewdrop, blossoms from the blood that flows.'

After a few more shanghais I was transferred to Shotts from Glasgow Sheriff Court where I'd appeared as a witness for wee Rab Leslie regarding the incident over the phone access.

Half Wit House

Shotts was billed as Scotland's new model prison, the answer to her troubled times. Still, it was a modern shithole and would have its own series of serious riots and troubled times. Though for a while, it looked like I wasn't going to get seeing any part of it.

'This is an absolute scandal,' the police inspector was saying to the PO. 'I have never heard of anything like this in all of my time. A life-serving prisoner with nowhere to go?'

'Aye, but it's no just any prisoner,' reminded the PO.

'Nevertheless . . .' We were sitting in the Cat-A-List van, stranded in the car park outside Shotts prison main gate. Locked out. The prison had refused to let me past their gate. There were six prison officers with me together with the full entourage of police cars, vans and motorbike outrider escort as was customary for an Cat-A-List in transit.

They'd phoned round all the prisons. Peterhead, Aberdeen, Edinburgh, Glenochil, Perth, Barlinnie. They had all refused to take me into those prisons. I had, indeed, nowhere to go except home. The inspector started figuring out a solution.

'There's such and such a mental hospital over there. Such and such a police station over there,' and set about trying to get me into one of those for the night. It had been four hours of this to no avail until the governor opened up three-way negotiations. The police inspector representing me, The governor representing Shotts prison and the Scottish Office on the other side.

I don't know what the governor got other than a peace pact with me but what I got was 1) Removed from the Cat-A-List 2) Use of the phone 3) A minimum of three two hour visits per week 4) Food supplied by my family as per the rights of an untried prisoner and 5) To wear my own clothing.

Finally they let me in. It wasn't much of a deal but they wouldn't accept my first choice – just to send me home. I was taken to E Hall, then a prison within a prison, opened up in the wake of the riots to house disruptive prisoners . . . who me?

They called it the Half Way House. I called it the Half Wit House because it seemed like some kind of weird lab-rat-trap experiment to me. The cells had this panel of buttons on the wall. Press the green one for this and the blue one to talk to the screw over the intercom. Press the red one and turn it twice like a screw to have the lock on your door electronically released. Provided that no other door was opened, you then had seven minutes in the corridor, sectioned off by a grilled steel gate at one end. You could then use the toilet or get hot water from the geyser to make tea. Back again and press the button turning it twice to lock yourself in and allow the next prisoner out for his ablutions. Whit! From dank and dismal dungeons to high tech hell. Nae Danger! It's bad enough having these screws lock me up with without them getting me to do it for them. I mean! What are they getting paid for anyway? Aye, but that would mean that no one else got out of their cell to use the toilet because of me. All my fault is it eh? This place was a maze of stupid little mind games designed to turn prisoner against prisoner instead of the screws. Aye right, Einstein, whit next?

Like, if you insist on having your visit then there is no staff to take the exercise hour. So? Fine then, we'll just have our exercise later. As for the door lark? Christ, I've been locked in solitary for over four years. Have I not learned a thing or two on ingenuity? I simply didn't use the system because as an innocent imprisoned there was no way they were getting me to lock myself up. I just invented my own plumbing system. A cardboard tube on a string hanging out of my cell window which worked just fine as a urinal. Amazing how it helped the grass to grow outside my window and those big mad looking mutant red daises too.

'Hey TC how the fuck have you got all that gairden an' floors oot there and we've got fuck all?'

'Aye well! You'll reap where you sow,' I'd say.

It was from this loony bin then that the torture trial started at Edinburgh High Court. All the screws and more from the assault trial gave their evidence again this time having to admit that they were team handed. Otherwise they stuck to the same script as in that case. That they had come to the door to tell me that my visit was cancelled and I had attacked. No one could explain why there had been so many of them but all ventured their theories as to how I may have come across such multiple and brutal injuries. I may have fallen on the bucket? I may have bumped into the corner of the bed? I may have suffered appendicitis? But no way did anyone of them strike a blow. They even denied having given a different version with regard to the numbers involved at a previous trial. But each one of them could confirm that yes, I was a dangerous prisoner and a mass murderer. So much for the impartiality of the jury then. Wee Spike and a few others gave their evidence of how they had witnessed the whole thing through the spy-holes on their doors across the way. Others had merely heard the click clunks of the riot gear and batons, the thumps and dull dunts of bone on stone amid the curses, kicks, growls and screams of pain. Some, like wee Ronny had witnessed their assembly outside his door and had listened to the chatter of their strategy following upon Governor McBain's order to do me.

Their case tried to make out that the like of Spike were liars. Saying that the Judas Hole, as they called the spy-hole, had a hatch which needed to be lifted open from the outside and closed again automatically under the force of gravity upon release. This only led to further evidence of dirty protests where, prisoners living 'on the blanket' would smear their walls and doors with shit. This explained that the spy-holes were often jammed open rather than closed because the screws would have to clean out the cells with a stem generator and, over the years of protest, all the metal had rusted. The spy-holes were rusted in the open position. There was no doubt that at least two prisoners, Spike and Dougie, had seen it. They had written petitions to the Scots Secretary, giving details in complaint at the time. These men were in solitary confinement and could not have got their heads together to devise a story fitting so accurately and independent of mine.

However, having petitioned the Scots Secretary they also tipped off the defendant in this case – the Scots Secretary. There was then evidence that the doors of those particular cells were removed and replaced with new doors with spy-hole gravity hatch in full working order. The more they tried to discredit the witnesses as liars, the more proof came out of the truth and attempts at cover up.

When I took the stand, it was plain to me that the only tactic they had was to call me names – Mass Murderer, Ice Cream Killer and so on in an attempt to turn the jury against me and to sympathise with the screws. As if to say, this evil killer of six men, women and children of the one innocent family got what he deserved. At least this gave me the opening to protest my innocence to that crime. Though I doubt if anyone would have believed me without a fuller detailed explanation.

Still, it was ironic that I was making a complaint of attempted murder and torture against the Secretary of State as head of the Prison Department. The Crown, now in defence of the Scots Secretary, were trying to discredit me by calling me a mass murderer while, at the same time, the same Scots Secretary, Malcolm Rifkind MP QC, presently had my case for appeal against conviction under Section 263 under his review. If that is not a conflict of interest, I don't know what is.

The medical evidence left no doubt that my injuries could not have occurred accidentally but could only have been inflicted by a brutal and sustained attack. The doctors spoke of how the gut was made of sterner stuff than we might imagine. It was strong and resilient, able to shift aside from under the pressure of a blunt blow rather than a rupture. In fact, the only way to cause it to rupture by a blow was first to trap it into position so that it could not shift. One way to do this is illustrated in my own description to doctors as to what had happened to me at the time. The body held in a semi reclining position as the blows are struck, traps the gut and causes it to rupture off the spinal column. This is the only plausible explanation which can account for such injuries.

Of course, this would also account for the double fracture to the transverse arch, fracturing the spine in two places under the same impact. There was also the boot print on the patient's T shirt and the multiple bruising. The cuts in the wrists from strain on overly tight handcuffs. The patient's account of events was the only one which fitted with the facts of the physical, material, medical evidence. Stick that in your pipe and smoke it!

There was a sense of pride in me at Edinburgh Supreme Court, crisp and clean in my civvy clothes and carrying my wee brief case. The voice over the tannoy echoing through all those corridors, 'Thomas Campbell versus the Secretary of State. Court such and such,' and everyone would stop in their tracks and turn to watch me stride by, thronged by a gaggle of screws.

'Guilty.' The bastards were Guilty said the jury. Not quite in those words but to the same effect. They had upheld the full writ without amendment or deletion. This included attempted murder, serious assault to the danger of life, torture, attempted murder by overdose of amnesic drugs and failure to provide adequate medical care.

I felt no elation or triumph, just a sense of quiet satisfaction that at last some measure of justice was being done. They had upheld the writ in full and that was all I wanted. The award for damages in reparation and costs was an irrelevance. Though it worked out at around seven grand for me including interest and whatever the costs were, I had no idea and didn't care. Those bastards had done the dastardly damage on me and had tried to get out of it by poisoning the jury against me by slander and more lies. Their defence was as darkly evil as the evil deed done. To me, this merely typified the calibre of the low lives in established administration.

Needless to say, the Scots Secretary refused to refer my case under Section 263 to the appeal court, even despite Love's sworn affidavits in confession to perjury. The Scots Secretary's argument then being that it was what the witness said in court which counts, not what he has said out of it. Fine then! I'm sure wee Ronny will be happy to hear that news then eh! Seeing as he is held innocent imprisoned to the opposite effect. The case TC-V-UK at Strasbourg on the censorship issue was upheld however. And censorship came to a stop. I will stand to fight again. The bloody beat goes on.

Then it happened again. Something to do with the slave labour assembly lines in the workshops down in the main institution. Being an ultra modern jail, they had these ultra modern control techniques. Or so they thought. There was these invisible barriers across the sweat shops where one part of the assembly line was divided from the other. Those on the one side of the line had no business on the other and were not allowed to cross from one side of the floor to the other. But they forgot, once again, to include human nature into their calculations and one brother crossed the floor to speak to his younger sibling when he was promptly leapt upon by the screws. The other brother, as you would expect, waded in to his assistance. Someone punched the riot bell, the second mistake for the fact that it has an adverse reaction on the psyche of the prisoners. More screws arrived and waded in and, therefore, so did the rest of the prisoners. The screws simply abandoned the premises and left them to it. Shotts had just had its first riot. A few more serious would follow but, meantime, this led to the entire jail being held on emergency lock down.

Gaggles of mutant cockroaches in full body armour and shields patrolling the corridor cell sections. Six to open a door.

'Up against the wall! Up against the wall!' they would scream on opening the cell doors. Once the prisoner did this, 'Face the wall!' they would shout before charging in and pinning the guy there with their riot shields, grabbing both arms from each side of the shield and twisting them into arm locks. Twisting the guy onto his knees then down onto his face on the floor. Bending his legs up and sitting astride them, bending them into the small of his back.

This allowed that man then to take charge of the prisoner, from that position, still holding him in arm locks while the rest of the squad backs back out the door leaving the prisoner's lunch on the floor. This for every prisoner at every meal time.

It seems that now that they had their new jail and new riot gear to play with, they wanted to test them out and to train the staff in the use of them. Who better to practise on than real prisoners? Thirty guys rear up and 500 are treated like this. If you didn't 'Get up against the wall' when ordered, they simply didn't come into the cell and you didn't get your meal. Suits me fine, I won't eat their food anyway. Thus I avoided the daily routine of torture and a few others followed my example. Wee Denny and Tam M, for example, nearly died of starvation. Communications where down and the siege was back in force. My own food supply was stopped along with the visits and the phone.

After four weeks of this, I petitioned to the Scots Secretary protesting about this treatment and of being held in solitary confinement again. Four weeks later I received an answer saying, in effect, that I was lying. That the prison had only been locked down on an emergency for 'two days' before being returned to the usual routine. The other prisoners' reaction to the news, read aloud from my cell window, could only be expected. After all, this was eight weeks into a lock down for the entire prison population, being officially denied.

As time passed, their problem then became that they couldn't open the place up again without eruption into serious incident in retaliation. They'd turned their ultra new modern jail into a stewing hate factory. Even the screws were ripping with paranoia. For not all prisoners had succumbed meekly to the daily torture routine but had resisted with equal force. For these men, driven half crazy in fear and isolation, besides the usual brutality, breath control tactics were applied. Simply, while the other screws tied and held the prisoner in knots, one would be assigned to suffocate him, smothering any resistance by suppressing his air supply, and controlling the air intake while the man in charge of the squad would call out numbers for various locks and holds. Pressure on, air off. Indicating when to allow a breath and when to stifle it. What they had not realised was that, instead of intimidating the prisoners, this treatment was driving them insane and the governor now had a prison full of crazy wild eyed maniacs to cope with.

Each time even a few prisoners were opened up together, they formed a mob. Screws where being attacked and taken hostage. So what did they expect? Cowering mice? These were real people with real lives and feelings and human dignity that they were doing this to. Putting sacks over their heads as they beat, brutalised and terrorised with great gusto.

People. Not fuckin lab rats.

Brian

So the siege was fully back in place and, while the mutant cockroaches in full riot regalia were still tying people in knots each mealtime, I was honoured by a visit to my cell by the principal officer.

'We've had a call from the social work that your son Brian has been assaulted and is critically ill in the Royal Hospital for Sick Children,' he said handing me a phone number before slamming the door shut again.

'Whit!' This was obviously very serious and alarming news. Brian was only five years old. A delicate fragile child suffering from chronic asthma, bronchitis and eczema . . .

'Had been assaulted?' . . .

'Critically ill?' . . .

'Was in hospital?'

What? Where? Why? When? Who? How, in god's name, was he? Questions ricocheting around my head in chaotic panic. Still they wouldn't open up the door again while the routine torture sessions were still in progress.

As soon as the cell door was opened again, I hurried out and headed for the phone to contact the hospital at the number given. Phone held in my left hand and 50 pence in the other. I am suddenly seized in a stranglehold from behind while my wrist is being gripped firmly to stop me from dropping the 50p into the slot. I'm gripped by the hair and pulled backwards away from the phone. Still holding the handset, our backward motion is halted by the limited extension of the steel cable attached to the phone. Someone is twisting my right arm up my back and trying to mug me for my 50p. Others are trying to prise the phone from my grip as I'm saying, 'I'm only trying to phone the fuckin hospital for fuck sake,' guessing they were trying to stop me from phoning the police or Press about their torture sessions. I was just letting them know that I wasn't.

'You're not allowed to use the phone,' the PO was yelling at me, twisting my arm, trying to thieve my 50p. They are all over me now. Four taking grips and half a dozen more crowding us in. They cannot prise me loose from the phone and the PO tries to reason. 'Look! you've not to be allowed to use the phone. Governor's express orders,' he says. The governor then was no other than my old antagonist Chief Cormack from Hell Block. Seems he was still intent on getting the boot in whenever he could.

'But y'know the social work . . . er con . . . tac . . .' I was gasping now, choking with fear for the safety of my child. 'Mah! My son . . . how, how is mah . . . my son?'

'Aye! Aye! I know, but the social worker will see you sometime tomorrow, now just let go of the fuckin phone,' he demanded.

'Naw! not till I know how my son is . . . Here then, you do it then, you make the call for me,' I said opening my hand and letting the coin fall into his, but, still he would not agree to allow any call to go through. 'PLEASE! FOR GOD'S SAKE,' I pleaded, 'It's only a bloomin phone call and it's me paying for it. I need to know how my son is.' I was in tears now, my heart breaking in my fear. I was beginning to suspect that there was something that they didn't want me to know.

'Just take him,' growled the PO and I was slammed

face forward into the wall by the phone, now giving them the leeway to twist my left arm up my back too. I was still gripping the phone handset when my legs were pulled away from under me, held in the air now facing down with my weight on both arms up my back. The PO was doing their numbers thing, 'HOLD . . . On . . . Off,' as my oxygen intake was controlled. Finally, only half conscious, I let go of my grip on the handset and was bundled down the back stairwell to the silent cell dungeons below ground.

Both my wrists were sprained, both forearms cracked, both elbows with a double fracture but what the fuck did that matter? What the fuck did I care? The pain was irrelevant and nothing in comparison with the absolute terror and anguish I now felt for the plight of my child. My wee Brian-Pie. Assaulted? Critically ill?

'Ya BAASTAARDS,' I could have torn the heavens down into hell only for a weapon to fight back with and to give these bastards their just due.

I spent that day and all through the following night in vigilance and in prayer to god to spare the life of my son and to take me in his place. From deep, deep in hell, from the ultimate isolation of that dark and silent cell with no windows, 'I would pledge my very soul to eternal damnation if only you would spare my son.'

Here in this nightmare within a nightmare world, sometimes I cannot distinguish which of the nightmares is the real world and which is born of fear. Here in this nightmare, dark and silent cell, left alone to wrestle with demons of dread, wrath and fear in a violent and bloody war for possession of my mind and soul whilst the same reflects itself in the material world. Scarred, weary and battle worn. Lost and forlorn, screwed up, bitter and twisted. I am not left unscathed by each horrendous encounter.

The smouldering residues of each psychic onslaught hover over the dreamscape battlefields of my mind like mysterious mists of ghostly gun smoke hanging amid the ruins of shattered dreams. Mud blood and splintered bones of naked trees entangled in the lost souls of the broken dead. By the setting of the sun in winters coldly still, no one escapes unscathed here in the hate factories of hell. Shit Street Shotts.

Psychic Storm

Each day I die a thousand deaths
Transfixed in constant exposure to the blast of the
    psychic storm
What must I become?

Occasionally, like a lighthouse beam coming round
    upon a solid rock of
reason, jutting out from the churning chaotic sea of
    madness,
My bewildered brain sees reason
And
In that fleeting moment of sanity
I behold the futility of reliance upon personal subjective
    perceptions of
our (so-called) reality
A reality born of the persistent endurance of pain
Where that which once was viewed as unacceptable and
    unreasonable
Becomes the norm

To the castaway stranded upon the rock in the roar of
    the tempest
The extreme of their usual everyday event becomes
    taken for granted as
the norm –
As the drowning man and the straw . . .

Yet what of those forgotten souls swamped in waves of
   psychic storm?
Where shock waves of fear and rage alternate
Churning hot and cold throughout the battered and
   bewildered brain?
Drowning in negative waves of fear, outrage and pain

What straw for them?

In the darkness of their starless night
Painting pictures of their fear in flight
And in their anger
Courting the danger

What battles rage beyond this page
As the sea of pain in waves of blame
Churns, the mortal mind, asunder

Give me back my life or let it end

> Rip off from the *Book of Passing Thoughts*
> by TC Campbell

Next afternoon I was taken back to my cell to see the
social worker who told me that Brian remained critically
ill and in isolation. Other children who had witnessed
the assault had spoken of 'a man' approaching Brian
as he'd been building sand castles amid the builders'
renovation materials strewn on the street. The man had
asked Brian if his name was Campbell and, when Brian
had confirmed this, the man had then thrown a handful
of powdered cement lime into wee Brian's eyes before
walking away. Inhaling the lime had triggered an asthma
attack and Brian had slipped into a coma. Barely alive,
fighting for his life due to complications with treatment
allergies triggering bronchial attacks.

This was not a revenge attack against me and mine as most people seemed to think at the time. The Doyle family would have had no part in any such lowlife, cowardly evil. This was a warning to me. A reminder that I still had family exposed in the line of fire. But, someone had just made a big mistake. Brian recovered but, from that day to this, still has serious eye problems. It is expected that he will eventually go blind.

Too Much to Ask?

Meantime though, I was back from hospital and in stookies. Arms bound at right angles across my chest, I couldn't move them to my mouth to eat nor likewise to wipe my arse. Housed in the prison hospital wing, wearing only a dressing gown, my own food was allowed but I couldn't eat it. My Complan mix would be made in a tub for me fed through an IV tube as a straw. Prison officer tells me that he is assigned to brush my teeth and wipe my arse for me.

'Aye right! Fuck off' I told him, resolved to resolving my own problem. Of course, the problem was soon overcome by my usual ingenuity. Simply by gripping the toilet paper in my teeth, unrolling it out to the point where I could snap off a length with my foot, I could then delicately lay it along the length of the rim of the bath. Mounting the rim as a horse, I could then kind of limbo dance in a disco or sexual motion along the length of the paper leaving skid marks along the way as evidence of applied genius. All very well in theory but of course the paper would, more often than not, stick to my buttocks leaving me with the tail of the donkey to show that I wasn't so smart after all. I would then have to protrude the offending tail under the shower and leave my arse out to dry in the breeze.

Not funny when your bollloks are itchy and you are left to scratch them on the corner of a table like Baloo in Jungle Book . . . 'those bare necessities' or something.

Here is where you find out who your friends really are.
You can't quite reach that itch which is driving you crazy.
Tamby the Bear was the surgery pass man employed as
a cleaner there. Old friend and co-accused at my trial,
convicted on the perjured evidence of Mr Love – comrade
in arms and all that – still there was no way I could
persuade him to help me out. No matter how I pleaded
for a hand to scratch that itch, he would always find a
sudden need to be elsewhere. Give him his due though,
he did come up with the brilliant idea of removing the
swab head from the mop shaft and standing back at
a respectable distance, from the bottom of the bed, he
would apply the extended . . . eh . . . backscratcher to the
delicate parts while I gave directions to his probing, 'Right
a bit, up a bit. There! Right there! That's it. Aaaah!' while
his face turned eighty shades of scarlet and the screws
rolled about in hysterics. Who cares. An itch must be
scratched regardless of whatever rules of propriety and I
would always be eternally grateful for his heroic efforts.

It took me many, many months before I could straighten
my arms out again to do these simple things for myself.
I couldn't wipe my eyes nor my arse never mind write a
letter in petition complaint. This also helped me see Jesus
Christ in another light too. For besides the lethal pain he
endured, I could see that crucifixion must indeed be the
cruellest of tortures to inflict.

I was soon back in the Hall and back to the screaming
nightmares of the living reality of the Half Wit Hoose of
E Hall. Needless to say my own food supply was once
again cut off along with communications . . .

The Angels Came

I was, once again, under siege. Hungering for Justice in a fast for freedom. After another sixty days without food and as the last man left in the Half Wit Hoose, I was carted over to the main prison digger. On arrival, I was given the standard treatment. The wee scurrying rat from Barlinnie was in his element here. Promoted in charge of the digger and now I'm weak from starvation he would have his sweet revenge. Bringing in his mutant cockroaches to beat me up, strip me naked and tie me in knots. The cowardly rat took the astride position over my legs, bent up and back to my buttocks and sitting there, started to buck, rubbing his crutch on my bare arse in a sexual motion to the great hilarity of his masked and hooded gang. They took away my clothes but, they couldn't take away my dignity. They took away my law books but they couldn't take away my knowledge. They took away my writing paper and pens, but they could not take away my voice. They took away the last of my civvy tea bags and, by doing so took away my fluids but they could not take away my will to resist. Thus after sixty days without food, it was another ten days without fluids before the angels came . . .

Maybe I was already dead. I don't know. All I know is that I couldn't breathe and didn't care. I had no expectation of ever seeing another dawn. My throat was closed, stuck tight and I'd not the energy to struggle to open it anymore. Then the angels came . . .

I didn't see them but I could feel them all about me and could sense their presence very powerfully within the chamber. Sweet, sweet choruses of angel song lifting me, filling me with peace and joy. 'Swing low sweet chariot, coming for to carry me home'. This wasn't an underground chamber. I was awake and could see the flickering shadows of cloud across the moonlight on the digger walls. My lips were touched like a tender sweet kiss pouring peace, like fluid through my weary soul. Energising and relieving from pain. I am not a religious person and would not have expected this but that touch on me was like a blessing. Like I had just been blessed. Nor was I hallucinating, I was simply hearing a heavenly choir and its song was lifting my soul from the pits of hell. The sweet, sweet blessing on my lips spreading like liquid love washing away my pain in a wave of peace. The dry sticky mess that had been my gullet opened up to let the air flow freely and I had the power to breathe again.

As the vibrations of the choir slowly faded, I was left with the sure knowledge that I was alive and that I shouldn't have been. I, Thomas the Doubter, who always demands corroboration, was left without doubt that I was, in fact, charmed. But why? Why me? Why not just let me be? Now, what price life? What task now lay ahead for me? What challenges and hardship to endure? I lay awake many hours till I heard the screws coming back on shift before drifting into a coma and wakening up in Law Hospital in Carluke and yet another form of angels there.

Scunnered, Scuppered and Skedaddled

A Right Scunner
(1991)

Big Arthur Thompson wasn't pleased. Not that you'd notice from his gable-end phizog, unblinking stare or shag-ruined rumble of a voice. He trained young and trained well. 'Give fuck all away especially when there is fuckin somethin tae gie away.' But he wasn't too damned pleased at all.

Arthur was meant to be in control of the streets of Glasgow – had been for decades. If it moved then he got a cut. If it stopped moving it was by his orders. Fuck sake, the Press had even started calling him the Godfather. Now this. A young upstart and a cowardly grass were giving him headaches. What was a man to do?

His troubles had started at home. His oldest boy, Arthur junior, known as Fatboy in the media and worse on the streets, had turned to dealing smack. Not that that bothered the old yin too much. He'd always known it was a moving market and you had to keep up with the times. It was just that, well, Fatboy watched too many gangster movies and Old Arthur worried that the boy thought life was really like that. His youngest son, Billy, wasn't exactly a chip off the old block. More like the missing link. Soft, easily led, hanging around with kids much younger than himself, thinking the world owed him respect because he was his father's son. In truth Arthur wondered about that sometimes.

The Welsh brothers were still a pain in the arse. Their

vendetta had been going on for years but the bastards were just too thick to know when they were beaten. They'd come close to giving big Arthur some serious jail time and that was something he just did not do. Even Get Me Beltrami had to work hard to get him off the murder charges. But good old Joe had worked the legal magic again. The pits came when the car blew up under Arthur's arse. Fairly rattled him but killed his mother-in-law outright. Drove his wife close to the edge so it had. When she led that night time armed raid on the Welsh's house he thought she'd finally cracked. He'd always known she was gemme but that's not women's work. Mind she'd given the brothers something to think about even if she had gone to prison for it.

Now he'd been getting a little unforeseen assistance in the Welsh direction lately. Young local boy, Paul Ferris, had been settling a few scores of his own. Just a wee bloke but with a big grudge against the same crew. When Arthur had heard about young Ferris scalping that Welsh bastard out on the street – well he'd always had an eye for talent and signed him up straight off. And the boy had proven an asset. Whatever Ferris had been asked to do he did it. As a bagman he was impeccable – always getting the dough regardless of the debtor. When Fatboy was ripped off for £50,000 on that deal – well, they just set Paul Ferris after the team. Fuck sakes, he'd hounded the whole mob across the city. And that was the problem. You couldn't let the help get too big for their own boots. Trouble was the boy Ferris just wouldn't lie down. God knows Arthur had tried. But now wee Paul had left him, walked out and set up on his own. Ferris would need watching.

Tam Bagan was another one. Christ, he was nearly family. Him and his brothers and sisters had been brought up by one of the Thompson clan. You'd think he'd show more gratitude. Mind he was a dangerous fucker.

Arthur had known that all along. Tam was all black leather gloves and shoot you for the fun of it. Had done just that on two boys from Easterhouse over – now what was it again? Nothing much anyway. Bagan was offski too.

If Ferris and Bagan had moved on to other territories big Arthur wouldn't have worried so much. But they'd gone the same way – Barlanark direction. And that's where the grass came in. The Craw wasn't much of a fighter, much of a crook, much of a brain but he was licensed. The Licensee, special licence as granted by Strathclyde Police for services rendered and rendered again. The fucker was trading bodies as fast as he could in exchange for immunity. Every dick on the street knew that if they worked with The Craw the bogies weren't going to bother too much – unless it was your turn for being traded. Mind you, you didn't have to work with the man to be given up to the police.

Was a time, street players wouldn't go near a grass. In fact they'd take him out on principle. But times were changing. It was the drugs and the young crew and fuckers like The Craw earning a good living as a full time Judas. There was no order anymore. No code. It was going down the stank and fast.

The Craw was getting too big for his boots. Trouble was he didn't negotiate like other street players. Arthur always had a sense there was somebody else in the room – the Dark Force, The Craw's own squad of policemen. Arthur had traded with the police often enough before – you did didn't you. Fatboy had even given them Ferris but the little shite was too smart for their moves. It was just that it was The Craw's speciality and he'd built up the dough to get involved big style in ice cream vans, pubs, taxis, property – everything legitimate that turned a buck. He was playing big Arthur's game and was good at that, leastwise his wife had the brains and he had the grass's gob.

The media had gotten hold of this notion that there was this Barlanark Team running crime in the east end of Glasgow. They were meant to be a big mob and a threat to Thompson, the Godfather. According to the media the Barlanark Team was run by Ferris, Bagan and The Craw and had a list of notorious characters as fully paid up members. At one time they even suggested that Fatboy Thompson was going to take it over.

'Wee cunt couldnae buy his way intae his ain hoose,' was his father's estimation though others were less charitable.

This was the Caravel Cartel, named after The Craw's pub – though his name was never over the door. Ferris didn't trust The Craw and The Craw was terrified of Ferris. Everybody knew that Tam Bagan was unreliable though deadly. These people worked to their own small groups. The Ferris crew was lined up with Bobby Glover and Joe Hanlon. The Craw relied on his brother-in-law, Snadz, and others he hired though mainly the police he traded with. Bagan was a loose cannon and worked alone as a rocket. It was Ferris and The Craw that worried big Arthur Thompson.

Ferris had some old time morality and was attracting a large following. The boy used his tactical brain and wasn't shy of taking care of people – whatever that entailed. It was a deadly combination. The Craw was a rat who would buy and sell his granny under police protection. It was a venomous formula.

Big Arthur Thompson was a worried man. It was unusual for him. A right fucking scunner, so it was.

Ballad of Jinxed Jonah

Then running through all this there was that mad cunt Jonah. Junked up tae the eyeballs, sure enough, but he was a storm trooper of the old school. A brain in his head and good with a tool in his hand when called on to do the damage. Problem was that he was a wild card, would do his own thing and draw alliances with anybody who would stand against The Craw. Y'never knew whit that mad cunt would do next.

In the late 1960s Jonah McKenzie was a defector from the Shettleston Tigers. He'd joined forces with the Bar-L because they were more suited to his style. In his mid teens he'd linked up with The Craw, Snadz, DeDe and that crew on posse parties raiding the local shops for cash rather than the stupid profitless gang warfare of the Tigers. The problem then was, in those days, most of the commerce focused around Shettleston and it fell under the territorial bounds of the Tigers. Therefore, the Bar-L night raiders would have to keep a scout out for the Tigers as well as the polis. Hence how the commando style tactics of this crew would evolve.

Jonah the Jinx was good for this. Known in the area as a Tiger, he could come out into the open while the others hid in the shadows of the railway embankments and hedging, and could thus avoid confrontations. However, there came a point in time when his defection became known and his cover was blown more than he then realised. The word got about that, if you see Jonah, the Bar-L would likely be somewhere close by in the shadows.

They all travelled armed in those days. Every teenager with any sense at all did. The territorial bounds were strictly drawn and 'Trespassers will be maulicated' was the code of the street. Finally, one night Jonah was spotted out in the open and the cry went up for the Tigers to assemble. There then followed a running battle with the Bar-L running into assembling packs of Tigers cutting off the Bar-L's escape routes to home ground. The Bar-L finally made the strategic decision, with the greater body of Tigers at their back, to confront the lesser body up ahead blocking off their last escape route. They fanned out and made a desperate dash in the open, every man for himself, in a bid to break out and break through their deadly encirclement.

The Craw had gone down under a hail of thrown rocks and bottles. By the time he'd stumbled stunned and dazed back to his feet, the Tigers were on top of him and his crew were little more than dots on the horizon. The Craw's tea was oot. History in the making but for one outrageous feat of bravado. The bold Jonah fullah had turned back for him. Charging headlong into the pack of Tigers in a feeding frenzy with The Craw cowering in a heap at their feet.

The Tigers broke rank. This was the Jonah they knew and knew he was not to be messed with. They reformed their ranks around their erstwhile member, giving The Craw the space he needed to make his own desperate dash for his life. He didn't hesitate and abandoned Jonah in his place to face the armed mob on his own.

Jonah was half dead when they found him. Stabbed several times and with deep cuts all over his head and arms. Worst of all, he'd lost an eye. The bold Jonah fullah had saved The Craw but he could not then realise the price he would pay for this act of ravado.

By the 80s Jonah had fallen out with the Bar-L and conducted a one man 'Police Grass' smear campaign against The Craw, joining ranks with Tam Bagan and Arty Thompson of the infamous Blackhill Toi. In 1983 The Craw would attack Jonah with a Bowie knife, almost severing his hand from the wrist, crippling him. Jonah would retaliate with a wee crew from Easterhouse, stoving The Craw's skull in with a pick shaft, also crippling his hand with a blade while he lay unconscious.

'An eye for an eye and all that,' Jonah would beam proudly but it wouldn't end at that. Jonah was still stirring things up, causing a police investigation into The Craw's activities on polis corruption. They then participated in a mad duel of cars. Trying to ram each other off the road, popping shots off at high speed. Finally ending with The Craw overturned on a football field and the Jonah fullah scrunched up in a wreck with a bus. Something had to be done. Jonah was drawing too much attention down on The Craw's activities. It had to come to some conclusion and fast.

Eventually, Jonah and Young Arty were set up on a drug deal in Barlanark. It's said that this was made possible by Tam Bagan's defection to the Bar-L. Certainly he was part of the deal set up with The Craw's planning to entrap Jonah in the police raid which followed but young Arty was caught up in the web too and, wasn't too pleased. Conspiracies to murder The Craw abounded but both Arty and Jonah were sent down for a long time leaving Tam Bagan free to join ranks with the formations of the new Caravel Cartel, the old Bar-L.

Jonah was the first back on the street. Cars were blown up, shots popped off as the tit for tat resumed.

A hand grenade rolling across the floor of the crowded Caravel pub. Armed police raids, dozens of firearms found. Eventually, Joe Banana's Hanlon and The Craw caught up with Jonah, doling out a severe butchering. Jonah having lost one eye in saving The Craw from just such a butchering, The Craw took his other eye, leaving Jonah blind. Led out of hospital blind, The Craw and his crew butchered him again. Thus Jonah became the walking pincushion for the Caravel Cartel.

'Before I die,' he'd say, 'put a shotgun in my hand and point me in the right direction.' But he would never be granted that last wish. Jonah McKenzie would slip into a coma and die blind and unavenged.

Arty Fatboy Thompson would be shot dead on his first weekend home leave from prison. The responsibility would be placed on the Caravel Cartel connection. Paul Ferris and his crew, Bobby Glover and Joe Bananas would be blamed. With Ferris powerless in prison, the latter two were betrayed, set up, kidnapped and tortured for information before being found shot dead in a car on the day of young Arty's funeral. Paul Ferris would stand trial for the murder of young Arty. Tam Bagan would be blamed for numerous attempts upon the life of the father. Naw! auld Arthur wasn't too pleased with these turns of events. Only The Craw was walking away unscathed while reaping the profits of his fallen comrades. In the longest criminal trial in Scottish history, Paul Ferris would be acquitted of the murder of young Arty and an entire indictment of gun and gangsterism charges when it emerged that the principal prosecution witness was a police plant, Dennis Woodman, amongst a raft of other aliases. Dennis the Menace, previously exposed in England as a serial perverter of justice, verballing accused people with false overheard confessions, now shipped up from the borders and planted beside Paul to do the dastardly deed but was exposed for the liar that he was.

It didn't end there. Gangsterism is always the old, old story of deception and betrayal. Many more people would be shot and many more would die as the struggle for control of the lucrative drug industry spiralled outwards into and beyond central Scotland.

But this was not my world. This was life on the outside world in the naughty '90s.

The Nutcracker Suite

Picture yourself in a small room, say a six by ten foot closet. Strip it down to its bare floor and walls as if for redecoration. Let's say this closet is at the top of a tower block or deep in the basement and, having closed the door, leaving the key on the outside, you find that you cannot now get back out again.

Then picture tomorrow. Picture tomorrow in your mind. The places you would normally go, the people you would normally see, food you would maybe eat, things you would do. Picture the wife or loved ones that you would normally hold in your arms, your bedroom, living room, TV you maybe watch. Your garden, your car, your friends and neighbours. All just in the normal routine of a day and cancel them. Just cancel them all. They are out of this picture for tomorrow.

Then do the same for the following day. Right on through, one day at a time for the entire week. They are cancelled. Add the following week to that. Make it a month. For the next month these walls, ceiling and floor of this bare closet is all that you have and maybe all that you will ever have again.

Take that through to the next month. It's maybe Christmas or Easter, someone's birthday or wedding. No matter. Cancel all appointments for this year in fact. Each minute of each hour of each day, every day of the week, every week of the month through the year. Every year of the decade. The decade? No! This is only the first decade and you are here for all eternity. This is it, this is all. Zero, zilch, nada. Your life has gone the way of the dodo. Simply solid gone. Kaput.

If you can begin to grasp even a fraction of the enormity of this situation, if you could, even for a moment, understand it – only then may you begin to comprehend the psychological effect that this situation has upon the prisoners in solitary confinement who endure it every moment of every day of their living reality for years without end. And, of those who have committed no crime to deserve it? When everyone just says, 'Heard it.' Where no matter how much you scream, there is no one there to hear you. No one is listening . . .

Most of my eight years in prison had been spent like this, between solitary and isolation, in exactly that situation and in the knowledge that this nightmare is forever. This is for real, the pain of my vision the outrage I feel. Then picture that door opening say, after ten years or so. And although you cannot now leave, others may now come in and see you. Sit with you. You may now finish that redecoration programme that you started all those years ago. Eat, sleep and see whoever you like provided they want to see you. You can now reorganise your life but only within the confines of this box you are in. That then is the Special Unit.

The unit was more like being confined to your own tenement building during the day and locked into your single end at night. When visitors called by any time of the day, it was for the prisoner to look after and cater for them himself. Tea, coffee and buns, or even with a meal to surprise them with after a long non-stop journey. Visitors would sometimes bring groceries or we could buy them ourselves from the shop at the bottom of the road just by making out a list with the cash.

Each Sunday I would cook everyone a huge Scots breakfast. Tottie scones or waffles, beans or plum tomatoes, square, round, link, beef, pork or soya sausage (or one of each), black pudding or haggis, bacon or beef ham, fried, poached, grilled, or scrambled egg with or without cheese. Very soon people began to realise that a Sunday morn was a good time to visit. Some dropping in from an all-nighter on the town for a breakfast at this most exclusive diner in town.

Very often we would get groups of visitors from universities all over the world. Criminology, psychology, sociology, zoology and ecology as well as law students and a variety of others of the ilk. These were all great people to meet with, talk to and show around. Very often I would be taken for the resident social worker whom they would take aside and enquire whether it would be safe for their students to mix with killers without any guards present. My reassurance that it would be fine and not to worry because I'd be there too, was always greeted with a sigh of relief. Some even took me as the resident psychiatrist and the regular visitor would get a laugh at this. Calling me the kindergarden con as they left their kids with mine for art class.

It was from this environment then that the Glasgow Two campaign for justice found voice. Developing into a properly constituted campaign with executive members of its board of the campaign committee. Chairman, press officer and so on. Printing out campaign committee releases for the Press, posters, flyers, statements of facts. Organising a counter propaganda campaign against the negative misinformation on the case to that point. For the first time we were able and in a position to answer back.

Arrival at the Special Unit in Barlinnie was a shock. More so initially that I'd arrived there at all. Made famous as the Nutcracker Suite from the early 1970s when it opened to house the like of Jimmy Boyle (*Pain of Confinement, Sense of Freedom*) Larry Winters (*Silent Scream*), Hugh Collins (*Walking Away*) and many more of Scotland's toughest nuts to crack.

Holding ten cells and two old arch type toilets on two levels, exactly the same open gallery design as the rest of the main zoo, this place was as old as the United States. A laundry room, kitchen, gym, and recreation rooms had transformed its old reception area. Utilising the Dog Boxes as dry goods and veg stores. Originally built apart from the main prison to house female prisoners it was now an ideal site for a prison within a prison. What later became its exercise yard was in fact the graveyard for executed prisoners identifiable only by the coded numerals chiselled out around the stone perimeter walls. In fact, a graveyard for the execution of those now sentenced to an eternity of years of existence in prison. The living dead.

This place was forever scandalised in the Press for its so-called soft line approach on hardened criminals. The fact that prisoners were allowed to decorate their own tombs at their own expense and were allowed the like of televisions if their families could afford to provide them. Such things were totally unheard of anywhere else in the system before this place.

In reality, it was a much more difficult regime to cope with psychologically than the usual prison jungle beat. The fact is, that by incorporating the simple democratic principle into the regime, every other fundamental principle of a community spun off from that. No less responsibility and respect.

Any changes in the regime and general running order of the unit were decided by democratic vote at group meetings. Of course, every vote could be rigged for the fact that staff including psychiatrist Peter Whatmore, psychologist David Cook, social worker, chaplain as well as governor, deputy governor and screws, outnumbered the prisoners two to one. There were usually around seven prisoners there, nine by the time I arrived, leaving only one cell vacant as a work room. This meant that prisoners had to actively campaign to win staff over to their point of view or position. Gradually evolving changes to the regime and earning the right to all that was achieved in all areas. For most of the people there, no less the staff, democracy was a totally alien concept within a prison environment, the repercussions of which must first filter through to the psyche of those concerned before they can be understood and utilised to maximum benefit and effect. Thus, the Nutcracker Suite became a community where every prisoner was responsible and accountable for the actions and omissions of each other and would move to resolve disputes and problems festered over in too many years of solitary, up against the proverbial Floydian wall.

The experimental system worked and worked well beyond all expectations. Here were the prisoners policing themselves for the sake of the harmony of the greater community. Not only did it calm the raging furies, not only did it untangle the psychotic knots of the screwed up, bitter and twisted, making them easier to cope with – it went on to actually transform them into model citizens with respect for the system of society and its authorities. For the first time in a life of violent crime and rebellion for many. Here was where the most violent, rebellious and unrepentant recidivists were tamed. Not by the boot and baton, whip em flog em in dungeon chains brigade, but by mutual trust and respect for human dignity. It was not her beauty which tamed the savage beast, it was her tender loving care.

Yet, as the Talking Heads once said, 'How did I get here?' The screws at Barlinnie, not for the first time, had refused to allow me to pass their prison gate. It looked like the Special Unit was a no go for me. Still, I had been voted in and in I would go. The unit itself being like a submarine in secure dry dock, I would first have to pass through Barlinnie's unholy soil to reach it. So it looked like, outwith being parachuted in, that option was out. Finally, I was brought to the Special Unit in the back of a van, not as an admission prisoner to Barlinnie, but as a package delivered to the unit as a Special Delivery. The van drove right through the prison, reversing up to the back door of the unit so that I could step directly into it without actually placing a foot on Barlinnie soil.

What a rude awakening. My first impression was that I'd been conned. I'd expected to see a plush, new, ultra modern suite but the unit had been starved of funding under Thatcher for so long that the very fabric of the building was almost in ruin. Wood, rock and the general trash of ages were piled everywhere. Recyclable material which, having been brought in, couldn't get back out of the submarine. My cell was like the old condemned cell over in Do-Lally D Hall. Filthy and stinking. It had been used as a store for dumping any old trash when there had been no room to dump it anywhere else. Iron bars, barbed wire, steel door, stone walls and floor. Heaps of old wood and bags of cement like a brick yard storage hut. It hadn't been cleaned out for me.

It took the whole day just to empty the cell. By 9 p.m. the door would be locked over and, as I looked around the cell I realised there was nowhere to sit. No bed or chair, no blankets, pillow or mattress. No piss pot, cup, cutlery, or plate. No light bulb. Nothing, zilch, nada.

Enquiring with the screws was even more of a shock. They just shrugged with an expression which said, 'Why're you asking me?' There in fact were no such items provided to nor by this unit. It provided for itself. Looking around at the other cells – carpets, curtains, shelved, decorated with panelling or wallpaper, furnished with bed, couch, Hi-Fi and TV – I could only wonder 'what the fuck is going on here?' The unit itself was a midden yet the cells themselves were absolutely immaculate bachelor pads.

I spent a long cold first night The harsh reminders in flashback to Peterhead digger, PH SC of Hell Block where I'd come from. Once upon a time.

Of course it gives you the inspiration and incentive to activate those brain cells left so long dormant over the years of solitary confinement. A new slant on shock treatment. Everything you achieve here, you achieve for yourself and there are no limitations nor restrictions as to what you may achieve from within the confines of these walls. Starting from scratch then you are left to rebuild the damaged and decaying fragments of yourself. Rebuilding your head in the practical world like some kind of Zen and the art of practical application or something. Piece by piece the picture begins to fall back into place. Recalling and redeveloping those lost skills of communication and application in a positively encouraging environment. The renovation of your cell, for example, becomes like a reflection of the state of your mind. Every scratch, bruise, bump and drop of sweat has its significant memory and the lesson learned.

It doesn't end there. Hating the sight of this place as the filthy old tenement midden that it was, I went on to try to inspire the other prisoners to get involved in extending the rerenovation and redecoration outwalls throughout the fabric of the building. We resurrected Jimmy and Sara Boyle's Phoenix project in an attempt to raise the unit from the ashes. This would go beyond merely clearing up and dumping the trash and re-decorating. It entailed re-rebuilding in areas and stripping in others.

Ronnie Neeson's co-accused, Toe Elliot, the Little Emperor, had a particular talent in the organisation of social functions. Art exhibitions and concerts, so that the motivation was always there to create and not stagnate. While women and children were always around as much as anyone else, this has its humanising effect. Especially children. Their presence makes you keenly aware of the environment and of the safety and cleanliness aspect of the areas of where they play. To guard your language and behaviour.

Of course there are always flies in the ointment. Some of the staff did not like, and couldn't handle the ultimate loss of control over the prisoners in their custody. One was the principal prison officer (PO). A loyal Orange Ulsterman we called Irish Jerry because we knew he didn't like it. There had been a particular decision of a group meeting which had gone to the full community meeting because it had entailed a fundamental change in the running of the unit and thus had to be ratified, amended or rejected by a full community vote. It had been ratified, almost unanimously, but with one exception. Irish Jerry.

The issue had concerned visitors and the question of whether they should be allowed entry into the unit to visit if they were, in any way, intoxicated by alcohol. The final decision of the community being that they should in fact be allowed in but only to the admission area where they would be sat down with the prisoner and staff. Given a cup of coffee and a talking to, they would be told that their condition was not acceptable and given the warning that any recurrence of this behaviour might result in them being refused entry and could well result in them being barred as a visitor entirely. In effect, they would be sobered up a bit before being sent home in a taxi at the prisoner's expense rather than just turned back into the street.

Billy Ballantyne was a lifer. His victim had bled to death after a drunken street brawl which Bally himself couldn't remember. About ten years or so into his sentence it had transpired that he could not in fact remember because he had been lying in a drunken stupor when the murder had been committed by his so-called friends who, in the knowledge of his blackout, had conspired to pin the blame on him. They had accepted a deal to cooperate as witnesses for the prosecution against him for their own immunity. Yet by the time they had finally confessed to this, it was already too late for the Bold Bally fullah. He had then served around ten years with about another twenty or so years on top for a series of riots and roof top protests.

Bally had serious problems getting his head around this turn of events in his tragic life. He had serious problems coping with the mountain of years on top of him. Serious problems of depression and bouts of psychosis as a result of too many years in solitary confinement. Incarcerated incommunicado. As result, he was volatile and closely guarded by the prisoners around him. One time he had taken a long running slam at the unit's outer steel door with his head. Knocking himself unconscious. He was fearless with a total disregard for pain. Of course, he was treated with sympathy and with gentle persuasion to good reason. This guy had given up on ever being free. He would actually have preferred the old jungle beat of the old regime so that he could then have this community responsibility lifted and fight the good fight in rebellion to the death. It was only this responsibility holding him in check.

He was definitely the wrong person for Irish Jerry to pick on. Or perhaps the right person for the purpose intended. For, from his perspective, who better to single out if you want to cause an incident and by so doing, discredit the unit regime once and for all by causing murder and, thus to snatch back totalitarian control.

Irish Jerry ordered that Bally's wife and children, regular visitors to the unit, be turned away at the gatehouse because of a drunken friend tagging along. Everyone knew that there would be a good chance that this might trigger a psychotic episode with Bally and that he would assume he was being singled out for a fuck about. That he would be only too pleased at the betrayal of the community by Irish Jerry and take up the challenge of confrontation head on if that was what was on offer.

To defuse the situation I called a meeting to have this issue reasoned out. We all knew that Irish Jerry was in the wrong. The minutes of the community vote were cited against Irish Jerry's demands that, 'No drunkards would be allowed entry on my shift.' But what about the wife and children? They hadn't been drunk.

The minutes of the community meeting were brought in and Irish Jerry read them out but there was something wrong. According to him, it had been his views which had been accepted and ratified as the final decision of the community.

Snatching the minutes out of his hand I was astounded to discover that there was a blue ink line scoring out the relevant typed lines of the final decision and, above that, it had been reversed in blue hand writing, 'To be turned away at the gate and barred.' Whit?

'Who wrote this?' I enquired. Irish Jerry had to admit that he had just done this when a meeting was called.

He argued adamantly that he was entitled to do this as it was he who was in charge here and not the community. His manner was demanding, totalitarian, aggressive. The exact recipe required to trigger an aggressive reaction from everybody else. He was spoiling for a fight, that much at least was obvious.

While Bally quietly wandered off in the direction of the kitchen unnoticed in the heat of the debate, slipping a fourteen-inch butcher's knife up his sleeve and casually strolling back. Keeping himself within close proximity of Irish Jerry but not taking part in the debate. I knew that he knew that Irish Jerry was trying to bait him. I also knew that Irish Jerry didn't know that Bally was aware of his strategy and was taking the attitude that if this bastard wanted to play games with him then he would duly oblige with fourteen inches of cold steel more than he had reckoned for. Daft Jerry hadn't yet realised that the incident that he was bucking for would kick off with him as the primary target in a blood bath.

Irish Jerry was on his feet, calling me names now, thrusting his face into mine. This was no longer a debate, this was a full blown flaming argument and, in turn, I duly obliged. Head to head now as we were pulled apart. Bally stuck like glue by Jerry's side, looking into my eyes, smiling and nodding his head slowly. He was saying silently, 'Just give me the nod, and it's no problem, honest!' Couldn't anyone else see that he was too calm? Couldn't anyone else see that he had a fourteen-inch butcher's knife up his sleeve and that he was zeroing in on Irish Jerry? That fucking idiot still hadn't tippled that I was trying to win the argument against him to save his life.

Then, right in the heat of this chaos, in walks my wife Liz with our little daughter Cheree Anne. Instantly recognising the rage in me, she hurries over and just plonks the wean into my arms. Stopping me and shutting me up dead in my tracks. The room fell suddenly silent as in walked Bally's wife Marie and the kids. Bally did a quick body swerve back to the kitchen area where he returned the blade to its proper place rather than in Irish Jerry's gullet.

The incident had been averted by community strategy. Marie, as part of the community, had been turned away at the gate. She had instantly recognised Irish Jerry's hand in this and had lingered outside until Liz had arrived and had about turned coming back in with her. On the other hand, the staff, also part of the community, had also recognised Irish Jerry's strategy and had gone down and brought in the visitors rather than confront a superior officer. They had realised that only the appearance of the visitors could defuse this situation and they had been quick to act.

Bally later admitted what had been his intention and had added the remark, 'Well, I may as well be doing a lifer for something,' but swore that he would only have produced the blade if any of the staff had drawn their batons. Well that was some improvement at least I suppose. You must take into account that this was the reason that Bally was there in the first instance. He was bordering on madness.

Yet there was no other place in the prison system where such an incident could have occurred and, in no other place could such an incident have been averted in the way that it was. For in no other place could the visitors have just walked right into the middle of it. Such were the dynamics of the place that people were pushed to their limits and beyond that they might then learn their breaking points and reactions and be forced to deal with them. No less so for the staff.

Sadly, Bally passed away soon afterwards. He died in his bed of heart failure. This was as a result of long-term heart disease which no one knew he suffered from. The

Press had a field day when Irish Jerry leaked his black propaganda that Bally had died of a drug overdose. All just part of his own campaign to stamp out democracy once and for all and to put himself back into totalitarian control. He would soon have his way when the Special Unit was closed down and he was promoted to governor. But in the meantime, the beat goes on and the campaign for justice, freedom and equality would have its day.

Changing Times
(Early 1990s)

Journalism is merely the posh word for scandal mongering. Journalists then are but scandalmongers. The word NEWS itself comes from the old public bulletin boards pinned up in the town square. The progress of the various wars from the North, East, West and South of the troubled land. Noting the advance or retreat of which army from where thus was of critical interest to the public for the fact that they had to know whether they were in the line of advance, and whether they were in the line of slaughter, or liable to fall under siege. Not a lot to do with scandalmongering . . . who's fucking the princess at the mayor's ball, exclusive in the private journals of Lady Muck, is more to do with the social rumour mills than with the essential facts.

Like the old busybody over the garden fence or the talk of the steamy – journalists too have their personal points of view, perspectives and prejudices. They swear no solemn oath to accuracy. Adding an emphasis or slant, propagating what they believe, or want to believe, or want you to believe is true is only human after all. Yet, rumour mongering for the propagation of personal perspective and opinion onto a wider scale is, in fact, propaganda whereby someone has the power to spread the word on the 'Authorised Version', be it that of King James, Pope this yin or that, William of Orange or the Koran. You'd better believe it. It's gospel. Swear to god, I seen it carved out on tabloids of stone. The ten commandments of I, Prince Buster.

Back in 1984, the Murdochs and Maxwells reigned supreme. Their tabloids had it all their own way and plenty of it under Thatcherism. Propaganda gone haywire and hardly a word of dissent. In Glasgow, the so-called ICE CREAM WARS were the source of creative sensationalism, a goldmine of journalists' dreams. For everybody's nightmare sells, sells, sells. Print and be damned . . . or be awarded journalistic accolades. Tales of gangsterism, conspiracy, mass murder and intrigue. The Yanks wouldn't have all the exclusives or all their own way with their Mafia stories. We'd have ours too. It's true, it has to be true, 'I seen it in the papers.'

Every tabloid racing to get one up on the story before and where better to get it than from the 'official' sources. The genuine and original 'Authorised Version' from the police themselves. Never mind the trial evidence, that's boring and doesn't work. Get the inside line from police sources. It's the best there is. All there is. After all, the subjects of the story are all locked up tighter than a drum, not allowed to talk to journalists as the rumour mill's conveyor belt trundles out the sensation towards glory.

Aye, well, that's journalism. I suppose it's a living but just a pity it reads as NEWS. The latest from the frontline kinda gets carried away with the story line as news is rewoven into propaganda . . .

If it is true, as Jesus says, that 'The truth will set you free' communications then are the key. To turn the propaganda one must first turn the key. Communicate, educate, propagate. The truth then, buried alive in Her Majesty's deepest darkest dungeons, has its own battles in struggle towards the light of the living reality. Communications are the key. Turn the key and let the truth set you free.

Between my fast protests, hungering for justice in a fast

for freedom and Wee Joe's audacious escapes from prison, crucified on the palace gates, we strove to communicate the one point. Simply that there was something wrong with the 'official line' and, somewhere over and through the clatter of the hot mechanical press in its churnings, people began to hear a penny drop and ask the question, 'Are these guys really serious? Do they really, maybe have something to say?' But more important, from the Special Unit, I was now in a position to say it. They had turned me loose from solitary confinement and, yes, I had something to say. *I Scream Justice* my Video Diary on BBC 2 was filmed from within the close confines of the prison. Whereas, Joe's Open Space Special, *Rotten to the Core*, telling the story of the case from Joe on the run, just about covered all perspectives. The BBC called it their ICE CREAM WARS WEEKEND transmitted back to back over two days. They broadcast William Love's first but not his last confession to perjury on television. Ending with Joe surrendering himself, this time upon the communications watch tower of Barlinnie prison in Glasgow after holding a press conference.

A third programme on STV's Scottish Report also featured Love's confession and told the story from Joe Granger's perspective. This featured Lisa Brownlee and Douglas Skelton as researchers and the authors of their recently published book on the case, *Frightener*, which title was based upon Love's assertion that he would never have thought to have used such a word if it had not been given to him by the police to tie in with their verbal evidence against me.

Our lawyer, John Carroll, with Lisa Brownlee and Douglas Skelton as independent witnesses, had secured yet another sworn confession to perjury from Love. This time, however, for the first time, he now confessed to having been the person responsible for firing a gun at an ice cream van and not, as he had testified in court, to merely having been the driver . . .

Times were changing. The public were beginning to see another perspective. The Press were coming around and the truth might yet set us free . . .

The Well Revisited
(The Govan Arms, 1993)

'They're at it so they are. They're aw at it aw the time.'

'Who's that then? Who's ittit noo?'

'They cunts, they fuckin coppers, ittit aw the time so they are. Hey! same again here, pal, an a packit a roasted eh . . .'

'Whit, zat you jist tippled?'

'Naw'm talkin aboot they two, TC annat wee Steely. Fuckin liberty that so it wiz.'

'Ye've changed yer tune?'

'Nah. D'ye see it oan the telly? A always knew there wiz somethin wrang there. Right ower the score so it wiz. They guys never even done it.'

'Aye neh'r they did but. A never seen it, wiz it any good?'

'Na'r wan oan the night again. Yeh want tae watch it so yeh should, yeh want tae see this guy TC, big mad beard an aw that, fuckin tryin tae light e's wee fuckin doot as e's talkin tae ye. Guy's bran new man . . .'

'Aye, A remember um, whit wiz . . .'

'Fuck sake aye! Yeh know'm don't yeh! Whit's eh like, man?'

'Fuckin big heid case. A told ye afore, done a power a debt that big yin. Jist goes right tae fuckin toon when ye start'm.'

'Aye well, ferr enough bit, dae yeh hink eh done it? A mean . . .'

'A told yeh, naw! A've never believed aw that crap the polis spun . . .'

'Dae yeh hink e's still the same? A mean, he didnae seem like a nutter tae me when A watched it oan the telly, A mean . . .'

'Nae worse than you, ya fuckin bam ye. At least HE settled doon an aw that years ago. You've still no grew up . . .'

'Whit ye mean? A've no done any real damage for dunkies noo.'

'Naw, no efter they jist missed ye weh that high jump indictment a few year ago. Shook the shite right oot o yeh eh! Gie'd yeh a taste eh whit ye were in fur so it did.'

'Fuck, man! That wiz aboot six stretch ago, an that wee cunt diserved it.'

'Well ye'd maybe jist gettin oot aboot noo if ye'd a got done for it, an anyweh, e'never diserved whit you gave'm for fuck all so it wiz jist doon tae yer para so it wiz. You'n yer fuckin speed balls, man. The wee cunt done fuck all but look the wrang weh. Yeh were lucky there so ye wur.'

'Aye bit, fuck sake, fitted up, man. Magin fitted up like that? Nae cunt wid fuckin believe ye . . . A mean, it's fuckin skerry stuff man, who'd want tae fuckin believe ye? Then they try'n fuckin kill ye cos you'll no fuckin jist lie doon tae it. They fuckin screws, man! Jist as well e's a fuckin hard cunt, that's aw A can say.'

'Whit else kin ye dae? Whit wid you dae? Wid you lie doon tae it?'

'Fuck that . . .'

Love's Affidavit

(1993)

'. . . Ha well! Ah can tell y' right now . . .' Love grins, beaming with pride '. . . A must've had a lot o hours in my day, eh! Like, A'm supposed to be in a pub in Duke Street with Tommy Campbell an all that. A'm supposed to be doin a robbery doon by the new Sheriff Court way with the lads . . . an A'm supposed to be in Garthamlock wi ma alibi . . . an all at the same time, eh! . . . Aye, well let me tell y'this . . . through all that time o the van gettin its windaes shot oot an all that carry on, Tommy Campbell never spoke two words t'me, no even wance. In all that time the man never even spoke wan word tae me . . . When that van got done, aye it was me. Me an another geezer A'm no gonny name. The guy was driving. We drove up and A drew oot a double barrel sawn aff shotgun an fired it at the ice cream van . . . A got back intae the car and we drove away, but as A've said afore, it was the wrang van. It was meant to be another Marchetti van. It was the wrang wan. It was meant to be Jimmy Mitchell's van that was fired at. A made a mistake. A thought it was Jimmy Mitchell's van. A mean naebidy was supposed to get hurt anyway, so like it was meant t'be Jimmy Mitchell's van but it turned oot tae be Fat Boy's Doyle's an this is why everybody jumped on the bandwagon as if it was Fat Boy that was the bad yin. If I'd seen anybody sittin in the front A widnae have fired b'cos A wuz'nae there to hurt anybidy, d'ye know whit A mean? A checked that there wasny anybidy in the front o the van. A couldn't see anybody b'cos the wee door to the back was shut o'er. A shot the van an got back in the car an drove t'wards Porchester Street. That's when A noticed that A'd done the wrang wan cos Jimmy Mitchell's van was actually sittin there on the corner as we came roon an A knew then it was the wrang van. That's how A knew it was the wrang van. That's when A tippled. Jimmy Mitchell's van was just sittin there . . .

'Aye but as far as it goes with me sayin the trial th'it was Tamby Gray that fired the gun. That's the way it was meant to happen. A was meant to say that it was him that done it. That was part o the deal, that he got nicked for that an the shotgun an' all that an, like he got banged up for it . . .

'A'm banged up in Barlinnie for the armed robbery an had just been refused bail. They took a crowd o us ower there to the Chief's office. We were all frae that area, to see the polis. A had nothin' to say. The next day was't see Norrie Walker (DCS) an' Mackillop (DI) came up an seen me in the Chief's office an like that's where they started talking tae me, started makin suggestions, what A should say an that, an that A shouldn't say this and like this is the way it happened an this is the way it's going tae be, an that A've got to make certain statements implicatin this yin and that yin, y'know what A mean? A was denying all knowledge of everythin, any knowledge of the shootin or any association with Tommy Campbell. They know A knew him but as far as they were concerned he was it, an fuck sake the suggestions they were makin . . . A wasn't involved in anything like that, A mean, A wasn't sayin that A was in a pub, the Netherfield, an these guys were all sittin roon tables discussin aboot lightin fires an pourin petrol through doors. It never happened. It was all put into my heed to say that. A don't think anythin A said

at the trial was the truth. Some o it might o been true but
the truth is that the truth wouldn't have implicated any a
thaim in anythin, except ma ain self. It was only the lies
that implicated other people . . .

'A was in for the robbery an by the time A went up for
that A was pinned to the statement. A was nailed to it.
The problem was that they had made me give it on oath
an A had sworn it in front o a sheriff. So if A backed oot
o't A was nicked for perjury. A made the statement an
A canny get oot o that wan noo can A? The prosecuting
fiscal was David Speirs an there was wan time A said A
wasn't going through w'it, no b'cos the deal, naw! It was
ucos A was scared o' what A was doin. A knew what A
was doin, d'ye know what A mean? A knew that A was
puttin big Tommy Campbell an Joe Steele an all that in
the jail, their ain hooses raided an getting turned o'er an
all that. They were going to the nick changed with murder
an all that carry on but that's when they started puttin
the pressure on me sayin, "Well if y' don't you've made
two police officers an that, you've said this an you've said
that, an all that. We'll nick you for all that." y' know?
But see, up at Barlinnie it was all matter of factly. A mean,
they spoke to me as if it was . . . as far as they were
concerned, they knew Tommy Campbell and Joe Steele,
an all the rest of them were guilty of this crime an that no
matter what nor how they done it, they were goin down
for it an that's just the way it was. That's the way it was
put to me. Like either A can cooperate with them an do
what they tell me to do an say, or A can go back to my
fuckin cell and end up gettin fifteen years up m'arse and
ma sister'll be charged with perjury. They believed that
they guys had done it an it was all o'er the papers that
they'd done it. Everybody believed it. They were sayin it
tae everybidy they spoke tae. A was told what to say, A
was told what to say in the statement an how tae say it.

Like the meetin in the Netherfield. Tommy Campbell's meant to have said all that? Fat Boy's gonny get it, an all that crap. But really at the end o the day, Fat Boy wasn't even important. He wasn't even that important enough to have come into any conversations in a pub. Andy Doyle didn't take any part in anythin, he never attacked anybidy. He wiznae . . . A mean, the guy only drove an ice cream van an probably got a tenner a night for it. A mean, he wasn't, he wasn't important enough for us to be sittin roon in a pub sayin Fat Boy's gonna get it an all that. He just wasn't that . . . He wasn't any kind of worry to anybidy like that, know what A mean? For anybidy tae say that . . . I don't think Tommy Campbell was even that interested . . . all that aboot frighteners an all that . . . This word Frightener right! A'd never heard it used in Glesca before that. A mean A wouldn't have expected tae hear somebidy turn roon an say "ach we'll just dae a frightener" . . . Where the fuck did thon word came fae? It was all made up anyway. A mean, as far as A can see it was the polis walkin in on him an like arrestin him an he's meant tae have said it was a frightener an all that an A'm suppose tae say he said it tae me so that it all ties in y'see? It was all just a carry on. Just wan big fit up o a case so it was . . .'

Free the Glasgow Two

Everybody knows TC. He's the serious one. The man you would look in on with a serious legal problem and the like. If he didn't know the answer, he'd look it up for you. A no nonsense type of guy but maybe a wee bit too serious.

The other half of the Glasgow Two is Joe Steele. The Myopic Mole, wee Joe, as he's better known, is the other side of the coin. Everybody seems to know wee Joe more fondly. Even the mention of his name provokes a smile. Easy going, witty and comical he is everybody's pal but don't ask him 'any of that legal stuff'. He'll tell you, 'Tommy does that.' He has no time for the abstract of principle or the rhetoric of what that may entail. Existing in the here and now his concerns are for the immediate material day.

If you ask TC why he never escaped to highlight their case as Joe had done he'll smile and say, 'Well they couldn't very well shoot wee Joe,' and it's true. This seems to sum up the difference in perceptions of the two. The police would, without hesitation, have shot TC on sight. Joe? They'd have given him his bus fare home. Why is that? There is no public perception that one is any more guilty, or innocent than the other.

In fact, Wee Joe escaped three times. Once to wave a banner in protestation of his innocence on the rooftops of his local housing estate while TC hungered for justice in a fast for freedom. It was the prison rooftop protesters who seized the news. Then once again, in a sensational public stunt, Wee Joe Superglued himself in a crucifix position to the palace gates in London, catapulting the dying campaign of the two onto the world stage. Within a week he was off again. 'Run, Joey, Joey run run, the cops are on your trail. Run Joey, Joey, run run, they're gonna take you back to jail.' How could it be that an alleged mass murderer on the run was applauded and supported by the public? Could it be that they knew something that the Crown did not? Or did they know it too? The police didn't seem too concerned either. Reassuring the public that he was not considered dangerous. So what the hell was going on here? Joe could go and in fact did go anywhere he wanted with impunity. As a celebrity, people wanted to say they had met him, had their picture taken with him, outside the prison gates or the Old Bailey and the like. He was never taken as any kind of threat to anyone.

Surrendering himself again in another splash of media hype. Scaling the communications watchtower at Barlinnie prison to hold a press conference live on the national TV news before being dragged back to jail, but wee Joe wasn't done yet.

Tried at Edinburgh High Court for three counts of attempting to evade the ends of justice by escaping from lawful custody he could get up to five years on each count. But first they would have to prove that he was detained under 'lawful custody' . . . exactly according to plan. But whose plan? Wee Joe was a fish out of water in a court of law. That half of the duo more in his element in that setting wasn't even called to court and, if he had any part in these escapades, it looked like a dumb and dead end plan, firing wee Joe in for another fifteen years just to make a point.

The first witness was called in proof of the lawfulness of the detention.

'Whose signature is on that document?' enquired the defence.

'What?'

'If you will address yourself to the last page of that document.'

'Yes.'

'Bottom of the page . . .'

'Yes.'

'Where it says signature . . .'

'Yes.'

'Do you see that?'

'Yes.'

'Whose signature is on that document?'

'Eh, there is eh, no signature.'

'No signature? Then it is not a lawful warrant at all then is it? It is just a piece of scrap paper is it not?'

'Eh, I eh . . .'

Wee Joe was acquitted. Not Guilty of evading the ends of justice by escaping from lawful custody because they could not prove that he was lawfully detained to begin with.

The nation thought it was hilarious. The national news showed flashes of Joe on the rooftops, on the palace gates and, on the watchtower while the newsreader, struggling to suppress a fit of giggles, announced, 'The High Court in Edinburgh found today that Joseph Steele had not in fact escaped from prison . . .'

The most daring and dramatic escape of all had just occurred right there before their very eyes. While wee Joe ambled easily with a grin he had trusted blindly in a leap of faith and, without hesitation or doubt, had taken it for granted that the safety net would be there to catch him. TC is that serious. He'll not tell you a lie. 'My name is Thomas,' he'll say, 'I require corroboration.'

'Where the fuck is he comin fae?' Joe retorts.

The Wills
of Justice Now

The Wills of Justice Now

While people in kangaroo suits pestered judges, the prison power supply went down at Shotts and Glenochil including the power to the electronic gates and security cameras. The Scottish Prison Information Network (Web SPIN) went down. Court buildings, bailiff and fine offices found their locks blocked by Superglue as did bank cash payout machines all over the country. As the Press sought out information and interviews with this new militant splinter group, operating under the name of JUSTICE NOW, the telephone contact number which they received responded with the simple recorded message, 'Glasgow Underground services . . . Which service do you require? Please press . . .'

Of course, I had no idea whatsoever who these people were. Whoever they were, I liked their style. Though I did hear a whisper of some link up between the Free Will Gray jury tampering case and the Cop the Clock case of Wullie Barbour, with the Glasgow Two Campaign. Perhaps then, it might be appropriate to explain who these people are . . .

Will Gray –
the Jury Tampering Case

Will and Marie Gray were at home watching TV with their daughter when trouble came through their door. Barging right into their ground floor semi without taking the time to knock. One of the uninvited guests was a friend together with his band of brothers and in-laws. Obviously in a hurry and alarmed, they had headed for Will and Marie's house as the nearest point of safe refuge from the gang of armed men in hot pursuit, brandishing knives and bats. It was thought that one was carrying a shotgun. The fleeing family themselves who were also carrying knives and baseball bats were not exactly, nor entirely, the innocent party to this affray. Will and Marie's house however was simply a convenient refuge from the chase.

The mob gathered its forces beyond the garden in the cul-de-sac chanting challenges and general abuse. Some members of the gang proceeded to demolish the two cars in the driveway with baseball bats. Marie, a frail and fragile woman, being the owner of one of the cars, dashed outside to confront the vandals, disarming one offender and proceeding to beat him about the head and body with his own offensive weapon and was herself instantly set upon by the mob.

Will was next to dart out of the front door in defence of Marie but, upon reaching the garden and realizing that he was bare footed and half naked and unarmed, stopped there in his tracks. The brothers Donahoe however, upon finally realising their duty, charged out past Will, yelling and waving their weapons, entering the affray in defence of Marie who, by this time, was staggering stunned and bleeding to the ground.

In the ensuing stramash, one of the brothers Donahoe battered one assailant with a baseball bat resulting in his death. The police arrived on the scene of the affray and Will was routinely arrested with the others and taken in for questioning. He was later arrested, together with his own brother and the Donahoes who had taken refuge in his home and charged with murder.

It soon emerged that this affray was but the latest in a long running vendetta in which the Donahoes were deeply embroiled. By the starting date of the trial, there were no less than ten accused of a variety of incidents of affray in a tit for tat vendetta stemming from an incident where the dead victim himself had been accused and acquitted of murder with a shotgun.

Approaching the close of the prosecution case, the Crown withdrew many charges against various accused, thus allowing half of them back out on bail pending the progress of the defence case. Five people – Will, Porky O'Rourke and two Donahoe brothers were still charged with the death – whilst another would later have that reduced to assault by the jury.

Unknown to Will and the court however, the bailed Donahoes had met up with and dated two female members of the jury. Had picked them up, wined and dined them and, although it was not known to the remaining accused at the time of the trial, illicit love affairs bloomed. It would emerge much later, during divorce proceedings against a female juror, that one of them had stayed overnight in the Donahoe family household, had met the mother and all the family at a party during the course of the trial and had a sexual affair with one of those bailed accused brothers yet on trial with Will.

It also later emerged that the foreman of the jury had passed a note to the trial judge complaining of the behaviour of certain female jurors but no action had been taken. It further emerged that jurors had visited the scene of the crime in their own time and outwith the evidence in court and had been able to provide further inside knowledge not given in evidence for examination in court. Cash was provided by the female jurors for the purchase of booze and the like for a party in the hotel during an overnight stay by the jury during their deliberations. All of which was ignored.

The trial judge, in his summing up, directed the jury that there was no evidence to say that Will Gray had struck any blow and that the only evidence was to the effect that the assailants had emerged armed from his door as he had stood, bare footed, half naked and looking confused in the garden. Will Gray was also identified as having shouted, 'That's enough Porky.' On this evidence, Will was convicted along with Porky O'Rouke with murder. The jury returned verdicts of the lesser charge of culpable homicide against two Donahoe brothers and reduced the charge to assault against a third.

It was an ex Scottish crime squad officer, George Thompson, then working as a private detective, who first uncovered the evidence of this affair and more. However, although he could speak with the parties concerned in relation to pending divorce proceedings against a female juror, the Contempt of Court and Juries Act prevented him from interviewing any jury member, as a member of a jury in relation to the proceedings and deliberations in Will Gray and Porky's case. This statute prevented any further enquiry in that area and any of those known facts from being fully investigated as grounds for appeal in that case resulting in the appeals against miscarriage of justice being dismissed without further ado and enquiry.

By July 2001, the Scottish Criminal Cases Review Commission had referred the issue of contempt of court to the High Court of Justiciary seeking a ruling as to whether they would in fact be allowed to interview jury members in these circumstances and in the normal course of their enquiries. For whilst it remained unlawful to speak to jurors with regard to the circumstances of the case, it would remain impossible to investigate any misconduct on the part of any juror or co-accused in the case.

The High Court ruled upon the exactitude of the meaning and parameters of the word 'deliberations' opining that word to refer to the point in time where the jury are set to deliberate a verdict at the close of evidence and that it was on this that they could not be questioned. Any other point in place or time, during the trial or at the hotel, prior to their sitting to reach a verdict, could be subject to enquiry by the Commission.

That enquiry is presently underway whilst Will and Porky await news on the progress.

Cop the Clock –
the Wullie Barbour Case

Wullie Barbour was the only one of three accused convicted of an armed robbery and sentenced to life imprisonment for allegedly discharging a firearm at pursuing police. I'm not exactly sure whether his campaign for justice is actually called Cop the Clock case or Clock the Cop case. For on close analysis, this mad pun thing seems to spin into endless avenues of probability until I'm unsure which way round is up anymore . . .

To understand this one must first appreciate that this is a pun spun on the slang terms for Cop which, besides policeman, also means Check this Out or Catch. Also, the word Clock, besides time, may also mean Dial or Face as well as Check this Out too. Thus, in the two words Cop and Clock you have the meaning of Check this Out twice which, together with the words Policeman, Catch, Dial, Face and Time, has spun a mean pun for, in this case, all meanings of the words are applicable in various orders. Both words invite you to check out not only the dial/face of the accused identified by the cop, but also invite you to check out the actual dial/face of the speedo clock of the car which the cop said he was driving at the time. The mileage clock on the cop car, said to have been part of the chase at the time, shows that the car was off the road at the time of the robbery, inoperable in the repairs shop. Could not have been part of the chase and therefore that those cops, allegedly driving it, could not have been there to have copped (caught) a clock (glimpse) at the robbers' clock (dial/face).

This may sound a wee bit obscure so let me try to explain the real circumstances of the case as briefly as possible.

Three or four armed and masked men held up and hijacked a security van loaded with nearly two million in cash on board. They drove it off road into a secluded wooded area and proceeded to offload the cash into a council water board van. However, the wooded area was not so secluded as they might have expected. For as it transpired, a pervert taxi driver had also taken a juvenile boy there and, in the course of tampering with him, had witnessed the transfer of metal cash boxes into the council water board van and had called it through over the air on his internal radio.

Thus, when the council van next appeared on the road, the police were onto it and gave chase but, under a hail of gunfire, withdrew to a safe distance and finally lost sight of the council van. The robbers, now aware that the game was up, abandoned the van and made off in various directions on foot. So far, nothing in this case is contested.

The dispute comes in when a cop in police car registration number such and such alleged that he pulled up behind the council van as the robbers abandoned it, discarding their masks as they did so to be later identified.

However, it emerged that all the police cars and their whereabouts in the area were accounted for with the exception of this one mysterious car which was not logged in as a participant in the chase. Nothing much could be made of this during the course of the trial and that identification was sufficient to convict Wullie Barbour of all charges.

This one unlogged car, however, became a crucial issue for investigation for appeal. Here, investigators discovered that not only was that cop car still in the repair shop but that it had been from some time before the robbery. That its mileage had been duly logged from the date when it was towed in some days before the robbery and that the mileage remained the same even after the trial. That car as the police alleged they had been driving during the chase, was the only car not accounted for during the chase because it was in the repair shop with its engine on the garage floor at the time. Could not possibly have been part of the chase and, therefore, those cops allegedly driving it – well you decide if they were there to see the robbers' van and the robbers remove their masks. Hence Cop the Clock case . . .

Check out the speedo dial of the cop who said he copped (caught) the clock (face) of the robber cop (check out) the clock (speedo dial) of the cop (policeman) who said he copped (caught sight of) the clock (face) of the alleged robber . . . or something.

Wulle Barbour is still doing time for it.

His Father's Son –
George Hynes

George Hynes' is one of the most blatant and tragic cases of police harassment ever recorded. Perhaps it would be more to the point to say, of family harassment for it appears that all three of the Hynes brothers were the subject of a police vendetta as a result of the actions of their father, Jimmy Hynes, an active justice campaigner whose activities had led directly to the arrest and imprisonment of a police officer. Roy Overend was convicted and sentenced to three years imprisonment for the crime of attempting to pervert the course of justice by perjury and planting false evidence. Upsetting the apple cart thus had brought the heavy hand of Overend's police colleagues down upon the family. This had led to his son, George, being sentenced to fifteen years imprisonment simply for being his father's son.

Jimmy Hynes Snr has little doubt that the circumstances of this travesty of justice stem from the earlier scandalous case involving the attempt to 'fit up' yet another of his sons, Jimmy. Young Jimmy Hynes had been arrested in the street together with two other young men. Whilst they were being processed into police custody on alleged breach of the peace charges, police officer Roy Overend was overheard responding to a phone call in respect of the finding of jewellery. The young men were later to be charged with and detained for the theft of this jewellery said to have been found in their possession upon the search of their persons by officer Overend at the police station.

It had been a matter of pure chance that the phone conversation had been overheard but this information had led to George Snr's campaign to find the finder. Posters, flyers and advertisements in the local press had finally resulted in the finder coming forward, 'It was literally only seconds before my client was due to appear in the dock at Hamilton Sheriff Court that the procurator fiscal told us that he was deserting the case. It was also literally only when we saw the statement of the policeman that my client learned that he was supposed to have been found in possession of jewellery at the police station. But as the evidence in court suggested, while he was being searched at the bar in the police station a call came in from a woman to say that jewellery had been found in the street. We immediately began a frantic search for this woman and it was the resultant advertisement in the local press which alerted others to irregularities.' So says solicitor involved for the defence, John Macaulay, a policeman himself for ten years in Glasgow before attending law school. He goes on, 'Regrettably what happened here is not isolated and that, sadly, is the bottom line. It has always been like that and it always will be. I speak from twenty years experience of seeing it from both sides . . .'

For some time following upon the conviction of officer Overend, the Hynes family's claims of police harassment did not go unnoticed by the community. Finally, George was arrested following upon an incident where people were assaulted in a disco club during a disturbance there. This incident was alleged to have carried on beyond the disco, to the point where armed and masked men had invaded the home of one of the bouncers concerned in the earlier incident. Once again, people were assaulted and a shotgun was discharged by one of the masked assailants.

The nature of the charge entailed that the only identification evidence, in the latter case, was that of general description as to build. 'A large fat man', for example, was charged and convicted, having been fully identified as part of the earlier affray. The evidence which convicted George Hynes, however, was that of the rather vague and flimsy statement averring that, 'He walked like one of the Hynes, like George only smaller.'

Although anyone who knew the Hynes might have taken this as a description of George's brothers, the jury were not aware of this. As the brothers were not named on that charge whereas George was, he was convicted and sentenced to fifteen years imprisonment because he 'walked like one of the Hynes', who, in fact, all walk like their father.

George has always denied any involvement in this incident for which he was wrongfully convicted. Even beyond the full serving of his sentence, he claims that the police and everyone else but the jury were well aware that he was innocent. The fact that he was not there at the scene of the crime and was not a witness to it, it was not therefore for him to point the finger of blame at anyone else. It is commonly accepted that George was only ever charged with this incident to apply pressure on the family to hand over the real culprit suspected, but never proven, to have been his brother Jimmy. Failing that, George, as the only suspect named, was the only one against whom charges could be brought in a court of law and would be the best, albeit second choice, candidate for a trial.

The jury were thereafter invited to reach a verdict upon the premise that,

If brothers and sisters I have none
and the man in the frame is
my father's son.
Who is it?

When the riddle of the Hynes should have read,

Of brothers three, I am one
and the man in the frame is
my father's son.
Who is it?

All I can tell you is that it was not George Hynes.

The Paw Print Clings Again
– Peter Ashbury

Marion Ross didn't deserve her brutal death. In the winter of '97, the fifty-one-year-old living alone in her Ayrshire home was said to be a wee bit eccentric, but harmless. An easy target then for the callous killer who thrust a pair of scissors deep into her eye socket before stabbing her in the throat, leaving her corpse to be found in her bedroom with the murder weapon still protruding from her gullet. Another horror story inflaming public outrage, focusing national scrutiny upon the local constabulary. The killer must be caught before the local residents in the home territory of Rabbie Burns could sleep at ease in their beds again.

Detective Constable Shirley McKie of Strathclyde Police played an important part in the investigation. She discovered an odd house shaped tin box in the home of one of Marion Ross' neighbours, Peter Ashbury, containing around £1,800 in cash. Could this be a possible motive for the murder? Constable McKie duly removed the item from Ashbury's mother's house and sent it off for forensic examination. The results which came through were the principal breakthrough in the case. The tin allegedly held Marion Ross' fingerprint. Must therefore have been in her possession as she had never been to Ashbury's house who, on the other hand, had carried out some DIY in her home. Ashbury was duly arrested and tried for murder at Glasgow High Court.

In his defence he claimed that the cash was part of his redundancy money withdrawn from the bank to buy a car in a deal which never come through. That the tin was always his, had been part of his mother's household for many years. This was confirmed by his mother and family members but how then could they account for Marion Ross' fingerprint on it? Ashbury's speculation that the police must have taken the tin to the mortuary to obtain the print from the corpse of the victim was ridiculed as highly improbable. No one believed him, least of all the media, but yet another fingerprint mystery was to emerge in this case. The fingerprint of Constable Shirley McKie was also found inside the bedroom doorpost near to where Marion's body was found. How could this possibly be? She had never visited the scene of the crime – officially. This would entail possible contamination of evidence with this officer apparently visiting both scene of crime and scene of alleged evidential discovery. In effect, could have removed the tin from the victim's home and planted it in the home of the accused – had Ashbury denied any knowledge of the tin. Luckily for Shirley McKie, he hadn't. On the other hand however, Shirley insisted that she had never visited the scene of the crime. Despite advice from superior officers that she should just make up a story about being in the house on a previous occasion, she refused point blank to lie on oath and was adamant that the fingerprint found at the scene could not be hers. She had never been there. Yet how could the fingerprint experts be wrong? They are never wrong. One fingerprint on a scene held the weight of evidence of two eye witnesses sufficient in proof and corroboration that the owner of that print was on that scene and no margin of error may be inferred.

Shirley McKie was cruelly ostracised by her colleagues and accused of jeopardising the enquiry and the trial evidence against Ashbury. That she must obviously be lying was surely apparent, thus tainting the alleged objectivity of the police enquiry. She had to be sorted and silenced once and for all the world to see.

Amid a media field day Shirley McKie was arrested and charged with perjury and her alleged previous errors of contamination were sinisterly and mysteriously leaked to the press. She was tagged as an irresponsible, rogue policewoman by her colleagues at the height of the media hype. Still she staunchly stuck to her position and, under enormous pressure, driven close to suicide, was forced to resign from the police force. Ashbury was convicted and was dragged away to serve his time screaming police corruption and fit-up. He immediately launched an appeal against his conviction from his prison cell whilst his antagonist, Shirley McKie, was bailed pending trial for perjury.

Come 1999 in defence at ex-Constable McKie's trial for perjury, two prominent, world renowned, American FBI fingerprint specialists, by the names of Wertheim and Grieves, blew the case against Shirley McKie right out of the proverbial water. The identification of the print in her case was 'no less than bogus' they testified. Over four days in the witness box Wertheim demonstrated to the Scottish public how the print could not belong to Shirley Mckie. Grieves, who trained FBI experts in Illinois, showed how the Scottish system of identification was archaic, unscientific, prone to error and cross contamination. That in this case, not only were the points of identification bogus, but also that in the instance of the related Ashbury case of the alleged print on the tin, the alleged points of reference did not match and could only be described as 'bogus'. Shirley McKie

was vindicated in her stand to refuse to commit perjury and was acquitted on a Not Guilty verdict by the
jury.

> SHIRLEY ACQUITTED, ran the repentant
> headline.
> FINGER PRINT EVIDENCE BOGUS
> SCOTS FINGER PRINTS IN THE DOCK
> FBI experts claim Scots' system was ancient and
> open to abuse at basic levels . . .

Now suddenly Shirley was the darling of the media but
what of Ashbury yet languishing in jail all but forgotten
in this clash of Titans?

Donald Findlay QC who had successfully defended
McKie was quoted as saying, 'If people cannot trust the
fingerprint bureau it should be scrapped and replaced
with a body upon which we can rely.' The veteran criminal lawyer, Joe Beltrami, went one stage further in considering the question marks now hanging over each of
many, many thousands of cases in which fingerprint
testimony had been led as the principal evidence, 'It's
mind boggling not to say extremely disturbing. There is
no doubt that this could have caused many miscarriages
of justice.'

A relieved Shirley McKie, whose father was a retired
police inspector, added her own warning, 'This could
happen to absolutely anyone. A normal person who does
not necessarily have a police background nor the help
that I had, would be in prison now.' Strathclyde Police
have yet to as much as apologise to their young female
ex-colleague. Not surprisingly, Shirley doesn't want her
job back but Ashbury wants his conviction overturned
and his life back.

After all . . .

Where the paw print clings
In the freezin snaw,
Does the paw print cling at aw in law?
Does the paw print cling at aw?

Does the paw print cling
Against the grain?
Does the paw print cling in the pourin rain?
Does the paw print point the blame
Where the paw print clings again?

Celebratory Note: In August 2002, David Ashbury was finally released from prison as having been unjustly convicted for the murder of Marion Ross in 1997. An inquiry is currently underway. The reason for his release? The fingerprints found at the scene were suspect. A polite way of saying they were not his. But how many others still languish in jail on the evidence of fingerprints – someone else's fingerprints?

Tragic Tales – the Special Unit and John Linton

Meanwhile, back in the unit, while my case against unlawful censorship of legal correspondence was being upheld at the European Court of Human Rights, our case for appeal under Section 263 to the Scots Secretary for reference to the Court of Appeal, including the new material, trundled on into its sixth year of enquiry. Our re-renovation programme carried on doing a great job.

My early Video Diary material included the new update renovation work, art exhibitions and concerts. Yet it was soon to become apparent why this work was never done before. For it transpired that, having opened the door to government funding, we had opened the door to closure.

A new young female governor was brought in together with her own team of deputy and female PO. Her name was Susan Brooks and with her came a review of the unit's practical and material functions and needs. Or so we were told. What we weren't told was that as the structural renovation drew to a close, the community itself would be part of the clearance programme. The space was now needed for Barlinnie's third new segregation unit.

There is not much can be said about this beyond the obvious that it was done slyly and with stealth. I remember the last of the community meetings when we were stabbed in the back with this news. The priest had tried to divert some of the flak away from the governor.

'No, she didn't lie as such, it's just that it was her brief and she was only doing her duty,' he said in echo of the Nuremburg Nazi defence.

'So you agree then, as a man of the Church,' said I, 'that just because we are prisoners, it's okay for the prison authorities to lie cheat and deceive us?' It was a question of what kind of trust and confidence in authority would that leave us with.

Brooks' report in recommendation of closure was no big deal. Just another step in the deception. It praised the Special Unit for its unique contribution, the way it was run and the benefits it had contributed to the system over twenty years. But it then went on to say that the area was too small for its purpose and that its principles should be kept intact to be transposed elsewhere to other more suitable accommodation.

This latter remark was a stealth reference to the newly operating Shotts Unit which, though built to design for the purpose, was less than a shadow of the real thing in its operational parameters. It had no democratic principle, for example. There were strict prison rules in force. It was in fact nothing but a soft option control unit with in-cell Sky television. Prisoners had to sign a contract of obedience to the rules of the regime and anyone attempting to develop its set limitations was immediately evicted. Its turnover was quite dramatic. The prison authorities, as usual, had taken all the wrong lessons from the Special Unit, believing that it had been the televisions in the cells which had tamed the savage in man. They took all the material lessons and by ignoring the psychological implications of its system, they murdered any notion of reform. Shotts Unit's total failure ensued as a result of this narrow reasoning.

So it was back to the old jungle beat of Shit Street Shotts for me. Right from entry at reception there was the usual hassle and confrontation. I wasn't to be allowed to wear my Glasgow Two, Innocent Imprisoned T shirts. They stole six of them from me but I'd still one on and refused to hand it over. So it was directly back into solitary confinement for me until I handed it over. It seemed that the Glasgow Two campaign was being closed down along with the Special Unit. In fact, many had believed that this was the main hidden reason behind its closure.

While in Shotts I wouldn't be allowed access to food supplied by my family as per the rights of an untried prisoner. It was back to the old routine. Strict solitary isolation. Hungering for justice in a fast for freedom. Under siege. In fact, I would now no longer even be allowed a visit until I surrendered the last of my Innocent Imprisoned T shirts. So be it then, Evil Bastards. Their siege strategy was pre-planned and well set in advance.

It's a sad and tragic reality that no one ever believes that any other person could go without food while food is available. Because they couldn't do it themselves, they impose the state of their own mind upon everyone else. It doesn't matter how many times you tell them they think they know better and that only their own delusions are real. So every new governor wants to be the one to test this theory out and to be the one to prove it at my expense and suffering. They think that all they have to do is isolate any person in such a way as they cannot cheat and get food on the side. That the tighter the isolation, the quicker the hunger striker will have to concede and swallow the crap handed out to them. They could not seem to grasp the fact that I was not a hunger striker. I was asking to eat, but just wouldn't eat what they give me. I was, in fact, under siege and the siege lines were strictly drawn.

Ode Note in Justice Name

They lock me down tight and they hold the key,
Innocent imprisoned in solitary
Isolation, sensory deprivation and enforced starvation –
but one more siege to me.

They have encroached upon my children's right
to see their father
They have imposed their evil will to spite
with their heavy armour.

They have inflicted their hate with men at arms,
They turned my children from the gate into the
    winter storms
and cut us deeply in their psychological mincing
    machine
But they cannot turn away our rightful outrage in silent
    scream.

They have enforced their perverse will with men
    at arms
To strip me of the very clothes I wear,
and left me, once again, in pain,
Sprawled naked, bound and bruised before them.

And when they came back to do so, again, I
    told them –
they would have to do so, once again,

Without any cooperation from me,
For they cannot strip me of my dignity,
Nor my human right to be free
To resist them,
In Justice Name.

Amen

From the *Book of Passing Thoughts* by TC Campbell

They kept me in strict sol con isolation for twelve weeks without as much as a visit never mind a bite to eat before I was transferred to Law Hospital in a coma. Down around seven and a half stone again. Even then, they were refusing to concede that they were wrong and it was only the prison gate protests and night vigils of my family and campaigners which finally forced the move.

Of course, by the time they had plugged me in at Law Hospital I had lost all desire to ever eat at all. Even when food was provided by my family, I didn't want it. Having gone through this hell so often before finally reaching a state of inner peace within myself. There then seemed to be very little point in returning to full health only to be put through it all again and again once the siege supplies ran out upon return to prison.

The doctors were saying it wouldn't matter anyway, as they reckoned that it was already too late. Blood samples taken had shown that besides high keytones and other vital deficiencies, my body was deficient in potassium. That without potassium it would make no difference what was taken in, I would die of heart strain as a result of vitamin deficiency anyway. My body was rejecting potassium and it was already too late. I was, apparently, beyond the point of no return. So it was a big 'Goodbye cruel world and Hello peace and oblivion' for me. So be it.

John Linton was a justice campaign storm trooper. A lovable rogue who was a shoplifter by profession. Yet to those of us who knew and loved him, he was as straight as the proverbial die. This guy would walk to the ends of the earth for a friend and he was a good friend to me.

John was a character. A get up and go-getter and a good earner. Nobody's fool. He was neither violent nor aggressive by nature but, like most of those young loners of the Gangland housing schemes, he was as hard and as wide as he needed to be to survive. The gangsters had learned to leave him alone. He carried a swivel blade as part of his designer accessories and had been known to use it when the going got tough. No big deal. Just par for the course in those areas.

The thing about John was that he had his ear to the ground and never missed a nuance of the rhythms of the jungle beat on the street. He also had a photographic memory with total recall of all the variations of contact alliances and control. He was a walking gold mine of information evolution and update.

He had done some pure excellent research work on our behalf. Infiltrating various camps and following the trail. Like a hound on the scent, once he had picked it up there was no stopping him following it through to its end. Coming up with new data and new leads on the Doyle fire murders not previously known. He was always there and always happy to oblige. Never looking for or expecting any profit for his efforts, he was always there when you needed him.

By way of a birthday surprise for me, approaching midnight on 4 November 1994, he had circumvented the security system of the House of Commons and, in the early hours of Guy Fawkes day used his swivel blade to carve out **FREE THE GLASGOW TWO** in bold letters on top of the private desk of the Lord Chancellor before distributing campaign leaflets throughout the in-trays of all the offices of government and law. But having spent too long in his woodcarving, John was eventually captured by armed police and spent the night in the Commons' dungeons before being released the following day.

Now laying in hospital some six months later wondering why John hadn't appeared with the Easter eggs for the weans as he'd promised, I wondered what could be wrong. It wasn't like him. Then the news came through that John had been shot dead. He had been lured by a Judas. Led like a lamb to the slaughter. Executed with shots to the back and the back of the head as a scapegoat for another's crimes and as a convenient excuse to silence him.

His loss was the severest blow which could have been struck. It was devastating to us all. The space he left behind him could not have been filled by ten thousand of the ilk who had killed him. Dirty low life cowardly creeps that they are. This became my reason to live and to fight another day. The space John left behind him was so great, I resolved that his killers would not have it all their own way with my death too.

I wasn't trying to eat. Not yet. I'd been here before and knew that any attempt to eat now would probably kill me. But I was letting the doctors do their thing with calcium and potassium boosters. With a more positive state of mind and determination to survive, perhaps they might just start the process of regeneration. They did. In the meantime, I bought Mars Bar Easter eggs for the kids. Someone got their thirty pieces of silver by reporting this to one of the tabloids who ran the story that I was scoffing Mars Bars on the sly. God save us. With all this going on, you'd think that they would have had better things to talk about.

No matter. The beat goes on . . .

The Wilderness

Voices in the Wilderness

Ten years in the wilderness. Ten years of struggle and strife, heartache and pain. Getting nowhere faster than we had ever been before. Our problem was due to the dearth of political will to address the controversial issues arising from this case. Some judge or other had been quoted that precedence dictated a definitive ruling as to the state of the law . . .

'This court shall never allow an appeal merely because a witness wishes to change their evidence.'

Convenient for various Scots Secretaries but effectively barring us from ever having an appeal heard, regardless of the fact that Love's confessions to perjury, with independent evidence in support, were a little more than 'merely'. Nevertheless, this opinion was held up and interpreted as meaning that a prosecution witness' admissions to perjury would never be allowed to form the basis for grounds of appeal under any circumstances and regardless of the fact that yet another, higher court had come to a different unanimous conclusion in the case of Robert Maltman . . .

Lord President (Clyde):
    'We are bound to make the rule for retrial *Absolute* . . .
    '. . . But it is an indispensable condition of the allowance of retrial that the new evidence should

be material to the justice of the cause; and it is inconceivable that it should be refused if it is seen to be such that to exclude it from the materials of judgment would prevent justice being done.

'It has been established, and one is thankful that it is so well established, that there is nothing that can protect the perpetration of a fraud in the obtaining of a judgment, for it will vitiate the whole proceedings, where it is alleged by one of the parties that the transaction was a farce, that it was not a bona fide transaction but a fraudulent one. No time probably would be held to be too late to open up such a transaction where it could be made out clearly and distinctly that the circumstances connected with the fraud had recently come to the knowledge of the party.

'Now where a prima facie case of perjury by a material witness can be made out, I refuse to say that this does not constitute "other causes essential to the justice of the case" for ordering a retrial, and I know of no authority in the law of Scotland which says to the contrary where it can be sufficiently and circumstantially averred that a verdict had been obtained or supported in material degree by evidence which is perjured. Then, in my opinion, if such a verdict would be allowed to stand it would be an affront to justice . . .'

Unanimous assent by Lords Clyde, Guthrie,
Migdale and Cameron, 1967

Common sense, of course, but such unanimous judgment by four judges, sitting once and for all 'to make the rule for retrial absolute' not being convenient to the administration's Hard Lines (Sucker) policy on law and new order regimes, was simply ignored in preference for the single judge's remark. Maladministration malfunctions, and they will simply choose whichever legal opinion best suits the policy of the day, holding it up as the definitive statement as to the state of the law – regardless of the interests of justice, equality and fairness, or even common sense. Their word is law and thy Thatcherite will be done, Amen. That our convictions and imprisonment were based upon the admitted perjured evidence of the witness Love, being plain to see, was of no consequence to this administration. There yet remained no legal mechanism by which to challenge our convictions in a court of law, other than that the case be referred to the court by the Secretary of State for Scotland. However, this being a Thatcherite government with only a handful of Tory MPs controlling Scotland, a tightly knit elite in dictatorial administration, they could not admit nor accede to any error nor flaw in their Hard Lines policy on Law and New Order regimes. They are but Crown lackeys pandering to the remnants of the monarchical and feudal systems of privilege and self-promotion for loyal services rendered to their liege lords. They will do as they are bid regardless, selecting their own and each other to high office. Granted privilege to walk all over the rights of their lesser minions ... One standard of law for the privileged and another for the poor is not an opinion nor mere political rhetoric. It is a statement of fact based upon a lifetime of experience at the wrong end of the Jackboot.

I cringe at the very idea of so-called Socialists being promoted to the House of Lords in Westminster. A Socialist Lord is a contradiction in terms, inherently paradoxical. For socialism necessarily entails the democratic function to be the true will of the people whereas these Lords are but remnants of the old feudal system. Tory wigs and lackeys, the very pillars of fascism. The very bricks and mortar to the Floydian Wall. Privileged and elite in their silken wigs and ermine gowns, dictating the new order of the day whilst the rest of us scrape and struggle in abject poverty, or rot in our dungeons of despair . . .

Voices from the Wilderness
(1995)

In 1995, after six years awaiting reply to our petition for reference to the Court of Appeal, we decided to take matters into our own hands and spur things on. The first step would be a petition to the High Court to try to seize previously undisclosed evidence such as the police statement which Love's sister Agnes had sworn on affidavit that she had given to the police at the time describing her brother's true part in the shooting but which had never been disclosed by the Crown as evidence. The point to this action being that we could then add such new material to our petition before the Scots Secretary seeking reference to the court and/or prepare the way for a civil action to prove our case.

Once again we were refused legal aid and John Carroll prepared the case for us to present personally to the court. It was heard approaching the end of the year. The task of reading out John Carroll's points of law and submissions was delegated to wee Joe. As there was more I had wanted to say for myself, over and above this, I had prepared my own wee speech for the occasion.

NOTE OF FURTHER SUBMISSIONS
PETITION 25.10.95
BY
THOMAS CAMPBELL
AND
JOSEPH STEELE
FOR
COMMISSION AND DILIGENCE

1.1. The Crown prosecuting authorities hold
    evidence relevant and pertinent to the
    petitioners case in proof of miscarriage of
    justice and, as result of their policy of non
    disclosure, the petitioners are denied access
    to the instruments and mechanisms of justice
    in a court of law.

1.2. The prosecuting authorities who hold this
    material in proof of the petitioners case for
    miscarriage of justice, have no exclusive
    right to assess and to make judgement upon
    what is, or is not, relevant and pertinent to
    the original defence of the petitioners. They
    have no right in fact to hijack with impunity
    those instruments and mechanisms of
    justice to the exclusion of all other interested
    parties. They are not objective nor impartial
    in this case.

1.3. With regard to the Crown prosecutions
    submissions that 'there is no obligation in
    Scots Law to disclose exculpatory evidence
    to the defence' I would submit that where
    Scots law has a tradition and, in fact, a real
    and commendable obligation of fairness and
    justice to an accused person then there can

be no place for such a scandalous statement which flies in the face of the fundamental principles of justice.

I submit that such a statement amounts to no more than an expression of archaic policy stemming from a time in history where in fact there was no obligation in law to provide even the basic facilitation for standard appeal procedures in miscarriage of justice cases. I give reference to the case of Oscar Slater and strike a note of warning that the Crown Office's policy practice stemming from such archaic and scandalous cases and times should not be misconstrued and misinterpreted as traditional Scots Law. For they have no sound foundation in Scots Law's true traditions of fairness and justice to accused persons before these courts.

1.4. I think that we are entitled to expect that today's courts would be somewhat more enlightened as result of the evolution of sound sense and reason.

1.5. For it would be more than a nonsense to assert on the one hand, that, 'the Crown Prosecuting Authorities have a duty to investigate all aspects of a case including that which may exculpate an accused'. Whilst on the other hand, to aver that however 'they have no obligation to disclose said exculpatory evidence to the said accused'.

1.6. I would further submit that, it is *exactly* from within such a biased and partisan approach in an adversarial system, that the

seeds of oppression are sewn and from within
which blatant double standards of justice,
that such injustices, as in the case of Oscar
Slater, and as in this case, inevitably stem
from the fruits of the poison tree.

2.1 Where, as the Crown Prosecution would have
it, that this court would uphold the Crown
Office's archaic and oppressive policy as
an ancient tradition of Scots Law. Whilst in
fact the truth of the matter is that there is
no obligation in Scots Law *NOT* to disclose
such evidence relevant and pertinent to
the interests of justice and in the particular
circumstances of this case.

2.2 We seek justice by access to the mechanisms
and materials of justice in a fair trial by full
disclosure of all the facts in this case for
consideration and judgement by the court. We
seek no more than is our just due and as is
now accepted as standard practice in England
following upon the cases of the Birmingham
6, the Guildford 4, Judith Ward and other
such miscarriages of justice cases resulting
from the Crown Prosecutions bias and
partisan approach in failure to disclose such
exculpatory evidence to the accused's defence.

2.3 We seek only justice and our just due in all
fairness to accused persons. There can be
no justice where there is no equality; and
where one party in any dispute retains the
archaic privilege of exclusive control of
the information, therein lie the seeds of
oppression. The result on non disclosure

is a miscarriage of justice in this case. The result of non disclosure is the allowance and retention of the privilege to impose double standards of justice upon those lesser privileged oppressed and downtrodden of our society.

2.4 If this Court of Law has consideration and respect for the principles of justice and fairness for all then it will grant warrant of this petition for full disclosure of all the facts of this case.

2.5 It not, and the innocent imprisoned are to remain wrongfully condemned as a result of the retention of the Crown Office's privileged and oppressive archaic policy, then I submit that would be just another blunder whose burden you would bear in history and our condemnation, instead of restoring the balance which you desire, which we all desire, would only sow new seeds of passion and disorder.

2.6 The cauldron of discontent, I tell you is full to the brim. We don't make it so, to overflow. (Zola. Dreyfus Is Innocent 1889)

Thomas Campbell
10 October 1995

The answer to this was, in effect, that the court cannot grant access to full disclosure for appeal whilst there is no appeal, nor mechanism for appeal pending nor existing. Not until or unless the Scots Secretary refers the case to the Court of Appeal would our petition be competent.

This may seem like a Catch 22 scenario – you can't get access to the evidence till you prove your case but you can't prove your case until you access the evidence. In fact, it is a Catch 22 but at least we had highlighted that anomaly, prompting the Scots Secretary to enquire deeper into what we had sought to access.

Professor Sutherland's committee report on their review of the Scottish criminal appeals procedures was making the news. Among other things, they recommended the setting up of an independent criminal case review commission to take that power away from politicians such as the Scots Secretary, Michael Forsyth MP for Stirling, who rejected that part of the Sutherland Committee's report, retaining the power and prerogative to dispense his opinions on justice issues, outwith a competent court of law.

One Man Stops Access to Courts

The Scottish Secretary's negative response to the Sutherland Committee's recommendations on dealing with cases of miscarriage of justice is of considerable interest to those of us still pursuing justice in the case of the Doyle Family murders of 1984. The response, which obviously poses a problem for us, is clearly of largely academic interest to lawyers but is a genuine cause for concern to the public.

Apparently the Secretary of State thinks that the present system, properly administered, could work well enough as it is. Our problem for a decade has been that it has not been administered properly at all.

Major legal and constitutional issues arise out of our case, a particularly scandalous and controversial one which has become a major embarrassment to the administration of justice. Despite the efforts of myself and my co-accused the issues have been swept under the carpet. There has been a cover-up.

Where there is no independent body to review the facts and circumstances of such a case on its merits there is no redress. We have been unreasonably barred and forbidden access to the courts by the legally incompetent and unqualified opinions of one man, not the

will of Parliament which has already accepted
and implemented such reforms in England
and Wales.

His refusal to sanction the creation of
an independent body which would curb his
powers to impose his partisan and singularly
unreasonable opinions as law is a matter of the
greatest concern to all Scots.

Thomas Campbell,
Innocent Imprisoned
HM Prison, Shotts.

Voices from the Wilderness
(1996)

The Sutherland Committee report had also recommended that a witness' change of evidence should be allowed as grounds for appeal where that evidence was crucial to the conviction and, provided that there was some adminicle of independent evidence in support, that it should be allowed to be heard. As in the previous cases of fresh evidence, such as that of Alan Church, Tam Moffat and others, a reasonable excuse would be required to be given by the appellants as to why this evidence was not brought before the jury at the earlier trial. This was a breakthrough for us. For besides Love's confessions to perjury, there was his sister's statement in confirmation of his perjury. The reason it was not heard at the trial was that Love had previous convictions as a serial perverter of justice and had set out to commit perjury, as a Crown witness, beyond our control, and, as a Crown witness, any attempt to dissuade him could have been interpreted as an attempt to intimidate or suborn a witness. His previous convictions as a serial perverter of justice, the terms of his alibi and his sister's statement to the police were never disclosed to the appellants at the time of the trial and could not reasonably have been known.

On 1 August 1996 the Scots Secretary referred the case to the Court of Appeal on the grounds of Love's confessions to perjury and his sister's police statement in support. 'That taken together, they raise questions on which it would be more appropriate for the appeal court to reach a final judgement.'

Innocents Abroad

Lib

Walking out of the court, bailed meantime, seemed perfectly natural. There was no sense of victory or triumph, only a sense of having finally achieved an overdue just due and of going home. It was like no time had passed between the appeal in 1985 until this point eleven years later. Twelve and a half in all. The oddest thing was that family, friends, the Press and the public had been removed from the court building and the corridors were empty. I had no clue of which way to go. The official court Press officer was there, walking with me, noting responses to questions, turning this way and that without thinking about it, leading me through the labyrinths into the light of day and the crowds. Free at last.

At home there were live satellite interviews outside the front door and throngs of Press inside. I was only conscious of the fact that oor Stephen was missing from the pictures, perhaps wisely avoiding notoriety, but I missed him. It was my son Brian's birthday and this had made his day and answered his prayers. There may just be a god after all. Party and celebration then. Exhausted and not really in the mood, feeling detached, but posing with the champagne for the Press anyway. In fact, I just wanted to be with the kids and to walk with them under the chill of the evening sky and to look at the stars.

Once the dust had settled, it seemed that everybody knew me. Like Sean Connery or Billy Connolly going about their normal daily business on the bus and at the shopping arcade, expecting to be anonymous. People pointing, waving, tooting their horns, stopping to wish us well. The warm and friendly welcome from the city astounded me. I had no idea that I would be so well known and so widely supported. I had stepped into the glare of publicity from a Sol Con cell and wasn't prepared for this notoriety. I had expected to be anonymous and to merge into the obscurity of the background as a normal citizen. It took some time to realise that it would never be as simple as that.

There was never a point where I was unhappy at home but in the passing of the first months it became apparent that Liz was unhappy with me. Not just me but with any man cluttering up her beautiful model home and changing things. It is difficult for a civilian to appreciate that any man coming home from twelve and a half years confinement in a stone box with little more than a radio and a piss pot for company, direly needs help and time to readjust to the new norms. For example, though I resisted the urge to sit on the floor to eat, this would have seemed perfectly normal to me as this is how we lived in the digger. Prison is an unnatural environment where normal is strange and the strange is normal. People are conditioned in an unnatural environment to accept the unnatural as the norm for the fact that it is the everyday to-day routine regime regardless of however abnormal that 'usual' may be.

As result of my difficulty in adapting to the free world and Liz's inability to adapt to me, within the first few months I had been asked to leave about at least as many times. Walking through the night in the rain and snow, looking for a friendly light in the glen, flopping on someone's armchair, soaked through and exhausted, trying to fathom what I was doing wrong. Arguments about which ashtrays are used and which not. Where I park my shoes, moving the Hoover, *Coronation Street* – it all seemed so petty to me and the results so extreme. There was obviously something else behind this and there was.

It was about control. For over twelve years she had controlled her domain, her sanctuary from Press storms and scandal, and she had become nervous and agoraphobic. I had just strolled back into her life and her domain and unconsciously taken over the controls and she couldn't handle that. I'd find myself tripping over the Hoover in the hall and without thinking about it, move it to a less obstructive position. I'd hear the theme tune of *Coronation Street* and switch over. I'd park my shoes next to my chair for easy access. I'd use ornamental ashtrays. The house was cold and I realised that the settee pushed up against the radiator was acting as insulation, keeping the heat from getting out and causing its thermal to trip. I moved the settee. I didn't discuss any of these things, I just did them without thinking.

'You keep changing everything,' she'd yell. It was about control and I couldn't see I was imposing on her private space and her holy sanctuary. I was imposing on her control and her security. It all seemed so petty to me but it was just that Liz wasn't used to a man around the house at all. Not just that it was me. Yet, neither could I take this kind of instability in my life when what I needed was stability.

After the last episode, walking the streets through the night in the wind and rain, I decided that I just wouldn't bother apologising. Tired of being Tommy Take-the-blame, I lived in my son Tommy's flat till I could get a flat of my own. It was in the same scheme as Liz, the same road, but it was a long road and at the other side of the scheme. An old tenement listed for demolition but at least the children could drop in on their way to and from school whenever they wanted. That was all that was important to me.

Liz seemed quite happy about this move nor was she upset, nor entitled to be upset, when I met another woman. Karen was more my age when I went to prison twelve and a half years earlier, a classic beauty, sweeping swathes of golden locks, huge bright, sparkling green eyes and a figure out of heaven. She was a godsend. We first met in my son Tommy's house and we went out for a drink, it was a great night, though sadly it ended in a typical bar room brawl, with Karen holding her own against the entire clan of the famous fighting females. We met up again when I returned her lost property, and our romance took off from there. She moved in with me and helped make a household a home. God bless her for her patience, understanding and guidance . . .

On the way down to see my brother in London I realised at Glasgow Airport that I still had Liz's house keys in my pocket. This would have presented a problem but for the bright idea of hiring a taxi to deliver them back home. Hurrying out to the rank, explaining the situation to the driver, he'd deliver them 'Nae problem' for a tenner.

'Good, lad. Good thinking, Batman,' I thought as I walked away and the driver taxied away with a fare. With a fare? It suddenly struck me that I hadn't given him my name or address. Rushing after him banging on the bonnet of his car,

'Hey! Hey! Hey!' He slowed for me to catch up, head and elbow out the window grinning.

'Aye! it's okay, Mr Campbell, I know where you stay. I seen it on the telly,' he waved as he sped away. Seen it on the telly? Is that why people were looking at me? I thought maybe my suit was out of style or something.

The London taxi driver tells me, 'You'll be heading for the Globe then, Tom?'

'Eh!'

'Seen you on TV. You'll be heading for the Globe then?'

'Eh ah don't think so,' said I not liking this notoriety one little bit and thinking, 'What the fuck would I be wanting with Shakespeare's theatre?'

'It's a Jockney pub,' he explains, making me wonder whether my thoughts were on air too.

Sure enough, I ended up in the Globe. It was like a visit to the old Barras. It was like a little Glasgow. Run by second generation Glasgow Cockneys, born under the chimes of the Bow Bells to Glasgow East-End parents, they were Jockneys. A warmer welcome there never was. This felt more like coming home than coming home did. These were more my kind of people than the people at home were. More old Glasgow than the present Glaswegians were, the London Cockney upbringing only adding to their charm.

Back on the plane on the way home it seemed that delay after delay on take off must be the norm. Baggage check after baggage check. It appeared that they had a bag without a passenger and were not too keen on taking off with it on board. Understandable after Lockerbie.

This young girl, maybe seventeen or eighteen sits beside me, introducing herself and her pal accross from us. I guessed that was the norm too. I thought, 'People are so polite nowadays.' Chatting away yet they seemed to be becoming more agitated as the delays persisted. Asking me at the window seat what was going on now down below, I was reassuring them that it was only a baggage check. My reassurances seemed to be having the opposite effect from the one intended.

'Are they checking our hand luggage?' and such. I was not born yesterday and know paranoia when I see it. These girls were up to something. I told them to settle down. They must have recognised my insight because, for some reason, they felt compelled to tell me that they were each carrying two kilos of coke a piece. WHIT! The plane takes off with them assured and me in a cold sweat. If these girls got done, who's getting done with them? Who would ever believe that we were strangers?

'Aye right! Heard it, aren't you thone TC character on the telly?' They wouldn't have done this on their own. Shit! Why does it always happen to me and how come they told me anyway? I could have been a copper for all they knew?

'You shouldn't have told me that,' said I. 'I might have been the polis.'

'Naw, TC,' says she, 'I seen you on the telly an that's why we sat here. We knew you were cool.' (Cool? Fuckin stone cold more like.) Hide in plane sight I suppose, whit next?

'Y'want t'go tae a party?'

'Naw thanks, sweetstuff, ahm busy.'

Off the plane, hurrying to get as far away from them as fast as I could. Still they kept up with me. I turns to say, 'Look just fuck off eh.' I got as far as, 'Look . . .' and she butts in.

'Aye there e's there.' The guy they were meeting shouts, 'Alright, big TC fullah,' rushes over and embraces me. Realising I knew this guy from old, by now I'm tripping out of my skull in paranoia, looking for the Knock charging in with guns and handcuffs. This could only be a fuckin set up if ever there was one. 'Seen y'on the telly, big man, y'want t'go t'a party?'

'Naw thanks, A'v got business.'

'So'v we. Ho! Ho! Need a lift?'

'Naw it's ok A'm cool, see ya.' Exit stage left.

'See,' I hears one to the other say. 'Told ya he was cool.' I decided to get a haircut and a shave. The beard had to go.

Free the Glasgow One

Oor Stephen was in trouble. He'd been arrested by CID as he left school and a parent was needed to sit in on the interview. I got down there to Shettleston sharpish. Notebook and pen at the ready. If it was admissible for the police, it was admissible for me. Turned out to be tape recorded though.

Stephen, at fifteen, was over six foot tall. Goldie blond hair and built like a honey monster. He also wore a white baseball cap. The exact description of one of the boys present when a bus driver had gotten some hassle from a group of four who had refused to get off the bus and, once ejected, had panned the bus window in with a brick.

The second incident had occurred the next day. Same carry on about refusing to get off the bus, same boys, same aggression. The tall blond one of Stephen's description had in fact been called Stephen. He had asked the driver, 'What's the magic word?' and on being told 'please' had exited the bus. The other three boys had continued to give hassle and the one with the leather jacket had stabbed the driver with a knife to his severe injury. Thus, what the police wanted from Stephen was the names of the other three boys and, in particular, the name of the one with the leather jacket. He was cautioned that he may be a suspect, acting in consort, on this crime.

'I don't know.'

'I wasn't there.'

'It wasn't me.'

'Don't know anything about it.'

He kept insisting. Stupid I thought, he should say who it was. He was in danger of being charged and for what? To stay loyal to some nut who goes about stabbing bus drivers? I know that at his age that I would have said and done exactly as he was doing now but the difference now was that I could see that I would have been wrong. He was obviously lying. I mean, how many fifteen-year-old, six foot tall golden blond honey monsters with white baseball caps called Stephen could there be at that school? He kept denying it point blank. I could see why the polis didn't believe him, I didn't believe him. They sent him home. Needless to say, he was severely grounded. Told me it was another Stephen by the same description. Aye right, heard it!

Next day I see him playing football down at the shops. 'Stephen,' I yells, annoyed for the fact that he was supposed to be grounded. He turns around and it is not my Stephen. It's another local lad, same age, same height, same hair, same cap, same name.

'Aye, Mr Campbell,' he says. 'Everybody does that. My name's Stephen tae,' he laughs. 'And, by the way, he wasn't there. It was me.'

Apologising to oor Stephen, he's full of big grins, 'See you wouldn't believe me, even after what has happened to you. You're not the only one y'know,' he's acting all aggrieved. Threatening to make placards and have his wee sister demonstrate in the garden 'Free the Glasgow One' heavy duty travesty of justice and all that.

'Okay, okay! I get the point.' Compensation of Big Macs all around was accepted and he, liberated to go get them but trouble never ends there. It always runs in chain reactions.

Stephen gets entangled in a gang fight up at the take-away. News reaches home and Liz sends Brian up to get him out of it and bring him home. I know Brian better than Liz does and I go up there too, via another route. Brian sees the two teams out facing each other, ready to do battle. Brian runs straight through the home team, right into the enemy ranks and the home team follow him, scattering the enemy like so much dust in the wind. Oh shit, echoes of madness from the distant past but what a different insight as a parent.

Brian comes sauntering back, saying over his shoulder to Stephen, 'You're wanted, you're in for it,' not seeing me approaching, taking him by the scruff of the neck, 'Naw, YOU're wanted.' Stern lectures only reminding me of what my Da had said to me when I didn't listen. From that perspective, I could only let them see that I see what is on their minds from what was on mine in similar situations when I was a lad. To let them see that generations of error had to be addressed and sorted out once and for all before they found themselves saying the same things to their own children.

So what am I doing lecturing teenage children? I'm too young to be lecturing teenage children. I'm not forty odd. They years in the jail don't count.

Sweet and Sour

Most of the best times are those normal and ordinary times that you only miss and appreciate from a prison cell. Simply walking in the street or the park with the weans. Bus trips and shopping expeditions. Nothing is simply ordinary anymore, everything is a novel delight. Just to be there, to be able to step in and to help out.

My daughter Cheree, for example, had never known me on the outside as a father and, as a result, unconsciously failed to consider me as an added advantage to her routines. Hearing her in the background bemoaning her big brother's lack of enthusiasm to escort her to the local Easterhouse swimming pool, it was a delight for me to pipe up, 'I'll take you.' I'd not seen a swimming pool for fifteen years and, being qualified as a lifeguard and instructor since my teens, I know how important it is that children should learn to swim. It horrified me that mine could not.

Suddenly then her brother Brian is keener to tag along with his pal, Cheree and her pal all bundling into the car, Brian giving directions. I may have been away a long time but I was sure Easterhouse wasn't this far away. In fact, Brian had directed me along the bus route to the Time Capsule out by Monklands way. A blooming wonderland to me with its waterfalls, spiral water shoots, tidal waves, woolly mammoths and, of course, burger bar.

Before I knew it, it seems I was appointed as the local

life guard-cum-swimming instructor and I was stuck with regular classes of up to half a dozen delighted school kids to look after. Not that I minded, as it was as much of a day out for me as it was for them. Karen would sometimes tag along too, but she was soon pregnant with our daughter Shannon and would only spectate from the gallery. The only sour note to these adventures came from Magma, a leggy blonde I'd known from old. She had been helping me to drive and get used to the roads and traffic again. In return I was to help teach her two kids to swim. Sadly this led to a scandal. She tipped off the Press who then covertly photographed us together, conveniently missing out the kids two steps in front. Luckily, the Time Capsule stewards prevented pictures being taken inside at the pool where Magma's close proximity had alarmed and harassed me.

I saw why the next day when the tabloids ran the scandal story . . .

TC GETS TLC FROM BLONDE NUMBER THREE. I hope it was worth the few quid for her. From then on I made sure I would never see her again.

And then there was Katie, my good friend and neighbour up the stair. Although she was the parent part of a one-parent family, going through a divorce and looking after the kids on her own, struggling desperately to make ends meet, still she was always cheerful, helpful, good for advice and a laugh. She came to my door with the news. 'Tommy, you have either got the polis or the social security snoops oot there in the bushes with cameras watching the hoose.'

'Zat right?' says I, picking up my own super zoomer and heads out there to see for myself who it could be. Little did we know that it was the Press on the snoop for more scandal.

Katie being Katie and full of carry-on, starts her twirling

and model posing at the top of the stairs leading into my close. Snap! Pop! the flash bulbs go off all over the place as camera men leap out of the long grass and bushes. Loving it, Katie starts an erotic saunter, hand on hip and the other behind her head as if she was some kind of superstar. They were reporters looking for scandal and had assumed she was Karen, 'How long have you known TC?'

'Oh! just since he moved in . . .'

'And how are yous getting on . . .'

'We get on just great, he is a totally fabulous guy.' They gave her £500 for the interview and the same again for the pose and her second name. She was delighted and more so when I wouldn't accept halfers.

She was furious then when the Sunday tabloids ran the story that I had got my neighbour, Karen McGuinness, up the spout. She was in the process of divorcing her man for infidelity, now he would be divorcing her and using this article and picture of her in those proceedings. She was soon spending her windfall on a lawyer and got the matter sorted out. Needless to say, my neighbours became very cautious about being photographed around me in case they too hit the scandal sheets. I was used to it. Liz didn't read the scandal sheets or believe a word they said anyway. Karen thought it was hilarious but I worried about the weans and had to draw the line when Cheree was approached by a reporter coming out of the primary school gates. Mimicking her mom she'd said, 'And he doesn't watch *Corry*, *East Enders*, *High Road* or nothing. He watches nature, about tigers and beetles and birds and floors and stupid things like that . . .'

So much for your scandal then, creep, eh! They didn't print it.

An Old Lag's Tale

I couldn't believe the stupidity of some people and was astounded at their presumption of stupidity in me in reflection of their own limitations.

So here was I, only just released in a blaze of publicity which never seemed to end, after twelve years in the jail. Yet here are people queuing up to try to persuade me to become involved in some serious criminal enterprise or another. I mean! As Groucho Marx once said, I wouldn't want to be any part of any club which would have me as a member. But, to have people intent on persuading me somehow didn't smell quite right. More than one such offer was for art and partners in armed robbery.

'Are they off their fuckin heads?' was my first thought until I remembered the Old Lag's Tale, way back there in the jail, and, somehow, it seemed more fitting . . .

He'd just finished a twelve-year sentence for armed robbery. Was out and about on his toes scouting out for a wee earner. He'd come to the conclusion that dope, Happy Jack in particular, was the only game in town.

'Everybody was doing it but nobody was admitting it,' was his way of putting it. He'd got to work then establishing his supply and market.

Strolling into one of his old haunts, The Caravel Bar in the old Bar-L, now under the new management of the infamous Licensee, better known to me as The Craw, he's approached by the local low life, now playing the part of gangsters. Here the new order of the day was laid down to him. That he was trespassing on their province. That they run the show now. That they would have none of his nonsense around here. That any earner he wanted to make, he could only do so through them. They would supply the kit, prices, punters and protection and, if not, he wouldn't be allowed to operate and would be promptly dealt with. He describes a scene out of *The Sopranos* before that series was ever even thought of.

Unimpressed by these, 'Halfwits and scumbags,' he'd risen to his feet and with finger pointed in their faces, had put them back in their places for the cowardly lowlife scumbags that they were. They had backed down and backed off.

In the week to follow he had suddenly found himself very popular and with scores of people queuing up to join up on his enterprise. He had shrugged it all aside, wasn't interested in taking on, nor taking over anything. All he was looking for was a quiet wee steady earner to keep himself ticking over on the quiet life. No big buys and no big deal but he was soon to discover the price of operating an enterprise outwith the Caravel Cartel's control.

Walking on the street one day, on his way to the Social Security in Shettleston, a car pulls up with three guys that he knew from old. He accepts a lift and enjoys the wise-crack along the way but, shortly thereafter, the traffic cops are on their tail-lights intent on pulling them over for routine traffic check. The driver puts his boot down and they bomb it to hell out of there. There then follows a mad car chase while the old lag gathers his wits about him. In his day, guys such as these were always hot on the trot for something or other. You ran with the desperadoes at your own risk. Assuming that either they themselves or the car couldn't stand a pull by the polis – he'd been in this situation before and knew the score, knew the procedure as sure as an old trooper knows the routine.

First sharp bend they came to, he was out of the moving vehicle and rolling to safety as the car upped through the gears again, speeding away. He was in the clear, in one piece, on his feet and running, leaping, jumping, tumbling grass embankments and garden walls and fences. Well out of the danger zone. Or so he had at first thought but, 'Fuck!' Those stupid coppers were coming after HIM. 'For Christ's sake! What's wrong with them? They fuckin rookies or somethin? Don't they know the fuckin score?'

It is generally accepted that traffic coppers will always pursue the car and the driver, not the passengers, but these coppers had drawn the car chase to a halt to pursue the passenger on foot. Very odd, beyond mere strange in the circumstances.

'So what the fuck is going on here?' he stopped to ask, still laughing that these rookies had pursued him and let the desperadoes get away. He knew he was well in the clear, without the car and driver, there was no way that they could rope him into whatever-the-fuck it was those guys had been up to. He was duly arrested anyway.

Driven into the local police station he's astounded to notice the fuckin car just parked right there, right outside the front fuckin door. The coppers just nod and smile at his recognition. But there would be a few more wee surprises in store for him yet to come. Inside the boot of the car they found a gun, masks, and a full layout plan for a robbery. He was convicted of conspiracy with person or persons unknown to commit armed robbery and sentenced to eight years.

'If you mess with that scumbag Caravel Cartel, big yin, you're messing with the fuckin coppers man!' was his thought for the day.

Sure enough. Even the coppers say so. A retired officer revealed that, at the time of the Doyle fire murders, The Craw was highly prized as a grass.

'There is no question about it. High ranking officers

kept him out of the frame and fitted up others to take the rap. In those days, fitting up was a way of life. He is like the Teflon Don. He has put more guys behind bars than I ever did and I was in the job for more than twenty years,' the polisman says.

So you can imagine how impressed I was with these strange invitations to go-a-robbing with these guys.

'Tell y'what though,' I'd say. 'Yous just go right on ahead without me and I'll be there, just happen to be there with my camcorder across the street. Just happen to catch it all on tape. Masked men in, masked men out and, fast getaway. I can guarantee I'll get more for the sale of the tape to the news room than yous'll get from the robbery and we'll split the difference, so how's that? We got a deal?' Strangely enough, not one of them ever took up my return offer, and, oddly enough, not one of those so-called cake walk robberies ever got done without me. Aye! so they keep telling me that things have changed. It seems that you don't get fitted up by the polis anymore. They simply get their Smack Jack partners to set you up instead. That way they can shoot you on the way out.

Well, I suppose that if you're daft enough to fall for it. Desperate enough to go for it or naive enough to believe in it. You might just get a little more than you bargained for. A long lie-in within one of Her Majesty's dungeons or permanent solitary on the last draft to hell.

Then they ask me if I want to go to work on the Happy Jack Track? Laying on close to a million in cash with regular supply of Happy Jack at wholesale prices. All ready, packed and sold, awaiting distribution. Everything any man could ever want or need right there at his say so. The ultra fast track to millionaire's row. Chasing Dragons and selling dreams.

'No thanks.' My only concern being, 'Deary me! the price for my head on the block is going up. Someone is getting desperate . . . I wonder who?'

The Thin Man

The thin man is an ugly wee queer hawk but like the bird that never flew ... A closet drag queen who likes to play with the big boys. Sells smack to school kids and kidnaps children to hold as ransom for the five ton which he reckons is overdue from a deal. Seldom seen unless you know that you're looking for an ugly bitch, for he moves in the guise of his sister. Talks like Al Capone to impress the shit out of the halfwits who carry out his bidding and do the dirty work. This eejit actually thinks he's a gangster. In fact, he is as he is, a petty crook without even the courage to come out of the closet. No harm in that, except that this bitch likes to play with the big boys and their toys. A little girl in a big bad world playing at being a gangster. As a result, he wreaks havoc and literally causes murder.

Still playing the same petty games since he was a child. Thievery is all he knows. Ripping people off and blaming others is all he has ever known. The difference now is that those others end up with a bullet in the back of their head, as he pouts proudly thinking that this is ever so clever.

So, I was telling people about her, putting them in the picture and him out of it. Fucking up his scene. I made no secret about it and she gave me a wide berth. She deserved so much more than that, but it was not my place to attend to it.

An old friend came to see me, badly shaken and deeply

concerned. He had quite a story to tell. One that I could see right through, even before the dawning of first light. The Bitch was playing her tricks again with the big boys and it appears that I was the target to her latest play.

Long time ago, myself and this old pal used to confiscate Happy Jack from the local dealers and flush it down the drain.

'No Happy Jack here', but things had moved on long since. Happy Jack was everywhere, big business and no concern of mine, yet it's never as easy as that. This ancient history was being used in a game play. My old friend had discovered that there was a hit out on both me and him for carrying out a recent confiscation order. He swears he knows nothing at all about it and I knew it had nothing to do with me. At first it appeared that someone had used us as an excuse for not paying their bills but close scrutiny uncovered that he was still working for the Thin Man who, having lost his street cred, was using this eejit as a front. It soon transpired that I was right. The Bitch was trying to put me out of the picture with her same old scam, fronted by someone else. Her problem was that she doesn't have the courage to say boo to a doo, can't confront me, but has to make a move to get back on the game. Shame, it might just have worked if I wasn't onto her, up to her old larks again.

Thus it was, just like the movies, cops with long lenses, zooming in on their target. The Thin Man's patsy was put under obs, checking and cross checking his every meet and move for a pattern, until I could predict where and when he would be at any given time. Choosing the best time to step in and say hello. Literally, I stepped into his car saying, 'Drive ya bastard.' He drove to my directions. Little girls want to play with the big boys. Fine! Let's go meet the big boys.

This poor patsy was fed misinformation to the point

that he believed he was living a real life godfather movie. By the time he met with the people he'd robbed, he expected to be sleeping with the fishes that never swam. Sobbing and blabbing, pleading for the chance to come clean. None of it was his fault, it was all down to the Thin Man he pleaded. The Thin Yin had fired him in to rip them off and to blame TC. To say that TC and his old pal had confiscated the goods and the cash due, so that they would never know what hit them when the shit came down. It was all his plan right from the start. None of what he'd told them was true. So how do we know that what you say now isn't just another story? He proved his story by spilling his guts on everything else the Thin Yin was up to. It had nothing to do with anyone else. The Thin Yin had taken the loot and the toot . . .

Problem solved but now what do I do with this dafty? The guy was just an idiot, a pawn in a petty poof's amateur play. So then we'll play him back. Simply to let him go would blow the cover of the paranoid illusions so carefully spun around him. So better that he be taken to the mysterious 'Factory' sinisterly stage whispered for him to overhear and draw his own paranoid conclusions before being allowed to escape. Which he did, with dramatic style. Taking advantage of a lapse in security, with screeching tyres, bent lamp posts and car bonnets, he bolted, like a bat out of hell. Good lad!

I hadn't struck a blow nor carried a weapon. Using only psychological manipulation, striking terror into his yellow heart to the point that the tales he would tell his associates in crime would have them diving for cover, under the bunker, awaiting an Armageddon coming down. Out of the picture, out of business, jumping at shadows for many a long moon yet to come. So ya wanna play with the big boys do ya eh! Yet even this pacifistic approach being so well organised and executed was to backfire on me for that very reason. Striking terror to the hearts of cowards is not difficult and no big deal, but the paranoid delusions created from their fear can spread and infect others where not intended. I guess that's Karma.

Kelly's Karma

Big Kelso was an old pal from the jail. An ex-lifer and one of the Bar-L who had been caught thieving a leather jacket from a party and, on being confronted, had stabbed his host to death in the fight which then ensued. Not a very sociable guy but, in fact, I always thought he was okay, even though nobody ever liked him because of his loud-mouthed arrogance. That didn't bother me, it's just the way he is and you just don't take him seriously.

He was sentenced around the same time as I was and here he had been out about a year having served around eleven years. It was a pleasant surprise therefore to find that he was now my neighbour, living one up above Liz's same ground floor flat where I'd been arrested from twelve and a half years earlier. Of course being a pathological liar, Kelso would never admit the truth about thieving a jacket from a party. Telling various tales to various people. Not good for the gangster's image y'see. Still, such character flaws aside, I thought he was quite a nice character when you got to know him but then I never was much of a judge in that area anyway.

He was another yin, how come they all come to me when they have serious trouble but never in good fortune? He was in deep shit. A hit had been put out on him by his own old crew, now known as the Caravel Cartel. I should never have got involved, not my problem and all that. Yet I couldn't just walk away when it transpired that the contractor turned out to be yet another long lost friend of mine. The least I could do for the guy was make contact and put forward a plea of mitigation. He agreed to meet with Kelso and I, the result of which was that the dogs of war were called off, at least in the meantime, as a favour to me. This meant that Kelso could come back out and walk the streets in the daylight, finally, free at last.

There was only one game in town, everybody was doing it but nobody admitting it, at least not publicly. In the long years of my absence the drugs scene had taken off like the proverbial magic dragon. Yet still there were clear lines drawn. Those who dealt in Happy Jack to build a stack and those who dealt in everything else but. Kelso's problem was that a large percentage of the Happy Jack came under the control of the Cartel and he was blackballed and boycotted by his old team. He literally was not allowed to operate or get a toehold in anything. Fine by me. I wanted nothing to do with any of it anyway. Yet his association with me meant that he could be seen around and meet people, friends of mine, with contacts outwith the control of the Cartel. That's their own business and none of mine what people do to make ends meet. This was like the roaring '20s Chicago style. Only now it was dope prohibited, not booze. Their business is their business and no business of mine. My concerns were more legit, laying the groundwork for buying and selling ice cream vans, but it never did get off the ground and the partnership dissolved once Kelso's source of income was unexpectedly and drastically exposed to me, with dire results.

Another old friend delivered a consignment of Happy Jack to me directly and, on confirming that I had no knowledge of any such order, had explained to me that as the news of this order had got through to his boss, the boss had become suspicious, 'TC doesn't do Smack.' He then had the consignment delivered direct rather than being picked up by Kelso who had been making the run for some time in my name.

I bumped into Kelso with a straight heed to the nose and a severe boot in the balls to dissolve the partnership. That should have been an end to our brief encounter, but it wasn't.

Kelso freaked out. He knew what had happened with the Thin Yin. The observation and organisation put into effect to close down an entire operation so effortlessly on my part. The stories he'd heard about it, were they true? They were in fact paranoid delusions but he didn't know that. Now he was expecting that such an organisation would be focusing on him. In fact, I was on my own now that our friendship was dissolved. This left him back in the line of fire from the Cartel where I had once stood as his shield. He freaked the freaker's freak. The whole world was conspiring against him and I was at the head of it all. His own contacts were coming to me. Kelso was armed to the teeth, paranoid out of his skull, checking under cars, under beds, behind bushes. TC was stalking him for the kill. He was trying to bug my phone, sitting out all night in the bushes waiting on me coming. He was eventually diagnosed as a paranoid schizo but, meanwhile, he was still on the loose and I the focus of his nightmares. He simply could not believe that I would let it go at that when in fact I never gave him a second thought. He wasn't worth a second thought, his delusions of grandeur were all in his head as a result of dabbling in his own product. I guess that's Karma. The problem with these eejits is that they want to play in the big league and roll in the dough but their heads can't handle the pressure and they crash back to earth with a thump. Tough at the top. In the end it was his greed that was his downfall. He had ripped off so many people in his hurry to build a mountain of cash that he was drawn deeper and deeper into the gutter.

I was getting news from the streets that he had been lifted, then again and again. The last news was that the police had taken him in and turned over one of his safe houses, which meant that they would have had to have caught him with something to warrant the search. However, he was out again that same day.

I went over to see my eldest son, Tommy, that day and was in for the shock of my life. Tommy was busy stashing parcels. Kelly had just been over and had asked him to hold onto these . . .

'WHIT?' I freaked out, hurriedly explaining that I had just heard that he'd got out of the nick. 'He's setting you up, he's trading you in,' and to dump the parcels in the midden. Quick before the coppers arrive. I got out of there fast, on the way out of the street passing the police on their way in, praying to god he would have it dumped in time before they put his door in. It suddenly struck me how close I'd come to being caught there with him and that in fact it was more likely that I had been the target.

Tommy had been quick enough to have dumped 90 per cent of it and was caught with the dross. In total there had been 16k of speed which had gone bad. The dirty big shit bag had tried to set him up and trade him in and had been so tight he tried to do so without any actual financial loss.

Fortunately corrupt police had been drumming out fake warrants on their PCs. Using them to raid non-Cartel dealers. Confiscating their kit and their cash, putting them out of business and selling the kit back to the Cartel. This hit the news when honest coppers, unaware that the warrants were fake had used them to make arrests which had fallen through on first appearance in court. Tommy had been arrested under one of these warrants and the case against him collapsed.

No such luck for Kelly though. His usefulness as an

undercover police agent reached its sell-by date when the good people of neighbouring Cranhill revolted against the dealers in death.

Cranhill had had enough. A ten-year-old boy had taken some of his father's Happy Jack and had gone to bed and died. The parents, out of their skulls on Kelso's kit, forgot all about him and the pit bull pups in the bedroom. Three or four days had passed before anyone found the body there. In between that time, the starving pups had been chewing on the dead child to survive.

The police had become involved, surveillance set up, catching Kelso making a delivery and had followed him home to his stash before pouncing and catching him with a couple of kilos of Happy Jack, gun, silencer, handcuffs, mask and gloves. An assassin's kit. Serious business for a murderer on parole.

Next I heard was Liz telling me that she had been asked to pose for a photo outside her front door, under Kelso's veranda to illustrate dimensions for Kelso's defence. The smack had been found on the veranda. What should she do? I advised that she should not go into the photo but that she should take the photo of Kelly's wife. If it was only for an idea of dimensions, then it wouldn't matter who was in the frame. Her offer to take the picture was refused. If she was not in the frame then it was no good. In fact, what he was trying to do was put my ex wife in the frame to show that a tall man such as myself could have reached up from her front door and put it in there – that, in fact, it was mine. Typical low life tactics to take his enemy down with him. Without Liz in the frame that particular defence was abandoned but he would try a few more before he finally went down for ten years. Whether he gets recalled on his life sentence beyond that is yet to be seen.

I don't need this crap. I'm just trying to get on with my

life and to clear my name. I shouldn't have to cope with these half-wits and greedy bastards dragging my name into their petty power plays and conspiracies. What am I supposed to do? Go to the police? And have my name all over the front pages again in some obscure slanted version in association with this nonsense? It was already all over the newspapers in connection with hit contracts out on me and even where the cash could be collected – from the so-called Licensee. The journalists and editors not only aiding and abetting a criminal conspiracy to murder by advertising the contract but actually being Art & Part in it by their direction on who will pay what price.

I can do without this garbage. My children can do without it too. Walking in the street with my son, Brian, the boy was jumping out of his skin with nerves.

'What in god's name is up with you, son?'

'But they're trying to kill you, Dad . . .'

It means so much more to him than it would to any other twelve-year-old. He was still in his mother's womb during the trial as she stood as my alibi. For every year of his life the family had the fire services at the door on the anniversary of the Doyle family fire directed there upon the emergency call, 'Woman and children trapped.'

This is simply a warning to me, the reminder that I have family exposed, literally, in the line of fire. So I don't need this crap from lowlifes and bitches playing games with my name. I have bigger fish to fry.

Nightmare

Recurring Nightmare

Tenth of February is one of those dates when something extreme or significant always occurs in my life. It was my lib date on my ten-year sentence into the winter of discontent, for example, and would've been my lib on this twenty-years, should that have been passed as a sentence. Now, once again, the day that my daughter Shannon was born, 3 February, I received the seven-days notice to appear at Edinburgh High Court of Appeal for a hearing on 10 February 1998.

The wean was a week old then when we drove out to Edinburgh – myself, Karen and a friend. It was a bright and pleasant day without a worry to spoil the view. I was reassuring the others that it was my impression that the court would not and, indeed, could not make any final decision at this stage. That this was just another procedural hearing. First, they would have to make a judgment allowing the hearing of fresh evidence or, rather, deciding upon whether it was competent in law to allow it to be heard – which it obviously was. Then set a date for that event and, once it was heard, to set a date for their final judgment which, at the very least, would entail a retrial. But it would be more likely that the Crown would not pursue this course and, in fact, were more likely to abandon the case from the point where the hearing of Love and his sister was allowed by the court.

My optimism was based on my understanding of the

state of the law as it then stood. This was that fresh evidence would only be allowed on an appeal provided that there was some reasonable excuse as to why it was not heard at the original trial (Alan Church-v-HMA). Our reason being that it was no fault of ours that the Crown's principal witness was serial perverter of justice and had made a conscious decision to pervert the course of justice once again in our case and had carried that out. There was not a lot we could do to prevent this as any attempt to persuade him to do otherwise may have been interpreted as an attempt to intimidate or suborn a witness. That we cannot be held responsible for whatever the distempered state of mind of the Crown's witness in his decision and determination to commit perjury against us. That he now admits to that perjury and that no such conversation had ever occurred on Charge 15 (fire murders) and that, in fact, he himself was the person responsible for discharging the weapon on Charge 9 (shooting the van) contrary to his evidence given at the trial. HIS excuse for his perjury being that the police had put him up to it as part of a deal in exchange for his liberation was not our responsibility and of no consequence to the pursuit of the facts and justice in our case.

That he now admitted the perjury on sworn affidavit, under caution to the police and on television, and that there was more evidence against the witness for perjury and more people having overheard him admitting to his perjury than there was evidence of his alleged overheard conversation against us at the trial.

Yet the law also required further safeguards to help ensure that what he was saying now was not just yet another lie. That some adminicle of independent evidence would be required in support of this new version and, although this was not required to meet the standard of corroboration necessary to sustain a conviction at a trial, nevertheless, some adminicle of evidence was required in support.

No problem. Besides his admission to perjury and besides the issue regarding the contradictions inherent in his alibi to his evidence, our main thrust would be the previously undisclosed statement to the police, affidavits and evidence of Love's sister, Agnes Love or Carlton. She had witnessed her brother firing the gun at Andrew Doyle's van mistaking it for Jimmy Mitchell's. This supported Love's confessions to perjury since he now admitted that it had in fact been he who had fired the gun at the van and not Tamby the Bear as he had falsely stated at the trial. Agnes Love then was not only evidence of who had actually fired the gun at the van, evidence of her police statement having been kept secret by the Crown, but she was also confirmation of Love's confessions to perjury in that respect. Would that adminicle be enough? Of course it would. It would be enough to convict him of perjury should the Crown make the decision to prosecute him in that respect. More than the sufficient adminicle as required by the Appeal Court and the law.

His evidence and credibility as a witness being fundamentally crucial to the Crown case there was no way then, in accordance to law, that the court could refuse to allow the truth to be finally heard. This appearance then would be no more than a procedural step. A formality. The formal announcement that the appeal is to be allowed to hear fresh evidence. A date would then be set for this main event.

Once that was over, Love's evidence and credibility as a witness against us dissolved in the light of the living reality, the conviction would either be overturned on the grounds of insufficiency of evidence in law or, as credibility of a witness is a point for a jury to decide, it would then be an issue for a retrial. Though highly unlikely that the Crown would want to pursue this latter option, it would, nevertheless, be the proper procedure and the correct course of action. Retrial on Charges 9 and 15 alone would suit me fine as my ideal.

Ignorance is bliss they say and it was in this state I strolled confidently into the Lions' Maw of the Appeal Court. There was some indication that something wasn't quite right. The Press were there en masse, unusual for a procedural step. They all had the same question, 'What if the court refuses the appeal?' and in my vain wisdom I wanted to explain the procedures of law and how that could not happen at this stage. Instead, I wearily tripped out the sound bite, 'In that case the fight for justice goes on,' never expecting it would actually come to that. I couldn't consider the possibility of the recurrence of that nightmare. In prison, I would only eat food supplied by my family as per the rights of an untried prisoner. The refusal of this appeal would negate that right and, in effect, amount to a death sentence for I would never surrender my right to protest and be free. I would die. Hungering for justice in a fast for freedom. Innocent imprisoned in pain. No! that wouldn't happen. It couldn't happen. It wasn't possible . . . unless they planned to refuse to allow the fresh evidence in support of our case to be heard? But there was no way, according to the facts and the law, this could be done legitimately . . .

Legitimately? That's the key word here. So how naive can one man be to have gone through trials that I have gone through and still expect a measure of justice might be doled out by a Scottish Appeal Court in a high profile, controversial case such as this? Human optimism, they say, is infinite. The drowning man will clutch at straws and, in the Nazi concentration camps hapless souls volunteered to dismantle so many unexploded bombs for the price of freedom, regardless that the odds against success were phenomenal and no one had ever reached the target. Still, each and every individual has the belief that they will be the one.

This is Scotland of the law which is held up to the rest of the world as a shining example and upon which the principles of the convention of human rights is founded. Its principles are, in fact, founded upon justice and fairness. But the fault doesn't lie with the principles of justice, it lies in the administration of the law. They just make up the law as they go along, chopping, changing and readjusting it to suit themselves in any given situation or new policy practices of the day. They believe their will is law and when close scrutiny bars them from changing the law to suit themselves they just change the facts to bar access to the letter of the law. Misinterpret the facts or change the meaning of a word. Like 'reasonable', for example, can now mean 'justifiable' if they choose to interpret it that way. Or they can disagree on the meaning of the word 'heard' to show off their rhetorical agility.

Lord Cullen, the new Lord Chief Justice Clerk, went into a long detailed dissection of the evidence in the case and, on Charge 9, brought the new Advocate Depute's arguments about Reynolds and proof of my alleged ownership of the car back into it.

'There was also evidence from a witness, Alexander Reynolds, who stated that later that same evening he found the co-accused Moore sitting in the car outside John Campbell's close in Craiglockhart Street. Reynolds then drove the car to his own close and the police seized it there that night. Reynolds also stated that on another occasion when he was in Campbell's house with Moore, Campbell told Moore that he owed him

a car because his, Thomas Campbell's car (the
Volvo), had been taken off Moore. Reynolds then
said that he would give Moore his car to give to
Campbell . . . In this respect the Advocate Depute
drew attention to the evidence of Reynolds as
linking Campbell to the ownership of the car.
He also submitted that Campbell's reaction to
the seizure of the car by the police, following
its identification as the car used in the shooting,
could also be regarded as significant. He did not
express any curiosity as to why it had been seized
or, if he knew the reason, any indication as to the
use it had been put to but merely told Moore that
he (Moore) owed him a car . . . However, these
matters were not mentioned by the trial judge in
his charge and, at this time, it is not possible to
know whether and to what extent they were used
in the Crown case against Campbell . . .'

This presumes that the car was accepted as mine when,
in fact, it was not. Reynolds had said no such thing at
the trial. The car owed by Gary Moore was due to the
missing wheel and hostage TV incident. Reynolds could
not identify the man to whom Moore had spoken and
had not entered the house, nor seen or heard the man
say anything. This was the submission of the original
Advocate Depute revisited by the new one. In fact, it
had been referred to in the judge's charge to the jury but
had been dismissed as the submission of the Depute and
not the actual evidence by the first Appeal Court when the
trial judge's earlier remarks on this issue were pointed out
in the appeal opinion of 1985.

'The same applies to Reynolds. Whatever you
may think of Reynolds' evidence none was given

by him upon which you could find in support of
the Crown allegation against Thomas Campbell or
Steele.'

Yet here, fourteen years later, the same Crown lies and
crap were being shuffled out again in support of their
case.

So why don't they LOOK AT THE FUCKIN TRAN-
SCRIPTS THEN? Instead of just accepting the Crown's
word for it.

So on and on like this, just a repeat of the last nightmare
with the Crown trying to justify their prosecution. None
of it was of any consequence to me. Just the usual trumped
up, one-sided set up but none of it was worth a fart in
the gale without the evidence of William Love. Try to
justify themselves all they liked to impress the shit out
of the Press and the public but without the evidence of
Love there was nothing but unfounded speculation. Cut
to the chase, Mister, let's go to it. How are you going to
get round that?

'Love does not admit or suggest that he was the
person who shot at the van or that he lied about
his part in the shooting,'

says Lord Cullen. Eh? What? That's a strange thing to
say since I sat here over many months listening to you
discuss and debate that very issue in exactitude of detail.
How can he make that mistake?

'Mrs Carlton is unable to give evidence which can
provide support for the proposition that Love gave
false evidence as a result of alleged inducement
and pressure . . .'

But that's Love's excuse for his perjury and not our concern how he tries to excuse his actions. Mrs Carlton is supporting evidence of his perjury, that's all that matters . . .

> 'She is able to give evidence which, if true,
> indicates that Love would have wished to minimise
> his own involvement in the shooting.'

Yeah? By blaming the others for the crimes which he himself had committed and as per his previous criminal convictions for serial perversion of justice. So, 'perjurise' becomes 'minimise' now does it?

> 'This could support the proposition that he gave
> false evidence as to his own involvement.'

He gave false evidence? Right! Fine! His evidence and his credibility as a witness being fundamentally crucial to the Crown prosecution case – that case then falls.

> 'But does not tend to show that he was induced
> and put under pressure by others to give false
> evidence on other matters relating to Charge 9.'

No? Does it not provide proof of the leverage upon which he could be prised and induced in these circumstances? Confirming his confessions? If he lied he lied, end of story. It is not for us at this appeal to prove, or for the court to try and disprove his excuses for HIS perjury. That would be for another court in another trial to deal with. He was a Crown witness – the excuses for his perjury are not our responsibility, nor our concern.

> '. . . let alone on Charge 15. In any event,

it does not provide independent support for
the explanation given by Love *since* he does
not say that he lied as to the extent of his
own involvement in the shooting. *In these
circumstances*, I am not satisfied that the evidence
which Mrs Carlton would give could support
Love's explanation that he was induced and put
under pressure to provide false evidence against
the Appellants in regard to the charges with which
I am concerned.'

Firstly, it appears that this judgment is founded upon an error of the facts. '*Since*' Love did not admit to the firing of the gun in the shooting '*in these circumstances*', Love's sister cannot support something which it appears (to Lord Cullen) that her brother has not admitted. This error of the facts gave access to the technical hurdles of the law to then refuse to hear the evidence of Mrs Carlton in support of her brother's confession to perjury. She cannot support something he has not admitted. Thus, without her evidence, Love's evidence itself cannot be heard as there would be no point to it without the independent support. I must ask myself, was this a deliberate error of the facts? I mean, what does he think the appeal is about? On what grounds was it referred to the court by the Scots Secretary of State to begin with? In fact, Love's confessions to perjury and, in particular, his confession to the shooting as well as his sister's independent support of that. How could he have missed the point in this, the highest court in the land, and missed that part of Love's confessions? Especially after many long days of discussion and debate precisely on that point. What does he think the appeal was about?

Secondly, he seems more intent on refuting Love's explanation of 'why' he committed perjury. Love's excuses are no concern of the appellants. Whether they are good excuses or highly controversial ones or not is no fault or concern of the appellants. The law is that the appellants are required to provide a reasonable excuse why his fresh evidence was not heard at the original trial. That the Crown's witness now admits to perjury is sufficient. Is it now the case that we require to provide two excuses? That our case stands or falls upon the excuse of the Crown's serial perverter of justice and perjurer? It is no fault of ours that he committed perjury against us nor are his excuses for that any concern of ours.

The problem here was that this court's opinion was now interpreting the law as that of requiring two 'reasonable excuses' as to why the fresh (in change of heart) evidence was not heard at the original trial. Our excuse that the witness deliberately committed perjury and, with the independent support from his sister, was in fact reasonable enough. However, that our excuse was now so indistinguishably linked to *his* excuse that the police had put him up to it, was just too great a controversy of wide ranging repercussions for the old guard to allow to be heard publicly in an open court. Everything else was just a farce and a cover up to put a gag on this being heard, even though that entailed that the interests of justice were being swept under the carpet and the carpet out the window and into the skip.

'The Advocate Depute maintained the argument that (without the evidence of Love) a retrial would not be possible, the Court should not quash the convictions unless it was satisfied that if the jury had heard the new evidence it would have come to a different result. Secondly, he submitted that the well known test set out in the opinion of Lord Justice General Emslie in Cameron was

to be preferred to the re-formation adopted by
Lord Justice General Hope in Church. However,
these are issues with which, in my view, I do not
require to deal with in order to resolve the present
Appeals; and accordingly I reserve my opinion in
regard to them.

In light of the view which I have expressed the
Appeals should, in my opinion, be refused.'

That there was not sufficient evidence in law to entitle a
jury to convict without the evidence of Love according to
the original trial judge. It appears now that the Crown,
having asked the court not to quash the convictions
because there would be no evidence, retrial was not
possible. Further, that the court should sit as a jury in
this case, giving a verdict before the evidence is even
heard, and that is exactly what Lord Cullen did. He
delivered his dirty dirk into the heart of Scottish justice
rather than allow the truth to be heard . . .

. . . immediately redeemed by Lord McCluskey:

'. . . In the present case, the new unheard
evidence attributed to Love is 'different' evidence
of the kind embraced by the words used in S. 106
(3c), paras (a)(i) and (b). The Appellants invite us
to hear Love, who was a most important witness,
give changed evidence which I may paraphrase as
follows:

'At the trail I lied on oath. I did so because it
suited my own selfish purpose to give evidence
incriminating both accused. Knowing that evidence
to be false. I lied as to my own role in saying
that I went to the police out of revulsion for the
murder. The police came to me. The explanation
as to why I gave the perjured evidence is this:

the police suborned me; they pressurised me
to give evidence against Campbell who they
clearly believed was guilty of arranging to set
fire to the Doyles' house; and I believed that it
would be in my own best interests to do what
the police wanted – because it would enable me
to avoid being charged myself with attempted
murder on charge 9 of which I knew I was guilty;
indeed I was the one who fired the shotgun; I
was willing to go along with this plan to present
false evidence; I also believed the police when
they held out to me the prospect of various other
advantages; they suggested what I should do and
how to do it; but ultimately it was my own choice;
I now wish to withdraw my incriminating evidence
against the Appellants on Charge 15; it is simply
not true . . .'

So, here then is a situation where the first judge is
contradicted and, in fact, corrected by the second judge on
a crucial and fundamental question of fact. Did or did not
Mr Love confess to firing the gun contrary to his evidence
at the trial? Lord Cullen says Nay and Lord McCluskey
says Yea. Such a crucial issue for the fact that it entails not
only his confession to perjury but the independent support
to that given by his sister, as required by law before it
can be allowed as evidence under the terms of the Act.
Fundamental because the whole appeal now turns upon
this issue and it was precisely on this issue that the matter
was referred to the court in the first instance. The question
now is, how can Lord McCluskey say this and, indeed,
quote from Love's confessions in that respect, while Lord
Cullen denies that Love said it at all? Who is right and
who is wrong? It is difficult to believe that Lord Cullen
flipped two pages over and missed that part of Love's

confession. Perhaps then this particular confession, of the many made by Love, is not the one Lord Cullen chose to address.

In fact Lord McCluskey was later shown to be correct when it was accepted that Love's confession, in that respect, had been before the Scots Secretary at the time of his decision to refer the case to the court and had, in fact, been lodged with the court from the earliest stages in the proceedings. That, however, Lord Cullen was not in error of the facts because that particular confession of Love's was not before him at the time his opinion was formed.

Yet still, we are entitled to a fair hearing of all the facts of the case, and any error in omission of the crucial facts means that we have not been given our right. Lord Cullen's opinion was based on that error of the facts since he believed that Love had not admitted to the shooting. *In these circumstances* depends upon an erroneous omission of crucial information. Lord McCluskey goes on in his opinion to show why he supports the appeal . . .

> '. . . Agnes Carlton, which is said to provide independent support is whether Mrs Carlton's statements, assuming them to be true, are not only consistent with Love's explanation for giving the evidence he gave at the trial but are also able to provide something which strengthens or confirms or supports that explanation. It is absolutely essential to keep in mind that there is only one competing explanation for Love's having given at the trial the evidence which he then gave; it is that his evidence at the trial was substantially true. I consider that there is considerable force in the argument that Mrs Carlton's evidence is more consistent with his

having lied at the trial than with his having told the truth. I choose to put the point this way recognising that the decision in *Fox v. H.M. Advocate* makes it plain that if the evidence is capable of supporting the explanation it does not even need to be 'more' consistent with Love's explanation in order to be corroborative in its legal character. There are, of course, detailed parts of Love's explanation that are not corroborated by anything now said by Mrs Carlton. For example, she makes no claim to have witnessed what was said or even discussed when Love met with two police officers, Messrs Walker and McKillop, on the occasions when, according to Love, they effectively scripted the evidence he was to give at the trial against the persons they considered to be the guilty ones. But *Fox v. H.M. Advocate*, in disapproving of the approach in *Mackie v. H.M. Advocate* 1994 J.C. 132 and distinguishing the well-known dictum of Lord President Normand in *O'Hara v. Central S.M.T. Co.* 1941 S.C. 363, makes it abundantly clear that all that is required to make evidence corroborative in character is that it is 'capable of providing support or confirmation in regard to *factum probandum* of which direct evidence has been given' (per Lord Justice Clerk). As Lord Coulsfield says in *Fox*, 'It is an everyday occurrence that juries are directed that corroboration of a strong piece of evidence may be found in a weaker piece of evidence which, *in itself, might not be capable of being described as incriminating*.' (emphasis added).

If corroboration that a crime has been committed can be found in such weaker and not incriminating evidence then inevitably the same

assessment must be made in relation to evidence
which is tendered by way of corroboration of or
'support' for a mere 'reasonable explanation'.

I must emphasise that in deciding the pure legal
question – the vital question at this stage – as to
whether or not Mrs Agnes Carlton's evidence is
capable, in law, of being regarded as affording
support for the explanation of Love's conduct at
the trial we must not take too narrow a view of
what that explanation is. I have summarised it
in one way; the parties have provided their own
formulations. But stripped down to the essentials,
the explanation is: 'I lied because I thought it
would advance my own selfish interests.' That,
in this context, is the *factum probandum*. It is
that which requires support. So, the crucial issue
here is whether or not Mrs Carlton's evidence
could provide support for that explanation. I
should not be prepared to hold, without hearing
Mrs Carlton's evidence in full, that it could not
provide support for that explanation. She provides
some support for the important detail that Love
was in fact guilty of using the shotgun in the
attempted murder which became Charge 9. The
importance of that piece of evidence is that,
if it is correct, Love was, in effect, lying so as
to minimise his role in the Charge 9 shooting:
instead of being the man who actually fired the
shotgun twice he presented himself in evidence as
merely the person who drove the gunman to and
from the locus. That was calculated to advance
Love's selfish interests, which principally lay in
obtaining immunity from prosecution. Mrs Carlton
also provides support for the assertion by Love
that a procurator fiscal was involved in something

underhand in connection with Love's giving of
the evidence he gave. In her affidavit she speaks
of being taken to court every day as a witness;
by then (September 1984) she had given a police
statement implicating Love as the one who had
used the shotgun in the assault which gave rise to
Charge 9. Her affidavit of 12 July 1987 includes
these passages:

'4. When the trial started I was cited as a
     witness. I cannot remember now how it all
     came about or who exactly it was for. I was
     there at the court every day for a fortnight.
     On the day my brother, William Love, gave
     evidence I was at home and two men came to
     get me. They said they were Sheriff Officers.
     I was taken to court and put into a room.
     The door of the room had a window in it. I
     do not remember the exact location. While I
     was there, two police officers came in and
     my brother William Love was handcuffed to
     each of them. My brother asked me how I
     was and I said that I was fine. That was all
     that was said. Shortly after that, my brother
     was taken into the court. A few minutes after
     they took my brother into court a man came
     into the room and told me I could go. I do not
     know who it was. I did not go back to court
     again after that.

5.   During the time I was waiting at the High
     Court in Glasgow I was sitting with my
     husband Ronnie. A man came in and asked
     me if I would come and see somebody. They
     would not let my husband come with me and
     I was asked to see the man alone. I followed
     the messenger and we went up to a room

at the top of the stairs and in the room was
a man with a black robe on. He was middle
aged. He did not tell me his name. The man
asked me if I would reconsider my statement.
He asked me if I would be able to say in my
evidence that the man who shot the van
was Thomas Gray and that my brother
William Love was the driver of the vehicle
that was involved in the shooting. I told him
I could not change my statement and that
my brother was the man I saw shooting the
ice cream van. The man said that if I did
not alter my statement my brother, William
Love, would get 15 years for perjury. I told
him that I was not prepared to change my
statement.'

Thus, the fact that Agnes Love or Carlton was sent home
by the prosecutor during the trial comes around again
to the issue of the difference between 'precognition as
opposed to police statement' in that the defence only had
a precognition from her and a precognition is not legally
enforceable. It cannot be put to a witness in court as a
previous 'utterance' and can be withdrawn or changed at
any time with impunity. But a police statement cannot.
It can be enforced and put to the witness who is held
to it at pain of perjury if they retract it. (Like Granger,
Hamilton and Reynolds for example.) Therefore, because
Agnes Carlton had been taken to see her brother and
the prosecutor and had then 'left the building' never to
return, it must be assumed by the defence that she was
not a willing witness. In fact, she had been nobbled and
got at by her brother and the prosecutor to change her
precognition. However, the defence were not aware of her
'police statement' to the same effect as her precognition. It

was not disclosed by the Crown prosecution at the time of the trial or for another twelve years. Therefore, the reason why she was not called as a witness at the time was this non-disclosure of her police statement, together with the prosecution's attempt to nobble her and, on failing to do so, sending her home. She leaves the court building. The defence, only possessing her precognition, must take her departure as a sign that she has retracted and do not pursue it further.

If the defence had been made aware of her police statement they would then have had the grounds to enforce it by citing her as a witness. Without its disclosure they had no grounds. The fault here is in the non-disclosure of obviously exculpatory evidence by the Crown in their dirty tactics designed to pull the wool over the public's eyes.

McCluskey

'Her whole evidence also suggests that Love, himself a villain with a long criminal record and deeply involved in the attempted murder of innocent people, voluntarily called in the police because of his abhorrence at the actual murder of other members of the Doyle family just does not ring true; she gives the lie to it. Evidence of the kind which she is now apparently prepared to give would, in my view, have passed the '*prima facie* material' test within the meaning of what is now section 268(2)(a) of the 1995 Act. It appears to me capable of providing 'support' for Love's evidence that he was under pressure, that he perjured himself, that he got instant tangible advantages from doing so and that the police and the procurator fiscal put pressure on him, as well as on her, during the trial to ensure that

Love stuck to the story he had provided when
precognosed on oath. It is capable of providing
support for the whole picture of Love's choosing to
act in a way that would advance his own interests
at the expense of others. It has also to be noticed
incidentally that she says that, much later, she
knew that her brother 'wanted it off his chest'.
This supports Love's position that for years he
has been trying to withdraw his trial evidence
and tell 'the truth'. One interesting feature of
this piece of evidence may well be that, before the
law was changed in March 1997, it would have
been *impossible* to place Love's altered evidence
before a court of law. The various lawyers acting
for Campbell and Steele must have known this
throughout most if not all of the time during
which Love has been saying that he lied at the
trial. It would be surprising if it was not just as
well understood by long term inmates of Scottish
prisons, such as Campbell and Steele and Love
himself. So it is arguably unlikely that Love or
anybody else involved thought that retraction of
Love's evidence would be likely to assist Campbell
and Steele. In my opinion, Mrs Carlton's evidence
ought to be heard. As I do not consider that we
could judge of the credibility and reliability of Mrs
Carlton without also hearing Love's evidence and
such other evidence as could be shown to have a
material bearing on the truth and significance of
the new matter said to have come to light since
the conclusion of the trial, I am driven to the
conclusion that this court ought to hear all the
new evidence that the parties can persuade us
may shed valuable light on any such potentially
material matter.'

Sutherland

"Turning to the requirements of subsection (3C) Love has advanced a number of explanations for his change of story. I do not consider that the possibility of obtaining bail can be regarded as a reasonable explanation. This would be an example of pure self-interest which could provide no sort of justification for committing perjury. He then maintains that he was told by two senior police officers what evidence they wished him to give and who put precise words into his mouth which he duly regurgitated at the trail. If this is true it might provide some material for him to think that the giving of false evidence would have some justification on the basis that if senior police officers were prepared to countenance, indeed encourage, such behaviour there would be no reason for him not to comply and I would be prepared to hear his evidence on this aspect. Your Lordship in the chair has mentioned the allegation that Love was threatened by the procurator fiscal that if he did not give evidence at the precognition on oath he would be charged with the attempted murder and that accordingly he was put in an impossible situation having told the police of his involvement after being told that he would not be prosecuted. For my part I very much doubt if this could constitute a reasonable explanation in the case of Love. In the first place it is not suggested that the procurator fiscal was endeavouring to persuade Love to give false evidence. As far as the fiscal was concerned he had no reason to believe that what Love was going to say would be other than the truth and it cannot be a justification for perjury for a witness to say that he was told that

the law would take its course if he declined to
give evidence. Secondly, Love was an experienced
criminal sufficiently well versed in the criminal
law to know that duress might provide a defence
to a charge of perjury and I have no doubt that
he would be well aware that statements taken
from him by the police, after a promise of
immunity, could not be used in evidence against
him. However, it may be that this would require
to be elucidated in evidence. I do not find in any of
the statements of Love any other explanations of
why he elected to commit perjury which could be
described as reasonable explanations. Accordingly,
in my opinion, at best, the only two explanations
which could be regarded as reasonable would
be that he was suborned to commit perjury by
the police and that he was forced to give false
evidence on oath because of the fear that he would
be prosecuted on the basis of the statements he
had given to the police under inducement.

The next stage is to consider whether there is
independent support for Love's explanation. This
was said to come from three possible sources. In
the first place, it was suggested that the evidence
of the police officers who interviewed Love in
connection with possible perjury charges could
provide support in that they could speak to Love
telling them what his explanations were. This,
however, could not be independent support as the
source of it all is Love himself. Secondly, it was
said that Mrs Carlton could provide independent
support. In this connection it must be repeated
that what is required by the statute is support for
the explanation and not support for the content
of the new evidence. The fact that Love said he

committed perjury is not in itself an explanation,
it is merely an assertion. What is required is an
explanation of why the allegedly true evidence
was not given at the trial and that therefore
calls for an explanation of why he gave false
evidence. The two explanations given by Love
which might be regarded as reasonable have been
mentioned above and it is these explanations
which require support. There is absolutely nothing
in Mrs Carlton's various statements which would
support the view that the police put words into
Love's mouth and there is absolutely nothing
which supports the view that the procurator fiscal
threatened him with prosecution if he did not
give evidence. There is accordingly nothing in any
evidence which she could give which supports the
only two explanations which could be regarded as
reasonable. It is perhaps not without that in her
statement of 26 April 1994 she says:

'I have no idea why he did what he did and
saying what he did in court,' which is the clearest
possible indication that she is unable to provide
any independent support for Love's explanations.
Finally, it was said that the facts that Love was
given bail and was not prosecuted could provide
support but in my view these facts are neutral.
If the evidence he gave at the trial was true he
would still have been granted bail and of course
having been used as a Crown witness could not
have been prosecuted. There is therefore nothing
in these matters to show that he committed
perjury, let alone what his reasons were for
so doing. For these reasons, I am satisfied
that there is no independent support for the
explanations advanced by Love and accordingly

the requirement of (3C) have not been met and
the new evidence from Love cannot be heard.

As far as the other matters raised in the
grounds of appeal are concerned I am in
agreement with your Lordship in the chair as
to their disposal. I therefore agree with your
Lordship that these appeals fall to be refused.

So now, according to this school of flawed reasoning, evidence of perjury together with independent corroboration of it is not enough. This court now requires evidence in support of 'why' the perjury was committed. Yet he was not 'our' witness. He was the Crown's witness. What then was their explanation?

How can it be? How has it now become that the victims of admitted perjured evidence (with independent corroboration of it) must now rely upon the quality of the defence of the perjurer in his excuses as to why he perjured himself against us? The administration of justice now appears to have been turned on its head to the point when a man pleading guilty, providing confession and corroboration of a crime, is dismissed out of hand by the court for the fact that he cannot provide a good enough excuse as to 'why' he committed that crime and the victim punished in his place as a consequence.

In fact, it has always been the law until this point that the 'reasonable explanation' was for the appellant to provide and earlier in Lord Sutherland's same judgment he concedes:

'Section (3A) provides that such evidence
may only found an appeal where there is a
reasonable explanation of why it was not so
heard. The first question therefore is what can
constitute a reasonable explanation. It was a

matter of agreement that it is for the appellant to
establish this explanation. Clearly the explanation
advanced would have to be accepted by the court
as apparently genuine before it could begin to be
established. Any explanation which is held to be
untrue is not an explanation at all.'

So, as it is a matter of agreement by all that the explanation stems from the appellant and not from the witness,
why then do they then go on to turn the case to reliance
upon the explanation of the perjurer whilst the appellant's
explanation was simply that he was in fact a perjurer and
admits it.

Thus, this subtle shifting of the onus for the explanation
from the appellant to the perjurer's excuses detracts
from the appellant's and misdirects from the appellant's
reasons as to why the fresh evidence was not heard at
the time, placing the victims of confessed perjury once
again into the hands of the defence of the perjurer and
his excuses for his crime. It never was a question of
'why' he did it. It is a question of whether he did it
as he said he did, or not. And, therefore, as to whether
there is any supporting evidence of his confessions to that
effect, or not.

All this then is a clever ploy, a rigmarole, an academic exercise in somersault semantics cloaking and side
stepping the issue that there is in fact direct evidence
in confession and independent corroboration that the
crucial Crown prosecution witness committed perjury.
What other explanation is therefore needed in proof of
miscarriage of justice?

This is an outright travesty of justice. An example of
the academia in high office convinced of their own superi-
ority, believing that the rest of us mere mortals are too
stupid to see through their subtle twistings, wringing the

law around to suit the establishment position, covering up for the follies of their fraternity.

I COULD NOT DEFEND MYSELF (AGAINST YOUR OPINION) BUT WHAT A BLUNDER WOULD BE YOURS IF YOU WERE TO CONVINCE YOURSELVES THAT IN STRIKING AT ME YOU WOULD ESTABLISH ORDER IN YOUR UNHAPPY COUNTRY. DON'T YOU UNDERSTAND YET THAT THE COUNTRY IS DYING OF THE DARKNESS IN WHICH YOU SO OBSTINATELY KEEP HER? THAT HER ANGUISHES ARE THE ANGUISHES OF EQUIVOCATION? THE MISTAKES OF GOVERNMENT OFFICIALS PILE UP ON TOP OF MISTAKES, ONE LIE NECESSITATES ANOTHER UNTIL THE MASS RESULT IS APPALLING. A JUDICIAL BLUNDER HAS BEEN COMMITTED AND, IN ORDER TO HIDE IT, IT HAS BECOME NECESSARY TO COMMIT A NEW OFFENCE EVERY DAY AGAINST SOUND SENSE AND EQUITY.

FROM THE CONDEMNATION OF AN INNOCENT MAN, FLOWS THE ACQUITTAL OF A GUILTY MAN AND, SEE! TODAY THEY BID YOU TO CONDEMN ME IN MY TURN, BECAUSE SEEING MY COUNTRY ON SUCH A TERRIBLE TRACK, I HAVE CRIED OUT IN MY ANGUISH ... SO! CONDEMN ME THEN, BUT IT WILL BE JUST ANOTHER BLUNDER WHICH BURDEN YOU WILL BEAR IN HISTORY AND, MY CONDEMNATION, INSTEAD OF RESTORING THE PEACE WHICH YOU DESIRE, WHICH WE ALL DESIRE, WILL ONLY SOW NEW SEED OF PASSION AND DISORDER.

THE CAULDRON OF DISCONTENT, I TELL YOU, IS FULL TO THE BRIM. I DO NOT MAKE IT SO, TO OVERFLOW ...

Emile Zola -v- The State, 1889. *Dreyfus is innocent*

Nightmare Revisited

The uproar persisted as we were led away once again in chains. This was a death sentence to me. The end of the world. How many times could this happen to the same people in one lifetime? A new beginning and a new life in ruin at my feet. A living, recurring nightmare.

Handing over what cash I had for Karen and the wean for the week's shopping. Cell phone, house keys, car keys to let her get home to the wean. The wean, Shannon, just a week old now. The end of my world yet a new beginning for her. Maybe I had achieved something worthwhile at least.

On to Edinburgh nick. Sat in a dog box. 'STRIP' is the first word of order uttered. 'FUCK OFF' the first reply in defiance. There was no conscious decision of nonconformity. To me I was still a free citizen and simply reacted to such a command uttered by any other in any circumstance. They continued to insist and I continued to refuse and ignore. It felt too much like a final concession. The last line in transition from citizenship to servitude and I simply could not take that step over that line of my own free will. Let them send in the cosh squads in their riot gear and shields. That would suit me just fine for they would have to kill me. Better than a slow death by starvation which was all that lay ahead for me anyway. So bring them on and we will take this struggle to the death.

There is a sense of freedom in the sure knowledge of

impending death, when all you have to live for is taken away. 'Freedom is just another word for nothing left to lose.' In this case, a bullet to the head would have been kinder. It is not quite that the knowledge of the inevitable impending doom stills the storms which rage within. It is more that the storms are no longer other than the norm. For it is more that the storms are all there ever is, ever could be or ever was. The storm is the norm. It wrapped itself around me like a shield. I am the storm, I have always raged thus. This is the norm. It fortifies like a force field wherein the 'I' remains still. Maybe they would call it shock but I was locked into the still tranquillity of the eye of the storm, nothing could touch me, and if they tried, they would bring the wrath of the storm down upon them. I see this now and analyse objectively from afar but, at the time, locked in the calm of the eye of the storm, taking on the riot squads and fighting to the death was as natural and took no greater effort or decision than breathing.

Joe was still prone to tears and my apparent calm seemed to puzzle him.

'It will soon be sorted out,' I told him in an echo of another time while thinking to myself, 'It will soon be over now,' embracing a death sentence. That I would soon be dead was my only comfort and consolation . . . And what of my children? What have yous done to my children? . . . Dirty scumbag, lowlife, evil bastards that y'are. You put the vanity and credibility of your fraternity above and before the interests of justice and equality . . . You inflict injustice before allowing the truth to be heard and, in so doing, corrupt justice from your position of trust for your own ends. May the wrath of god fall upon you . . . Such thoughts transcend the mere idea in the face of the living nightmare.

Joe was taken aside and offered a deal. He had insisted that it should be recounted in my presence for my reaction and/or opinion. That he could remain there in Edinburgh's Saughton prison and would be granted category C, trustee status, within six months in the top wing. Transferred to an open prison before the end of the year. Weekend leaves, home visits, he would be liberated around his fifteenth year, just a couple of years hence. His year plus on the outside had shown that he presented no danger to the public. Blah Blah Blah-fucking-Blah.

Joe had matured a great deal and had come a long way since his late adolescent Myopic Mole mentality. He was now a responsible mature adult with a different outlook on life. He had, in fact, called me into this little conference not only for my opinion, but because he had known instantly what it had meant. That these governors were offering him a deal and not me, nor us both together, entailed that I was to be stamped upon and ground down. But first they would have to drive a wedge between us. Divide and conquer. Joe had wanted me to know what was going down and what was in store. Always insisting, 'And what about Tommy?' The silence in answer to that question had said more than enough and so he had insisted on my presence to hear it for myself.

Now, in answer to Joe's question in my presence, I was offered a similar deal, just a little behind Joe's schedule. Perth prison, C cat within the year. Open prison after two years of that and liberated after a further three. Right on the twenty year mark. All that would be required of me was that I was to play the game, cause no fuss nor controversy. Accept my sentence and get on with it, play the game and obey the rules.

'This is not a fuckin game, Mister. I'm not playing your games. This is for real and I'm fuckin serious. Deadly serious. You can stick your fuckin deals and your system where the sun doesn't shine cos so far as I'm concerned this case is not closed, and I'm not yet dead,' said I.

'Same here,' Joe said, grinning happily like a Cheshire cat. 'You heard it.'

I was led away to the digger still in my civvies so that they could go to work on Joe as originally intended. This deal was never intended for me to begin with, it was intended for Joe. If only they could get one to accept it they could then crush the other under their jackboots. 'Fuck it,' I thought, 'Go for it Joe.' I was already dying anyway. Day one of the final count down. How long can this body last?

The digger was just the same. The same dank dungeon with the same smell and filth. The same nightmare revisited from my first appeal over a dozen years earlier. Same rancid smelling pisspot in the corner. Filthy army blankets and shells of dead cockroaches. At least Dirty, the resident rat, was in his element and well fed. 'Wonder if I'll see him tonight,' I thought. He used to come out tentatively, nervously testing the reaction of the resident lodger, before more boldly entertaining with his antics and cockroach kills. He welcomed a lodger to his domain, this would mean new crumbs and titbits if the human didn't freak out. He was a well kept secret among the long term residents of the dungeons. He didn't appear. Must have had some hard times with the shorter stay residents, only the cockroach shells to show that he, or his offspring, still frequented this exclusive diner.

Taking off my shoes, tie, jacket and folding my suit trousers, using my coat as a blanket, I settled down to the longest day, into the long cold night of vigilance. Thinking of others, Karen and the children. How they would be coping with this nightmare. How they would be hurt and confused by it all. Till somewhere in my living nightmare I tumbled into the blissful oblivion of sleep . . .

Awaking with a start, reaching out for the cot and the

wean beside the bed to feed her. Only for the living nightmare of my dungeon, like a dagger in my heart, to pen-
etrate my reality. Groundhog day. Repetition. How many
times had I done this before? Every few hours throughout
eternity, awakening to feed the baby, awakening into a
nightmare reality.

'Ah well,' sigh I. It won't be long now. Day two of
the final count down. Shipped out to Shotts and Joe to
Perth. Seems that 'new deal' is the order of the day. New
improved versions from various governors. 'No thanks.'
The beat goes on. But so many people seemed so intent
on having us accept a deal of some kind, it made me
wonder if this had been preset, arranged even before
our court ruling. Perhaps as part of a grander plan and
that our refusal to conform with it was not included in
the calculations. New civvy clothes delivered for me to
change into and hang up my suit for better days.

Over to the halls and to many old friends still there is
less than a comfort in the circumstances. Everyone wants
to talk, see me all right, but I'm too preoccupied to focus
directly on the babble around me. By now, as I knew it
would, my brain is churning up and displaying anomalies
and inconsistencies in the judgments. Lighting them up
like neon signs in my head . . .

If one verbal corroborates another as this judgment
now says, then that would open up new areas of fresh
evidence in our case. What's good for the goose is good
for the gander . . .

'Only sufficient proof that perjury was committed, but
not sufficient reason as to why.'

'Love does not admit that he fired the gun . . .'

At least I would live long enough to see the judgment
in writing and make my reply. It would be some weeks
before it finally came through but, in the meantime, there
were some points I could make from memory.

Phoning home. Click! The phone cuts off. Nipping upstairs to the next landing to use that phone. Click! That is cut off too. The entire hall is cut off without their pay phones. The screws assure me that it is a fault on the line and that they don't know what is causing it.

Next morning I'm taken before Assistant Governor Patterson. He accuses me sternly that I was, 'talking about your case on the phone,' and warns that it will not be tolerated. Not part of the deal. I've to buckle down and play the game. I've not to talk about my case 'at all' far less on the phone. Blah Blah-fucking-Blah! Seems that nobody told this guy that I wasn't playing any games and had not accepted any deals. Yet, that not being in the reckoning of the grand plan, here he was crashing in like a bull in a china shop, trying to enforce it as if it was all agreed. I wasn't to try and deny it, he had it all on tape and transcribed. I was talking about my case and I know fine well that this is strictly forbidden.

'Do you mean to say that you cut off my phone call home yesterday?'

'Yes, you are not allowed to talk about your case to anyone and you know that fine well.'

'First I've heard of it . . . You mean you cut off everyone's access to the phone, the entire hall, because I was using the phone?'

'You were talking about your case, don't try and deny it,' he spluttered.

'Excuse me, I am allowed to talk about my case to who ever I like and you have no right to try to stop me. This case is not closed and it is not for you to try to close it. This is a properly constituted campaign and I am as entitled to talk about it as you are to talk about the weather. Don't you tell me what I can't or cannot talk about and I want to know what makes you think that you have the right, not only to cut off my call, but the entire hall because you say I'm not allowed to talk about my case.'

He was not that hall governor, he was a trainee hall governor. It appears that as he could intimidate and bully protection prisoners he had made the mistake of assuming that all prisoners were the same. There was no reasoning with this guy. He decided, on his discretion and without any disciplinary report of any kind, that I was barred from using the pay phone ever again.

I ended up trashing his office. Trying and failing to pan the office windows in with my fist because they were Perspex. I tried again with a fire extinguisher before being dragged away to the digger by the mufti. Not bad, I'd lasted almost three days in the system before confrontation with the ignorant idiots who run it. Governor One, McKinlay, accepted that Patterson was in the wrong. That he could not bar me from the phone without a formal disciplinary report hearing and that, in fact, I was allowed to talk about my case, just not to the Press. He was wrong to cut me off from my first call home and the use of the phone was restored 'Under strict monitor'. I was sentenced to fourteen days solitary confinement in the digger for assault. One of the mufti said that the extinguisher had accidentally brushed his shin but no injury received.

The fourteen days run on to forty odd. The digger was the ideal place to observe and therefore to begin a hunger strike while keeping the lid on the information leaking out. It didn't matter to me where I was. One cell is as good as any other to die in.

Nothing is ever quite as easy as that. The campaign held protests, demos and vigils at the prison gate. Sparking the prisoners into protests of their own. The digger flared up again and again and the incidents throughout the prison were becoming more frequent and difficult to contain. I refused to go to hospital and they moved me to the prison hospital wing. Still this body doesn't know how to die.

Eight weeks into the final countdown and a glimmer of
hope when the courts written opinion comes through.

'The judgment is fundamentally flawed,' I'm told. Ha!
as if that was news! Yet Lord Cullen's error in omission
of the fundamental facts can be referred to directly on
record. And, as this entails the very issue upon which
the case was originally referred to the court on the first
instance, the Scots Secretary, Donald Dewar, would have
no option but to refer the case back to the court to be
properly dealt with in accordance with law. Fuck it! I
have heard it all before. You can carry on with Joe
without me. I'm not coming back just to be put through
that nightmare again. Yet what of Karen and the weans?
What of those who walk up and down outside the wall?
Tommy Sheridan and Governor McKinlay had a solution.
As Section 263 to the Scots Secretary was headed as a
'Further provision as to appeal' then as the petition was
now before the Secretary I could be considered as having
the entitlement to the rights of an appellant. Family would
be allowed to provide food as per the rights of an untried
prisoner. But too late, I had already gone beyond caring
and was only looking forward to oblivion. It was Karen
who enforced this compromise by going on a hunger
strike herself. Saying she wouldn't eat until I did. And
so I live to fight another day and the case is reactivated
under yet another new enquiry.

We were married on 23 April 1999 and Karen was
beautiful. Shannon made a lovely little bridesmaid. Just
a quiet family affair for the fact that only family were
allowed anyway.

The Very Merry Pranksters

With Tommy Sheridan, the Scottish Socialist MSP, at the helm of the Justice Campaign Committee, the campaign for justice for the Glasgow Two swung back into action. Thousands of posters printed, leaflets, flyers, statements of fact in official Campaign Committee releases. Justice marches and demonstrations with live music from the schemes.

At one point they demonstrated down the street of Donald Dewar, then Scots Secretary of State and later to become the First Minister of Scotland's new Parliament – Prime Minister by any other name. They then occupied the offices of Henry McLeish, then government minister in charge of prisons who went on to be the First Minister of the Scottish Parliament. They had a merry time there, drinking all the expensive booze from his hospitality cabinet, waving banners and distributing information leaflets over the veranda and via the Internet from his office PC web site. Whilst Tommy advocated caution, good behaviour and restraint, the very merry pranksters made good-natured celebration of their victory.

'Here's tae us, wha's like us?'

Sadly, old Donald Dewar passed away but not before finally enacting the Sutherland Committee recommendations for the setting up of an independent miscarriages of justice review commission previously rejected under the Tories. Then, after fourteen months of inquiry, he referred our case back to the court of appeal, for full and proper hearing of all the facts and circumstances of the case, to the new Scottish Criminal Cases Review Commission (SCCRC) in April 1999, as its top priority case for review.

High hopes then for some and some cause for optimism for many but, from my point of view, it was just another wasted fourteen months imprisoned. The commission would have to start again from scratch. Yet it was reckoned, with the case records so well documented and with various enquiry reports already prepared, all expectation, even from the SCCRC, was that the case would be done and dusted by December that year. We would be home for Christmas, almost two years from the point of the last Appeal Court's crucial error about the essential facts regarding Mr Love's confessions to having committed perjury at the original trial in 1984. Sixteen years earlier. So we told them again and again in the form of a leaflet, telling the world what no one else was telling them.

Free the Glasgow Two

In October 1984 **Thomas Campbell** and **Joe Steele** were wrongfully convicted of the Doyle family murders upon the evidence of a serial perverter of justice who has now admitted by recorded interviews, sworn statements, on television and under caution to the police, to having perverted justice once again in his evidence at the trial of the Glasgow Two in exchange for bail and immunity from prosecution on his own unrelated offences of armed robbery, attempt to pervert the course of justice and attempted murder, respectively.

In August 1996, the then Scots Secretary, Michael Forsyth MP, referred the case to the Court of Appeal. This reference was based upon the witness Love's confessions to perjury at the trial which evidence to an eavesdropped conversation in a public house was crucial to their wrongful convictions. Lord Kincraig, trial judge, noted:

Now there is no evidence to say that these accused were near or at the scene of the crime at the time the crime was committed and so the evidence is that of inference from the evidence before you which is that of the witness Love's evidence regarding the conversation in a public house . . . There is insufficiency of evidence in law to entitle you to convict without this evidence . . . The Crown case stands or falls upon his evidence. It is therefore crucial that you believe him . . .

It should be noted that the witness Love's evidence to

an eavesdropped conversation in a pub was not corroborated by any evidence nor supported by any witness in that respect. Furthermore, it was in fact refuted by three accused and two prosecution witnesses. Now countless more witnesses, TV viewers, sworn and recorded confessions etc speak clearly to having overheard HIM confessing that he lied. His first confessions were from 1986 . . .

'There never was any conversation about that fire in that pub nor anywhere else mate. That was just something that was put into my head by the police for me to say that as part of the deal . . . It was all just one big fit up of a case . . . It was me who fired that gun at the van, I was the one, not Gray. I took a double-barrel sawn off shotgun and fired it at the ice-cream van.'

Love's sister, Mrs Agnes Love or Carlton, is further independent evidence in cross check to her brother's confessions to perjury. Not only did she witness his attack on the ice-cream van, but she had also provided the police with a full detailed statement of his part in that incident at the time of the attack in 1984, but which crucial evidence remained secret and undisclosed to the defence until 1996 when the case was referred to the court by the Scots Secretary. As a result of this failure to disclose such exculpatory evidence Thomas Gray and others were wrongfully convicted upon the basis of Love's evidence at the trial in 1984, blaming them for his crimes. Mrs Carlton states . . .

'It was my brother Billy, I seen him from my window. He had come to my house with a double barrel sawn off shotgun about 'that' size and said that he was going to shoot up Jimmy Mitchell's van to give him a fright. 1 seen him do it from my window, but it was the wrong van . . .'

The Scots Secretary's reference to the court regarded

(1) Love's confessions to perjury and in particular, the significance of his admissions to discharging the firearm at the ice-cream van. That taken together with (2) his sister's witness and statement to the police to that effect, were sufficient to raise concerns on issues of which it would be more appropriate for the Appeal Court to reach a final decision.

However, at the Appeal Court in February 1998, the Lord Chief Justice Clerk, Lord Cullen, appears to have somehow managed to overlook Love's confession in that respect and at page 52 of his opinion states . . .

(SLT 940H) *'Love does not admit or suggest that he was the person who fired the gun at the van, nor did he admit that he lied about his part in the shooting . . .'*

Lord Cullen returns to repeat this crucial error of the facts at page (SLT 941 K) . . . *'Since he does not say that he lied as to the extent of his own involvement in the shooting,* **in these circumstances** *I am not satisfied that the evidence that Mrs Carlton would give could support Love's explanation that he was induced and put under pressure to present false evidence against the appellants.'*

Thus on the basis of this error of the facts, Mrs Carlton could not 'confirm' something of which it appeared (to Lord Cullen) that her brother had not admitted. Therefore her evidence was not allowed to be heard which was the independent support of her brother's confessions to the shooting incident and therefore to perjury at the trial. Further, as the law requires some such independent support, there now was no point in the court hearing the confessions of the witness Love without her evidence to support it. Thus the appeal to have the evidence of perjury heard by the court was refused by Lord Cullen based upon an error of the facts of the case.

Yet the very next judge to give an opinion was Lord McCluskey. In his most excellent opinion in support of the appeal, he confirms that Love had indeed confessed to discharging the gun at the van as his sister had witnessed and contrary to his evidence against Gray and others at the trial. Lord McCluskey paraphrases Love's in-depth confessions in that respect . . .

(SLT 948K) *'Because it would enable me to avoid being charged myself with attempted murder, of which I knew I was guilty because I was the one who fired the shotgun, I was willing to go ahead with the plan to present false evidence . . .'*

On the basis that his sister's statement to the police supports this, he supported the appeal to have the evidence of the perjury and supporting evidence of his sister, heard by the Court for full examination under oath . . .

'For should it be confirmed in evidence then that would entail that a serious miscarriage of justice has occurred . . .'

The third judge, Lord Sutherland, opined that . . .

(SLT 955A) *'The fact that Love said he committed perjury is not enough, it is not in itself an explanation, it is merely an assertion. What is required is an explanation of 'why' the alleged true evidence was not given at the trial and that therefore calls for an explanation of 'why' he gave false evidence . . .'*

On this basis, Mrs Carlton could not support any evidence given by her brother as to 'why' he gave false evidence and the appeal to have the evidence heard by the court was refused by Lord Sutherland.

It now appears that the administration of justice is stood upon its head to the point where a man pleading guilty, providing confession and independent support in corroboration to his crime (of perjury) is dismissed by the court for the fact that he cannot provide a good enough excuse in explanation as to 'why' he committed that crime and his victims were punished in his place as a consequence. How can it be that his victims of admitted and accepted perjured evidence must now rely upon the quality of the defence of their perjurer? And upon his excuses as to why he perjured himself against them?

Since the Appeal Court ruled two to one not to allow the evidence of perjury at the original trial to be heard, then 'In these circumstances', Lord Cullen's patent error of the crucial facts became one of the essential points upon petition to the new Scots Secretary, Donald Dewar, to have the matter referred back to the Appeal Court to be properly and fully dealt with by the court in accordance with the facts and the law. The Scots Secretary confirmed that Love's confessions to perjury and, in particular, his confession that he was in fact the one who had fired the gun at the van, contrary to his evidence at the time of the trial, WERE in fact before him, as with the previous Scots Secretary and WERE before the court from an early stage in the proceedings as was quoted by Lord McCluskey in the same Appeal Hearing. Nevertheless, the Secretary stated that Lord Cullen was not in error of the facts because due to some clerical oversight or other, the witness' confessions in that respect were not seen as included within the list of documents before Lord Cullen at the time his opinion was formed. The Scots Secretary went on to impose his own opinion in presupposition of that of the court, averring that . . .

'Even if it had been, it is irrelevant and would have had no bearing upon his Lordship's rejection of Mrs Carlton's evidence as independent support of her brother's confessions to perjury in that respect.'

The Secretary was referred to Lord Cullen's opinion 'in

these circumstances' and after further deliberations, the Secretary of State could . . . *'make no final decision'* and referred the case to the newly formed Scottish Criminal Cases Review Commission in April 1999 after four-teen months of enquiry and sixteen years of wrongful imprisonment.

Yet where there is proof and supporting evidence that the **Glasgow Two** are wrongfully convicted and impris-oned upon the evidence of a serial perverter of justice, then to continue to hold these men in prison whilst refusing to allow the fearful facts to be examined under the scrutiny of an open court in a public trial, is a scandal of epic proportions and a gross travesty of justice entailing a crime against society for the fact that the cover up is called 'justice' in our name.

Justice cannot be done for the Doyle family, nor in the public interests while the innocent are imprisoned in pain. One injustice does not correct the imbalance of another, and after seventeen years of cruel travesty, the struggle for justice does not wane.

Where the court and the course of justice stumbles upon such errors and, as a result, fails to address those very issues upon which the case was originally referred in the first instance, is it therefore reasonable, just or fair to hold these men in prison rather than publicly admit the gross travesty of justice perpetrated against them in our name? For, through no fault of their own, but by the perjured evidence of a serial perverter of justice and misdirection and error in the administration of the law, these men have suffered seventeen years of a living nightmare, innocently imprisoned in our names and in the name of justice.

It has been three years since the crucial error of the essential facts in the opinion of the Court of Appeal. Three years of further wrongful imprisonment for the **Glasgow Two** whilst the Scottish Office and Scottish

Criminal Cases Review Committee's *'intense and urgent'* priority enquiry can come to no decision upon what to do in this case. In the meantime, justice delayed is justice denied, but justice prevented is justice perverted and, when this is exacerbated by the legal administration's refusal to cooperate, it becomes more than a miscarriage of justice. It is an outrage and an outright affront upon the public. As Thomas Campbell says . . .

**'Where God hath given,
man taketh away
In boundless arrogant vanity
Lord's temporal date proclaim
God's given law as their
domain.'**

By any account it is neither reasonable, just nor fair to hold these men in prison without a full and fair hearing of all the facts of the case for another single day. The SCCRC have a duty and responsibility, not only for these men and their families, but also the victims and their families and in the public interest, to ensure that justice is restored by the reference of this case back to the Court of Appeal for a full and proper hearing of all the facts and evidence of the case. In the name of justice, equality and fairness for all and, though the heavens fall, let justice roll on like a river, righteousness in an ever flowing stream . . .

Free The Glasgow Two

Justice Denied is Justice Delayed

December 1999 came and went with the Commission initiating one new inquiry after another. It seems that they were taking nothing for granted and nobody's word for anything unless they could acquire that data for themselves. Fair enough but that left our time dragging on and on in prison whilst they took yet another, fourth sworn statement from Mr Love. Seeking out and reinterviewing everyone concerned in the case for themselves.

Week upon week, month upon month the case enquiry dragged on and on with one impediment or another getting in the way of the Commission's inquiry. Finally they initiated a legal action against the police and the Crown Prosecution Service in an attempt to take possession of all documented evidence of the original investigation. This action itself ran into many court sessions and many more months dragging by awaiting its final outcome with the Crown Office contesting any form of disclosure every step of the way. Leading to the press headline . . .

CROWN OFFICE IN ICE CREAM WARS COVER UP

. . . telling the story of the Commission's struggles to access the original trial and inquiry evidence in the face of the Crown Office's blatant refusal to hand it over.

The court's judgment was finally issued on 11 September 2000 – more than two and a half years from the point of the Appeal Court's original error of the essential facts. The court held that all material evidence relevant to the original inquiry should be handed over to the Commission in pursuit of their own enquiry but, apparently, the Commission would be required to seek the Crown Prosecution Service's permission and consent before they could use or disclose any such evidence publicly in their final decision. So much then for the alleged independence of the Commission. This judgment would leave the Commission subject to the discretion, decisions and policy practices of the Crown Prosecution Service. However, should the Crown Office refuse to grant their consent for the usage and disclosure of such evidence, the SCCRC retained the option to take that back to court.

And so, the Commission began the examination of seventeen boxes of seized documentation previously held exclusively by the Crown Office and police. Once again, December 2000 was given as the probable date of the Commission's decision. Postponed till February 2001. Bringing us up to a further three years of inquiry and into our seventeenth year of imprisonment. Three years to sort out a single but crucial and fundamental error of the facts by Lord Cullen which can be seen at a single reading of the court's opinion in their judgment of 10 February 1998.

Still it drags on and on. Now into November of 2001. Once again it is proposed that a decision will be reached by December and that we will be home by Christmas. But I won't 'squander my resistance for a pocket full of mumbles. Such are promises. All lies'n jest, Lie L'lie . . .'

Approaching December, Wee Shannon, just seven days old when the Appeal Court done the dastardly deed and dug their dirty dirk into the back of Scottish Justice, is almost four years old now. My children – Tommy, Stephen, Brian and Cheree Ann – have all grown up without me but Shannon, at least, has a chance to know her father outside of prison. Joe's son, John Paul, the same age as my Stephen, two when we were imprisoned, is himself now a father with a daughter at that age. Joe's son Joseph Jnr is the same age as my Shannon. They all expect us home this Christmas. They have all expected us home for too many Christmases. Every day of every week of every month of every year we wait for justice but it never comes.

I feel that these people are not aware of the travesty exacerbated in the passage of time. They are not aware and don't want to be aware that they are dealing with

real people, real pain in real time . . . Concerned only
with the academic exercise of the abstract rhetoric. They
do not see and do not understand that they may never
know the ultimate truth with any degree of certainty with
their heads buried deep in ancient archive records. The
truth is out there, beyond the cobwebs of those ancient
spun illusions. The truth is in the living reality that we
are innocent and we have a right to be free.

I'm afraid to admit to myself that it's getting though
to me, wearing me down. It's not so much the eighteen
years of constant struggle for justice. It's more these last
four years to sort out an error of the facts by the court
and which should have been sorted out in four minutes,
four hours, four days, four weeks or four months at
most. Yet they have dragged it on four thousand fold
beyond the time that it should have taken. What are
they doing? Why are they doing this to me? My mind
screams in horror and in pain. I guess that it is just that
my psyche is weary and battle worn in constant exposure
to the psychic storms . . .

Poem

From the valley of the shadows
Beyond all shades of doubt
When the bloody battles over and
The minions of hell cast out
What moves the last man standing
So to shout?

When the signals from the mountain Keep
Proclaims triumph to the sky
The bloody war is over but,
What victory have I?
What moves the last man standing
So to cry?

What victory have I who gave
My life and soul to war?
Seen noble comrades to their graves
Amid the bloody gore.
What moves the last man standing
So to roar?

Now the bloody battle's over but,
What victory remains
In this land of desolation
Upon these fields of pain?
What moves the last man standing
So to proclaim?

Am I the last man standing?
Have my comrades fled the field?
Were my standards too demanding
Upon this sword I wield?
And when I stumbled wounded
Did law stand as my shield?

Am I the last man standing?
Has the enemy fled the field?
Am I left alone, but commanding
The Reaper's sword to wield?
If not for truth and justice then
But blood is the crop I yield.

Am I the last man standing?
To cross the Rubicon
and to gain a Pyrrhic victory
Cut deep to the bone.
If I am the last man standing,
I am damned.

Waiting and Waiting and . . .

Our case was referred back to the Court of Appeal by the Commission by letter dated 28 November 2001. It had taken almost four long years to sort out the simple error of the facts by Lord Cullen just to get us back to where we had originally been.

The Commission's report was very much a whitewash but it didn't matter. They went on to raise a point of issue in respect of the false police verbal evidence and this could now be added to the original points for appeal regarding the perjured evidence of the witness William Love. This part of the Commission's report reads as follows . . .

The Commission Speaks at Last

On 7 June 2002, the Commission instructed an opinion from Professor Brian Clifford, a forensic psychologist based at the University of East London, on certain aspects of the trial evidence. Specifically, Professor Clifford was asked to consider the evidence of the four police officers who arrested Campbell and who testified that he had made an incriminating remark which implicated him in both the murder and the shooting. The Commission sought Professor Clifford's opinion following receipt of an opinion on the same issue by Dr Peter French, a forensic linguist, who was instructed on 22 December 2000.

Transcripts of the evidence given at trial by all four officers were sent to Professor Clifford as well as copies of various statements produced by each of them prior to the trial. The Commission was advised by Strathclyde Police, and Crown Office at an early stage of the investigation that none of the original police notebooks had been preserved. Nor in terms of the list of productions attached to the indictment, does it appear that the relevant excerpts of the notebooks were lodged at trial.

Campbell's arresting officers were Detective Inspector William McCafferty (now deceased), Detective Sergeant

Andrew Hyslop and Detective Constables Alexander
Geddes and Ian Cargill.

According to the evidence of these officers, on entering
Campbell's house on the morning of his arrest, a
summary of the contents of the petition warrant was
read out to him in the living room. As Campbell was
not at this point charged with murder, the details of
the warrant referred only to the shotgun attack on
the van as well as other alleged offences including
breach of the peace and malicious mischief. After being
informed of these details, Campbell was told that his
house was to be searched. According to the officers, it
was at this stage that he made the following remark:

'I only wanted the van windaes shot up. The fire at fat
boy's was only meant to be a frightener which went
too far.'

According to the evidence of all four officers, the
remark was noted by each of them at the time. As well
as Campbell, there were two other people in the house
that morning: Campbell's partner, Elizabeth Donaldson,
and a friend, Archibald McDougall. However, according
to the police evidence, both of these individuals were
still in bed when the admission was made. This was
disputed by Campbell and Mrs Donaldson, both of
whom claimed in evidence that Mrs Donaldson was
present in the hall when the officers entered their
home. Campbell denied that he had made any such
remark and claimed that none of the officers had taken
any notes while in the house. Mrs Donaldson confirmed
that Campbell had made no such comment to the police
while in her presence.

With the exception of DC Geddes, who was able in his
evidence to recollect the alleged remark from memory

(he claimed to have looked at his notebook immediately before coming into court), all the officers referred to their notebooks prior to giving evidence of the alleged remark. In terms of the trial transcripts, the words noted by each officer are by and large the same.

The version of the comment given in evidence by DI McCafferty is as noted above. The versions given by DS Hyslop and DC Geddes are identical to this, only the word 'windows' appears in the transcript instead of 'windaes'. DC Cargill's version is also the same except that, instead of 'windaes shot up', the phrase 'windows shot out' is recorded in the transcript.

Under cross-examination by counsel for Campbell, DI McCafferty stated that he noted the comment while sitting in front of Campbell in the living room. He denied that the only thing Campbell had said to the police following his arrest was when he challenged them for taking a sum of money which his wife needed to buy stock for her ice cream van. DI McCafferty did not know whether DC Geddes had noted anything said by Campbell as he was too busy writing his own notes to know what anybody else had done. Although DI McCafferty regarded the remark as significant, he had not asked DC Geddes back at the station whether he too had noted it. It was put to DI McCafferty that where only one officer manages to note a comment made by an accused it is quite common and proper, once back at the station, for the other officers to look at that officer's notebook. In response, DI McCafferty explained that he only knew what he did in such situations and re-iterated that he had taken his note of the comment at the time. DI McCafferty did not read the comment back to Campbell nor ask him to initial his notebook to confirm that he had noted the

comment correctly. He claimed that he never asked
people to initial the contents of his notebook.

DI McCafferty explained that he had not reported
Campbell's comment that day to the officer in charge
of the investigation, Mr Walker, and said that this was
because he had spent the rest of the day examining
letters which had been taken from Campbell's house
following the search. He could not remember when he
had told Mr Walker about the comment. DI McCafferty
was then asked to confirm that he had never consulted
with DC Geddes about the comment and that he had not
reported it to the officer in charge of the inquiry until
the following day. He responded in the following terms:
'That's right. I did not tell him that day. There's no
doubt about that.'

In re-examination, DI McCafferty claimed that
there was no urgency whatsoever to transmit any
information regarding Campbell's arrest to Mr Walker.
He had provided a report on the matter to Mr Walker
the following day.

Under cross-examination, it was suggested to DS
Hyslop that Campbell had made no such comment. DS
Hyslop denied this and claimed that he had taken his
notebook out as soon as the comment was made and
had noted it in the house. He could not recall whether
DC Geddes had his notebook out at the time. He denied
the suggestion that the police evidence of the comment
was part of an effort to build a case against Campbell.
He was not asked in evidence whether he had
compared his note of the comment with those taken by
his fellow officers.

DS Hyslop was present when Campbell was charged
with the murders ten days after his arrest and

confirmed that Campbell had made no response to
caution and charge. He accepted that on being charged
Campbell had become very agitated and had asked
the bar officer to note specifically that he had made
no response to caution and charge. He denied the
suggestion that Campbell was being 'fitted up' by the
police in respect of the comment spoken to by the
officers.

In re-examination, DS Hyslop re-iterated that there was
no truth in the suggestion that the police evidence was
perjured.

DC Geddes stated in cross-examination that he was
certain that Campbell had made the remark. He was
not asked whether he had compared the note he had
taken with any of the other officers.

Under cross-examination, DC Cargill denied the
suggestion that Campbell had made no comment
following his arrest. He was aware that DI McCafferty
had noted the remark but did not know whether the
other officers had done so. He was asked whether,
when he got back to the station with the others, they
had checked with each other whether they had noted
the response correctly but he denied this. He agreed
with the suggestion that there had been 'no comparison
at all'. He was asked whether he regarded it as
unusual that all four officers had noted the remark
and responded that 'it could be unusual, other times it
is not'.

The police statements submitted by each of Campbell's
arresting officers were also examined as it was
considered that these might better reflect what each
of them recorded in their notebooks. Some support for
this view is contained in a letter from the Deputy Chief

Constable of Strathclyde Police dated 6 June 2001 in which he states that it is 'common and best practice for comments made by an accused person to be noted into an officer's notebook. Thereafter, any statement prepared would include the direct quote as drawn from the notebook entry.' The letter concludes that 'it would be my expectation that notebook entries involving comments made by an accused person would be accurately replicated within any statement thereafter prepared.'

Aside from some minor differences, the versions of the comment contained in each statement are identical to one another. For example, the version contained in DI McCafferty's statement is the same as that contained in DS Hyslop's statement except that the latter contains the words 'the Fat Boy's (sic) while the former refers only to 'Fat Boy's (sic). In addition, whereas in evidence, DS Hyslop and DC Geddes are recorded as using the word 'windows' as opposed to 'windaes', this distinction does not appear in their respective statements, which both contain the word 'windaes'.

In the Commission's view, it is unfortunate that the police notebooks have been destroyed as these would have disclosed the exact words each officer claimed to have noted at the time. While each officer's evidence of the comment (which, aside from DC Geddes' evidence, was given following notebook consultation) provides a generally reliable account of the words noted by the officers, there is clearly the possibility of inaccuracies occurring as a result of the transcription process undertaken by the shorthand writer, or even by the possible reluctance of the officer concerned to recount in evidence the vernacular terms used by an accused (for example, 'windaes'). The same inaccuracies can occur during the preparation of statements which, although one might expect would accurately reflect the contents of an officer's notebook, often require to be typed into final form by someone other than the officer concerned. Nevertheless, in the Commission's view, despite the absence of the notebooks, the accounts given in evidence and in each of the statements provide a generally accurate reflection of what each officer recorded in his notebook.

In summary, while DS Hyslop and DC Geddes were not questioned on whether they compared their respective notes of the comment made by Campbell with their fellow officers, it is clear from his evidence that DC Cargill did not do so. In the Commission's view, DI McCafferty's evidence also suggests that he did not compare his own notes with that taken by DC Geddes nor with any of the other officers. Accordingly, the Commission considers that in terms of the evidence the only officers who may have compared their respective notes of the comment made by Campbell are DS Hyslop and DC Geddes. The remaining two officers, it may be assumed, managed to note the comment independently.

In order that their views on the matter could be obtained, it was decided that those officers who were not questioned in evidence on whether they had compared their notes of the comment should be interviewed. Given that the officers were being asked about events which took place over seventeen years ago, it was recognised that they might have difficulty in recalling specific aspects of the case.

Mr Hyslop (now retired) could recall the general circumstances of Campbell's arrest. He recalled that Campbell had said something like 'the fire at Fat Boy's was a frightener which went too far'. He believed that he had noted the comment immediately after it was made but this belief was based not upon specific recollection but rather the practice he adopted at the time. To the best of his knowledge he had not compared his note of the comment with any of his fellow officers. According to Mr Hyslop, generally speaking, no such comparison takes place between officers. Indeed, any such comparison was considered by Mr Hyslop to be inappropriate as he beheved it important for each officer to give his best evidence in his own recollection of events. If an officer fails to note a comment made by an accused then, in Mr Hyslop's view, he must stand up and tell the truth about this in court.

DC Geddes (now Inspector) could not recall whether there was a collective check between Campbell's arresting officers as to the comment made by him. However, he explained that he would not have consulted with his fellow officers, as normal practice in such situations is to rely on one's own note of the comment and not to compare this with colleagues. If, for some reason, he had been unable to note the comment he would not have consulted with any of his fellow officers. In any event, as he had taken a note of Campbell's comment at the time there would have been no point in later comparing his version with the other officers, as by that stage he could not have altered it. Inspector Geddes believed that it would be inappropriate to copy from another officer's notebook

unless that officer had specifically been given the task
of taking notes of everything uttered. However, as
in these circumstances the recollection contained in
his own notebook would not be his own, in Inspector
Geddes's view, it would not be permissible for him to
give evidence of the comment. In any event, as he
had given evidence of the comment made by Campbell
it was clear that this was what he had noted. He
would not have compared his note with any of his
fellow officers. This, he said, was not something done
then or indeed now. His notebook contained his own
recollections and no one else's.

Accordingly, although neither officer was able to
recollect specifically whether they had compared
the note they had taken of the comment, both considered
that to do so would be inappropriate on the basis
that any subsequent evidence given by them would
not represent their own specific recollection of the
matter.

Opinion of Professor Brian Clifford

General
Brian Clifford is a professor of cognitive psychology at
the University of East London whose research interest
lies in pure and applied aspects of memory. He has
published four books and a large number of articles on
the subject and, in particular, the field of eye witness
memory in which he has an international reputation.
He was a founder member of the Division of
Criminological and Legal Psychology (now the Division
of Forensic Psychology) of the British Psychological
Society and is a chartered forensic psychologist.
He has also undertaken numerous consultancies
for solicitors and defence barristers in England

in connection with various aspects of eyewitness identification.

As indicated, Professor Clifford was instructed to examine the evidence of Campbell's arresting officers in respect of the comment and provide an opinion on whether this can be considered reliable. In order to answer the questions put to him, Professor Clifford required to conduct a number of controlled experiments using voluntary participants.

Prior to describing the various studies, Professor Clifford provides in his report a summary of the existing literature on memory capacity. The chief characteristic of short term memory, he explains, is its very limited capacity. Although there is some debate on what that capacity is, most psychologists agree on an upper limit in the region of 7–9 items. However, in circumstances where the items can be organised or 'chunked' by the memory (for example., as a result of the words being in the form of meaningful sentences) the number of items capable of recall can increase. This increased ability is, however, dependent upon the size of the sentence and it has been found that memory span decreases with larger 'chunks'.

In Professor Clifford's view, the existing theories of short term memory capacity suggest that as far as memory of sentences is concerned, this is likely to be greater than 7–9 words but not much greater. Also, while humans are able to comprehend and recall the meaning of such sentences, they are unlikely to be able to remember them verbatim.

Accordingly, as regards the comment made by Campbell, Professor Clifford anticipated that participants would display an inability to recall this verbatim and would also omit one or more semantic units into which the comment can be divided.

The Studies
As Professor Clifford emphasises in the report, his opinion cannot assist in determining whether the comment spoken to by police and denied by Campbell was actually uttered, as clearly this is known only to those who were present during the arrest. Similarly, only the officers themselves know for certain whether the manner in which the comment was recorded by them was as described in their evidence. Nevertheless, he considers that through experimentation, an opinion may be offered as to the reliability of that evidence. To the extent, therefore, that the participants in the studies were found to have the same ability to recall the comment as that seemingly possessed by Campbell's arresting officers, one could, in Professor Clifford's view, be fairly confident that the accounts given by them in evidence are reliable. However, in the event that the officers' apparent comment was found to be greater than that of the participants, or than theoretical expectations, this may in turn cast doubt upon their accounts.

As indicated, the notebooks produced by Campbell's arresting officers have been destroyed. Accordingly, the Commission has required to rely upon the versions of the comment recorded in each of the officer's evidence as well as their respective statements. The approach taken by Professor Clifford to the various studies was to look upon the versions of the comment given by each officer in evidence as to all intents and purposes, verbatim identical allowing for 'mis-translations' between notebook and statement;

statement and evidence; and evidence and transcript. In Professor Clifford's view, such an approach is justified by the fact that the slight differences between the versions spoken to by the officers are not such as to alter the meaning of the comment. For example, the phrase 'at the Fat Boy's' is semantically identical to 'at Fat Boy's'. Further reference to this issue is made below.

(a) Study 1
Professor Clifford conducted two studies in relation to the comment attributed to Campbell. Study 1 involved a participant sample of 54 male and female professional employees, all of whom were English and spoke this as their first language. The participants were divided into two groups: the Informed Group (IG) and the Non-Informed Group (NIG). The IG were told by Professor Clifford that he had been asked to look into a case involving an alleged miscarriage of justice and that a potentially important issue in the case concerned memory capacity. They were told that the case involved 'arson' (the word 'fire' was not used as this appears in the comment made by Campbell) and the 'discharge of a weapon'. In order to convey the importance of the study, the IG was also told that the person involved was currently serving a lengthy prison sentence. The NIG was told by Professor Clifford only that he was interested in verbatim memory capacity.

The IG was intended by Professor Clifford to simulate to some degree the knowledge possessed by Campbell's arresting officers at the time the comment was noted. This was, in his view, in important allowance to make given that prior knowledge of this type (ie knowledge of the nature) of the offences of which Campbell was suspected can often aid the recall of long sentences.

Participants were presented with five comments individually (Campbell's comment and two from each of his co-accused, Joseph Steele and Thomas Gray) and were requested to recall each of these by immediately writing them down verbatim. Participants were instructed to indicate any words or phrases they could not remember by inserting dashes where they believed the words or phrases appeared in the utterance. In order to replicate as far as possible the circumstances in which the comment was made by Campbell, the voice used was that of a 45 year old Glaswegian male. The voice was tape recorded and the contents then transferred to a computer in order to reduce background noise and to ensure that presentation of the comments in each study was standardised.

The participants' recalls were 'scored', firstly, for verbatim correctness and, secondly, for semantic completeness (or meaning). Verbatim correctness was calculated by giving one point for every word correctly recorded, irrespective of whether the participant's recall altered the meaning of the comment. For example, if a participant recalled Campbell's comment as '*He* only wanted the van windaes shot, the fire at . . . frightener . . . too far', this would score 12 out of a maximum of 24 (the number of words contained in Campbell's comment), even though by introducing the word 'he', the actual meaning of the comment was changed.

Professor Clifford considered that this form of scoring was the best means of testing the officers' ability to remember the comment in its entirety as well as its exact wording. In his view, if it was shown that the participants could recall the exact number of words uttered by Campbell, in exactly the form in which they were uttered, then the almost identical recalls presented by Campbell's arresting officers in evidence could be regarded as reliable. If, on the other hand, participants recalled less than the maximum and/or altered the wording, then the evidence of the officers may be viewed as less reliable.

So far as Campbell's comment is concerned, the mean verbatim recall for the Informed Group was 9.6 words and, for the Non-Informed Group, 7.2 words. These figures represent approximately 40 and 30 per cent of the total words available for recall. The actual range of verbatim scoring achieved among the participants in the Informed Group was between 4 and 14 words, while in the Non-Informed Group, between 2 and 14 words. Accordingly, no participant came close to recalling the number of words which Campbell's arresting officers seemingly achieved. In these circumstances, Professor Clifford concludes that verbatim recall of a sentence containing 24 words is not possible.

Professor Clifford also tested the ability of four-person groups within the sample to achieve identical recall between them. Groups of four persons were chosen to reflect the number of officers involved in Campbell's arrest . . . key segments of the comment were missed by all participants in the four person study. Significantly, within any group of four participants, no two achieved identical verbatim recall. These findings, Professor Clifford suggests, are not entirely, unexpected in terms of results produced by previous studies.

Professor Clifford concludes that sentences of more than 10–12 words in length will be very difficult, if not impossible, to recall verbatim. While the ideas contained within a comment may be recalled on an 'all-or-none' basis . . . exact wording will be very difficult to retrieve. Indeed, he found that attempts at verbatim rather than 'gist' recall sometimes resulted in participants abandoning the task altogether. Professor Clifford considers it 'very improbable' that four officers would be able independently to produce identical verbatim recalls of Campbell's comment.

(b) Study 2

The second study conducted by Professor Clifford was designed to assess whether the results of Study 1 occurred not through a genuine inability on the part of the participants to recall the comment in question, but rather their lack of familiarity with the Glasgow accent. Professor Clifford considered that before the findings of Study 1could be accepted, a further study involving Scottish participants would require to be undertaken.

The Scottish sample consisted of 74 participants in the main from the fire and police services and the nursing profession. Whereas the sample in Study 1 was divided into Informed and Non-Informed Groups, Professor Clifford decided that no such distinction should be made within the Scottish sample and that all participants in Study 2 should be given the same information as the Informed Group in Study 1. This, he considered, would encourage maximum possible recall among all participants.

The participants in Study 2 were presented with the same series of recorded voices as those in Study 1 and were asked to recall each comment verbatim in writing.

As in Study 1 recalls were 'scored' for verbatim and semantic correctness.

In the event, the results of Study 2 varied little from Study 1. The mean number of words recalled verbatim in the Scottish sample was 9.6 out of a total of 24. The minimum number of words recalled by any one participant was 4 while the maximum was 17. Again, no participant came close to recalling all the available words.

In the light of these results, Professor Clifford concludes that the low verbatim recalls observed in Study 1 cannot be explained by the inability of the English sample to understand the accent in which the comments were spoken. Rather, the results reflected the difficulty of the task itself.

(c) Semantic Analysis
Professor Clifford also attempted to assess the participants' ability to remember the actual meaning or 'semantic units' contained within Campbell's comment. According to Professor Clifford, it is these units which are stored and retrieved in the memory when the length of the comment in question exceeds the capacity of the short term memory. Participants might therefore be expected to find such units easier to recall than the precise words spoken.

Professor Clifford considered that Campbell's comment comprised four semantic units:

1. Shooting at van windows
2. Fire at Fat Boy's
3. A frightener
4. Going too far

It was found that of the total 131 participants tested, not one recalled all four semantic units. This leads Professor Clifford to conclude that the probability of any random four police officers managing to recall a sentence of 24 words in identical format is 'infinitesimal'.

As highlighted above, the evidence given by DI McCafferty and DC Cargill suggests that neither officer consulted with one another or with their fellow officers to verify the accuracy of what they had noted. Professor Clifford was therefore asked to assess the likelihood of DI McCafferty and DC Cargill being able to note the comment in such similar terms in the absence of subsequent collaboration. In his supplementary report, dated 29 July 2001, Professor Clifford points out that in the light of his finding that not one of the 131 participants recalled all 24 words, the probability of any two officers achieving total verbatim recall was 'very low indeed'. While there were a number of slight differences between each officer's account in evidence ('windaes shot up'/'windows shot out'), even if one were to remove these words from the overall total, the best verbatim 'score' by any of the participants would be 14 out of 21, which is still short of the verbatim recall ability seemingly achieved by the officers concerned. Moreover, Professor Clifford explains that if one examines the recalls of the highest scoring participants their written records are characterised by variation in terms of the actual words and the order in which they were recalled, not similarity.

As indicated, DS Hyslop and DC Geddes were not questioned in evidence on whether they had compared their respective notes of Campbell's comment. It is therefore possible (despite what each claimed at interview with the Legal Officer) that they did so. Professor Clifford was therefore asked to assure that both officers had collaborated and that this was the reason why their respective accounts of the comment in evidence were so similar. He was then asked to consider the likelihood that both officers were able to recall the comment in almost exactly the same terms as their fellow officers who, as mentioned above, denied in evidence that they had compared with any of their colleagues.

Professor Clifford re-iterates in his supplementary report that, in terms of the findings, it is extremely unlikely that any one officer was able to note the comment verbatim, far less two. In the scenario described above, Professor Clifford considered that there would be three different versions of the comment: one produced jointly through comparison between DS Hyslop and DC Geddes and two produced independently and without comparison by DI McCafferty and DC Cargill. In terms of the test results, the independently produced versions would differ both from the jointly produced versions and from one another.

In Professor Clifford's view (as expressed in his supplementary report as well as his additional submissions dated 10 September 2001), the most that one could expect in terms of the results of the studies is that two out of the four versions would be similar (ie the two versions which were compared). Even assuming that comparison took place between DS Hyslop and DC Geddes, the likelihood of them producing between them such a similar version to those which, in terms of the evidence, were produced independently is, according to Professor Clifford, 'very low indeed' and, in terms of the experimental data, 'non-existent'. He concludes that the only logical deduction which can be made in these circumstances is that at some stage, all four accounts must have been compared and brought into close alignment, or worse, were created together.

Professor Clifford also considered whether there was any merit in the proposition that due to training and the type of work in which they are engaged, police officers have a greater ability than the general public to recall details of what they see and hear. As indicated, Study 2 included 14 police participants who were tested alongside participants from other professions including fire officers and nurses. While it was found that the police officers performed (marginally) better numerically than some of the other groups, Professor Clifford found that these results did not translate into 'statistically, reliable differences'. In other words, by analysing the results statistically, it was found that the greater ability displayed by the officers in the study would be unlikely to re-occur if the study was repeated. In support of this finding Professor Clifford makes reference to other studies whose findings reflect his own.

Professor Clifford concludes that in light of this, 'the memory performance that apparently was exhibited by the police officers in the case under review must be seen as truly remarkable. So remarkable, in fact, as to be doubtful.'

Summary
In Study 1 Professor Clifford found that not one of the 54 participants involved came close to recalling verbatim the number of words seemingly

achieved by Campbell's arresting officers. Those participants who were given prior notice of the background circumstances recalled approximately 40 per cent of the total number of words while those who were denied this information recalled approximately 30 per cent of the words. In respect of the four person groups within the sample, key segments of the comment were missed by all participants and no two within any group achieved verbatim recall.

These findings were replicated in Study 2 which involved a purely Scottish sample. It was also found that out of the total 131 participants tested, not one was able to recall the various semantic units contained within the comment.

With regard to the evidence given by DI McCafferty and DC Cargill to the effect that neither compared their respective notes of the comment, Professor Clifford found that the likelihood of both officers independently achieving total verbatim recall was very low indeed. Similarly, assuming that DS Hyslop and DC Geddes did indeed compare their respective notes of the comment, Professor Clifford considered there to be a very low likelihood of both officers producing a version of the comment so similar to those produced independently by their fellow officers.

Opinion of Dr Peter French
As explained, Professor Clifford's report was instructed by the Commission following receipt of an opinion from Dr Peter French, a forensic linguist based in York. Dr French was formally instructed on 22 December 2000, but his report

was not received by the Commission until 6
April 2001.

Dr French is an independent forensic consultant who
specialises in the analysis of tape recordings, speech
and samples. He is a founder member and current
chairman of the International Association of Forensic
Phonetics and is co-editor of The International Journal
of Speech, Language and the Law. He has published
widely on matters relating to language texts, speech
and tape recordings and has been consulted as expert
witness on many occasions. He has appeared as an
expert witness in numerous cases in England and
Northern Ireland, acting for both the Crown and
defence.

Like Professor Clifford, Dr French was provided with
copies of the transcripts of evidence given by each of
Campbell's arresting officers, as well as their police
statements. The questions on which his opinion was
sought were broadly the same as those which were
eventually put to Professor Clifford. Specifically, Dr
French was asked to assess the likelihood that all
four officers who arrested Campbell were able to note
the comment in such similar terms, given that two
out of the four officers gave evidence that they did
not compare their respective notes with their fellow
officers. His response to this question is as follows:

'I consider the possibility of all four officers
having contemporaneously and independently,
without subsequent cross checking or consultation,
recorded Campbell's alleged 24 words in their
notebooks with the very high degree of cross-textual
correspondence one finds here as remote in the
extreme.'

In support of this conclusion, Dr French refers
to various psycholinguistic experiments which
have shown that people process language very
quickly and tend to store the gist rather then
the exact form of words to which they have been
exposed. He also refers to an experiment which
he conducted for the Crown in connection with a
previous appeal in England, *R v Nedrick* (1986
Cr App R 267 – no mention is made in the report
of the experiment) which demonstrated that
absolute verbatim recall is not possible even under
optimally advantageous conditions. The experiment
consisted of live dictation to 8 subjects, 4 of
whom were professional transcribers of tape
recorded conversations. All subjects were given
time to finish writing down each utterance before
the next utterance was dictated. In Dr French's
view, the conditions created by the experiment
were very much more likely to obtain verbatim
records and cross textual convergence than
those which perhaps applied within Campbell's
house on the morning of his arrest. Dr French
found, however, that even under the optimum
conditions of the experiment, the written records
produced by the subjects diverged both from what
was actually dictated and from one another. In
Dr French's view one would expect to find very
substantial cross textual variation in the much
less favourable 'real world' conditions appertaining
at the time of Campbell's arrest. In the light of
this, Dr French stated that he had very serious
doubts regarding the reliability of the evidence
given by those officers who claimed to have
noted Campbell's comment without subsequent
collaboration.

Following receipt of his report, the Commission wrote to Dr French in order to query the basis on which his findings appeared to have been made. Primarily, the Commission was concerned at the lack of detail in the report and the fact that, although Dr French had indicated that his findings would be based upon experimental studies designed to the specific facts of the present case, these appeared not to have been undertaken. These concerns led to the Commission obtaining a second opinion from Professor Clifford.

A further report was received from Dr French on 6 September 2001, in which he re-addressed the questions originally put to him, this time basing his conclusions upon experimental studies designed specifically to the facts and circumstances of Campbell's case.

In the report, Dr French claims that, due to memory limitations, notes taken by police officers of remarks made by accused persons are unlikely to be verbatim, even though the officer concerned might insist, or genuinely believe, the opposite. Previous experimentation has shown repeatedly and consistently that under most circumstances verbatim memory is extremely short-lived.

Dr French expands in the report on the previous experiment conducted by him in connection with *R v Nedrick*. The experiment involved the dictation of a text consisting of 554 words to a group of 8 subjects. The content of the text was based loosely upon a disputed confession which featured in the case. Four of the subjects were employed as professional transcribers whose daily work involved the production of verbatim records of audio recordings. The remainder did not work within this occupation. The text was read to subjects at 'dictation pace' and each was instructed to write down, to the best of their abilities, the exact words spoken.

It was found that all subjects made errors, including the omission and addition of words as well as the replacement of words with other words. Across all participants, a 3.5 per cent average error rate was found to have occurred. Among the transcribers the average incidence of error was 3.1 per cent while among the non-transcribers the rate was 3.9 per cent. In addition, it was found that subjects' records of the words dictated differed widely from one another. Dr French highlights that, although the error rates appear low, the experiment reflected the best possible conditions for achieving a verbatim record of the text. In Dr French's view, one would expect the accuracy of police officers' records to be very substantially worse.

For the present case, Dr French devised an experiment involving 12 subjects of mixed occupational background, including two serving CID officers who had experience of transcribing tape recordings of conversations. Subjects were played audio recordings of 5 comments. Item E was based upon Campbell's comment while items B and C were based upon comments made by Campbell's co-accused, Thomas Gray. Items A and D consisted of utterances unconnected with the present case. As all subjects were familiar with 'Yorkshire English', any words of Scottish or Glasgow dialect within utterances were removed and replaced with Yorkshire terms. Campbell's remark was altered as follows:

'I only wanted the van windows shot up. The fire at

Del Boy's were only meant to be a frightener which went too far.'

A period of five seconds was allowed to elapse after each utterance was played, following which the subjects were instructed to write down exactly what they had heard, word for word.

Each utterance was scored in terms of the number of subjects achieving an accurate record of the linguistic form (in other words, the ability to record the right words in the right order). This was done in two ways. Firstly, account was taken of whether the subject had correctly noted any linguistic 'contractions'. Thus, where a comment contained the contracted form of 'do not' (ie 'don't') and a subject wrongly recorded the extended form, but otherwise correctly recorded the utterance, he would be scored as having accurately represented the remark. The second scoring criterion was more stringent and involved marking subjects in terms of any failure to note such contractions.

Dr French found that, with regard to Campbell's comment, none of the subjects achieved formally accurate records under either scoring criterion.

Dr French also examined the extent to which subjects recorded identical versions between them, irrespective of whether these were formally correct. Again, records were analysed using two criteria. In the first of these, for records to be regarded as identical to one another, they required to be formally and stylistically identical. This required the respective versions to have the same words in the same order and the same punctuation (ignoring full stops and question marks). The second criterion was less stringent and took account only of subjects' ability to record the same words as one another in the same order.

It was found that using either criterion no two subjects recorded Campbell's comment in the same way. In other words, there were as many versions of the comment as there were subjects.

Dr French concludes in the report that, given the similarity of the versions of the comment contained in the statements and evidence given by DI McCafferty and DC Geddes, it is unlikely that the comment was recorded by each of them entirely independently.

Dr French also considered the likelihood that all four officers were able to note the comment in such similar terms without comparison or collaboration (in other words, taking account of the positions adopted at interview by DS Hyslop and DC Geddes). In assessing this issue, Dr French assumed that the comment as it appears in each officer's witness statement was extracted from their respective notebooks. This assumption is based upon the terms of the letter received by the Commission from the Deputy Chief Constable of Strathclyde Police referred to . . . earlier. Taking account of the experimental data, together with the spelling and word omissions shared in the statements of' DS Hyslop and DI McCafferty, Dr French found it 'incredible' that these two officers could have recorded the remark independently of one another.

Overall, Dr French considers the possibility that all four officers independently achieved such similar recall as displayed in their oral evidence and witness statements as being 'extremely remote'.

Both conclusions lead Dr French to have very

serious doubts about the evidence of DI McCafferty
and DC Cargill that they noted the comment without
comparison,

The Issues at Trial

The credibility of many of the police officers involved
in the case and, in particular, those who arrested
Campbell, was clearly a significant issue at trial.
The officers who attended Campbell's house were
extensively cross-examined on the basis that their
evidence regarding the comment and the map had
been fabricated. It was suggested to DI McCafferty
that much of the evidence the police spoke to finding
at Campbell's house had been 'planted' in an attempt
to form a case against him. Counsel for Campbell also
appears to suggest during his cross examination of DI
McCafferty that a number of the words and phrases
contained within the comment (for example, 'Fat Boy'
and 'frightener') were known to the police prior to
Campbell's arrest, either as 'investigative features' of
the case or as a result of information provided by the
witness, William Love.

Further, it was suggested to DS Hyslop during cross-
examination that when Campbell was subsequently
charged with murder, he approached an officer
unconnected with the case whom he asked specifically
to note that he had made no response to caution and
charge. DS Hyslop accepted that this had occurred but
claimed that he had already noted that no reply had
been made. Campbell explained in evidence that he had
done this because he was concerned despite his silence,
he saw one of the officers writing in his notebook. It
was also suggested to DS Hyslop in cross-examination
that the police were 'fitting up' Campbell in terms of

the comment attributed to him and the map found in his house.

This theme appears to have been continued by counsel for Campbell in his speech to the jury, which is commented upon as follows by the trial judge in his charge.

'Now, in this case an attack has been made by counsel on the credibility of Love and Ness and many of the detective officers involved in investigating these crimes . . . So far as the detectives are concerned, Mr Macaulay delivered a vehement and sustained attack upon the integrity of a number of the detective officers involved in this case, some of considerable experience and in superior positions, some with less experience and in lower positions. He used words such as 'rotten', Strathclyde Police 'rotten' and you will remember he used such expressions as 'There are good policemen, bad policemen' and then reference was made to 'the ugly'; and they have been submitted to be 'liars and bullies'.

Indeed, a little later in his charge, the trial judge presents the jury with a fairly stark choice in relation to its assessment of the police evidence.

'It is only if you accept the evidence of the accused and the others to whom I have referred that you could agree with Mr Macaulay's submission. If you do, you must consider what follows. What follows is that you are saying that not one or two or four but a large number of detectives have deliberately come here to perjure themselves, to build up a false case against an accused person, and they have carried this through right to the end; a conspiracy of the most sinister and serious kind. They have formed this conspiracy to

saddle the accused wrongly with the crimes of murder
and attempted murder, and murder of a horrendous
nature. If so, it involves them making up and
persisting in a concocted story, concocted statements
attributed wrongly, falsely, to the accused. Now, what
do you prefer, ladies and gentlemen? It is up to you:
you saw the witnesses in the witness box; you heard
how the questions were answered. You have to make
up your mind what you believe.'

In convicting Campbell unanimously of murder and
serious assault, the choice which the jury eventually
made is clear.

The Possible Impact of the Opinions

While the findings made by Professor Clifford and
Dr French cannot determine conclusively whether
the comment was actually made by Campbell, in the
Commission's view they nevertheless tend to cast doubt
upon the reliability of the officers' evidence on this
issue. This would appear to be in two respects. The
first concerns how, given the findings produced by the
various studies, the officers involved were able fully
to recall the comment at all. In terms of the studies
carried out by Professor Clifford, not one of the 131
participants was able to recall the number of words
seemingly noted by the officers who arrested Campbell.
Nor were any of the participants able to recall all the
semantic units into which the comment was divided.
These findings are to some extent reflected in those
made by Dr French. While the Commission accepts
that police officers cannot always be expected to note
down the precise words spoken by an accused, even if
one assumes that the officers who arrested Campbell
noted down only the 'gist' of what was said this would

not explain why the versions each officer spoke to in
evidence were almost identical.

Secondly, the findings cast doubt upon the evidence
given by DI McCafferty and DC Cargill, both of whom
resisted suggestions made to them in cross-examination
that they had compared their respective notes of the
comment. Professor Clifford found that the possibility
of any two officers having independently achieved
verbatim recall of a comment of such length was
very low indeed. This conclusion is supported by the
fact that in Study 1, no 2 participants within any
group of 4 achieved the same verbatim recall as the
other. Indeed, it was found that even among those who
achieved greatest recall, the wording of the comment
and its meaning varied significantly from one to the
other. Dr French found in his study that none of the
subjects was able to recall the comment verbatim and
the majority was unable even to recall a version of the
comment which both fully and correctly represented its
semantic meaning.

Given the similarity of the versions of the comment
spoken to by each officer, in terms of the findings of
both studies it would not be unreasonable to conclude
(despite the positions adopted by DS Hyslop and DC
Geddes at interview) that comparison took place
between all concerned. As described above Professor
Clifford makes such a finding in his supplementary
report. The Commission considers that at its most
favourable, this suggests that perhaps one officer,
possibly more, may have given evidence not based
wholly upon his own recollections but rather upon
those of his colleagues. At worst, it suggests that the
evidence of DI McCafferty and DC Cargill in respect
of their resistance to suggestions that they did not

compare notes was untruthful. In these circumstances, given the strength of allegations made against the investigating officers at trial by Campbell's counsel to the effect that they had pressurised witnesses and fabricated evidence, it is possible that the jury, had it been exposed to the findings of both experts, might have regarded any apparent dishonesty on the part of Campbell's arresting officers as supportive of these claims. As indicated during cross-examination on whether he had consulted with his fellow officers on the comment allegedly made by Campbell, it was suggested to DI McCafferty that it was not improper for a police officer who fails to note a comment made by an accused to refer to a colleague's notebook entry. In the light of the above issues, it is possible that the jury, had it been aware of Professor Clifford's findings, might have inferred that there was perhaps a sinister reason why he refused to accept that this had occurred.

While the Commission accepts that police officers may frequently be reluctant to admit that such comparison has taken place, perhaps due to fears that such an admission will be met with allegations of collusion, it is clearly important that evidence of admissions made by an accused is given honestly and accurately. This is particularly so in circumstances where allegations of impropriety have been levelled at the officers involved.

The Commission also considers it notable that at interview DC Geddes claimed that, as he had noted Campbell's comment at the time, there would have been no point in subsequently comparing his note with those of his fellow officers, as by that stage he would not have been able to alter the contents of his notebook. The Commission understands that the

obligation upon officers to take notes of an accused's
comment 'at the time' requires them only to do so as
soon as reasonably practicable. However, in terms of
the evidence of DI McCafferty and DS Hyslop it is clear
that both noted the comment immediately after it was
made. As indicated, Professor Clifford found that in the
4 person group analysis all participants omitted key
sections of Campbell's comment and no 2 participants
in any 4 person group achieved recall of Campbell's
remark. If one accepts that in terms of these studies
all 4 officers must at some stage have compared their
respective notes of the comment, the findings tend to
cast doubt upon the evidence of DI McCaffertty and
DS Hyslop that the comment was noted by them in
Campbell's front room. Such an inference assumes,
of course, that none of the officers altered their
notebooks after comparison with their colleagues.
In terms of the evidence given by DI McCafferty
and DC Cargill, of course, no such comparison
occurred.

In these circumstances, the Commission considers it
arguable that the contents of the two reports constitute
potentially important and reliable evidence which would
have been likely to have had a material bearing upon,
or a material part to play in the jury's determination
of a critical issue at trial, namely the reliability and
credibility of the evidence given by the officers who
spoke to the comment. Had the jury heard evidence
of the kind which the two experts can now give it is
possible that they would have assessed the credibility
and reliability of the officers involved in a different
light. On the other hand, it is possible that they
would still have preferred the officers' evidence. The
Commission does not consider that a proper view can

be taken of the evidence without the benefit of hearing this in full, assuming of course that the court deems it admissible and material. This issue is dealt with in the following section.

Admissibility/ReasonableExplanation

As part of the instructions given to both Professor Clifford and Dr French, each was asked to consider whether, to their knowledge, the type of evidence they could now give on the subject of witness memory was widely known at the time Campbell's trial took place in 1984. Professor Clifford was also asked whether any research conducted prior to 1984 is likely to have been widely known to anyone uninvolved in the field and, in particular, whether he was aware of any previous case in England or elsewhere in which evidence of witness memory capacity had been led. This information was sought in order that the Commission could consider whether there was a reasonable explanation as to why such evidence was not heard at Campbell's trial, in terms of Section 106(3A) of the Criminal Procedure (Scotland) Act 1995.

Dr French in both his reports concludes simply, that, to the best of his knowledge, no one in the United Kingdom was practising in forensic linguistics in 1984 and that, therefore, evidence of the type contained in his report could not have been led at that time.

As a psychologist, Professor Clifford approached the question from a different discipline than Dr French. In section 7 of his report he explains that the theoretical background to his own research in the present case was fairly well established in 1984 and could have been led in evidence at that time. However, in his

view, courts in many jurisdictions have been unwilling
to admit evidence from experimental psychologists
whose work has traditionally been looked upon as lying
within the common knowledge and experience of the
jury. Accordingly, evidence of the type produced in his
report is, he suggests, commonly deemed inadmissible
as expert witness testimony.

In support of these views, Professor Clifford refers to
the decision of the Court of Appeal in England in *R v
Turner* (1975) QB 8,34, in which psychiatric evidence
to the effect that the accused was likely lo have become
enraged following a confession from his partner that
she had had sexual intercourse with two other men,
was held inadmissible on the basis that it fell within
the common knowledge and experience of the jury.
In that case, the following remarks were made by
Lawton LJ:

'An expert's opinion is admissible to furnish the court
with scientific information which is likely to be outside
the experience and knowledge of a judge or jury. If on
the proven facts a judge or jury can form their own
conclusions without help, then the opinion of an expert
is unnecessary . . . The fact that an expert witness has
impressive scientific qualifications does not by that fact
alone make his opinion on matters of human nature
and behaviour within the limits of normality any more
helpful than that of the jurors themselves . . .'

Later in the opinion, Lawton LJ makes the following
remark:

'Jurors do not need psychiatrists to tell them how
ordinary folk who are not suffering from any mental
illness are likely to react to the stresses and strains of
everyday life.'

Professor Clifford suggests in his report that this
apparent reluctance on the part of the courts to admit
evidence of the kind contained in his report may
provide an explanation as to why such evidence was
not heard at Campbell's trial.

The approach in *R v Turner* has been followed in
number of other jurisdictions. In *R V Smith (1987)* VR
907, a single judge of the Supreme Court of Victoria,
Australia, held that evidence sought to be led by
the defence from a psychologist as to the processes
and possible problems associated with eyewitness
identification was inadmissible. This was on the
basis that the evidence in question was concerned
with a 'normal human process' and, as such, was
something which it was assumed could competently
be addressed by the jury without expert testimony.
Reference was also made by the court in *Smith* to a
previous decision by the Court of Criminal Appeal in
Queensland in *R v Fong (1981)* Qd. R. 90 in which
it was held that evidence of research conducted by
psychologists in relation to human memory was also
inadmissible. The trial judge in that case expressed
the view that aspects of human memory are 'every
day matters well within the field of knowledge of
juries'.

There appears to the Commission to be relatively
little Scottish case law dealing specifically with the
admissibility of expert testimony, although what there
is seems consistent with the approach adopted in *R v
Turner*. In *Ingram v Macari* (1982 SCCR 372) it was
held that expert psychological and psychiatric evidence
on whether indecent publications were likely to deprave
and corrupt was inadmissible and that it was the duty
of the sheriff to make up his own mind on such issues.

This decision is consistent with the earlier case of *Galletly v Laird* (1953 JC 16).

In *HMA v Grimond* (29 June 2001), which involved alleged child sexual abuse, the complainers had failed to disclose certain allegations against the accused during a previous police investigation. The Crown sought to lead evidence from a clinical psychologist experienced in such cases, the purpose of which was to explain that delayed revelations of the kind made by the complainers are a common feature of child abuse cases. The evidence was therefore intended to counter any suggestion by the defence that the complainer's evidence in respect of the fresh allegations lacked credibility. The defence objected to the leading of such evidence on the basis that issues of credibility were for the jury to determine, and not an expert witness. In sustaining the objection, the trial judge (Lord Osborne) referred to the following passage from *MacPhail on Evidence:*

'It is thought that it would be wrong in principle to admit such evidence. The credibility of a witness is a matter for the tribunal of fact to determine, and to introduce the opinion of another witness on the subject, and perhaps further evidence for and against the grounds of opinion, would confuse and prolong the enquiry' (paragraph 16.19).

Reference was also made in the course of the opinion to the following passage from *R v Turner:*

'We adjudge *Lower v The Queen* (1974) AC 75 to have been decided on its special facts. We do not consider that it is an authority for the proposition that in all cases psychologists and psychiatrists can be called to prove the probability of the accused's veracity. If any

such was applied in our courts, trial by psychiatrists
would be likely to take the place of trial by jury
and magistrates. We do not find that prospect
attractive and the law does not at present provide
for it . . .'

In the Commission's view, the evidence sought to
be led in *Grimond* is arguably different from that
contained in the reports upon which the referral of
the present case is based. In *Grimond*, the evidence
consisted of an analysis of the mental states of the
complainers with a view to enhancing their credibility
before the jury. However, in the present case the
evidence consists of an assessment, not of the
state of mind of the officers concerned, but rather
the reliability of their evidence concerning certain
potentially material facts. In the Commission's view,
such evidence is arguably distinct from that concerned
with the mental state of a witness and its possible
impact upon his/her credibility. Some support for
this view can be found in the passage quoted by
Lord Osborne from *Walker on Evidence* (paragraph
1.6.2):

'Apart from the statutory rules, it is thought that
evidence of facts affecting the credibility of a witness,
apart from the evidence of the witness himself or
herself is generally inadmissible *unless the facts are
also relevant to the questions at issue.* This is not
because the facts are irrelevant, but it is inexpedient
to spend time on the investigation of collateral issues
concerning persons who are not necessarily parties to
the cause' (emphasis added).

As explained above, one of the major questions at issue
in Campbell's case concerned the credibility of the

police officers involved in his arrest and, in particular, whether their evidence of the comment made by him had been fabricated. Accordingly, in the Commission's view Lord Osborne's opinion was arguably concerned with evidence of a different kind from that in the present case.

While the Scottish cases cited above suggest a firm view against such evidence, in more recent years it is arguable that courts in England have adopted a more relaxed approach than that evident in *R v Turner*. Most of these cases have, however, been concerned with evidence regarding the accused's mental state. Nevertheless, by narrowing what is considered to fall within the common knowledge of the jury, some courts have been prepared to admit evidence which in terms of *Turner* might have been looked upon as being concerned with 'everyday' matters. In *R v Emery* (1993) 14 Cr. App. R. (S) 394, while the English Court of Appeal did not abandon the *Turner* rule altogether, by allowing evidence of 'battered wives syndrome' the assumption that all forms of human behaviour apart from mental disorder fall within the common knowledge of the jury was not applied.

It should be highlighted, however, that in the case referred to by Professor Clifford in his supplementary report, *R v Hersey* (1 December 1997), the English Court of Appeal supported a trial judge's decision to refuse to admit evidence from a defence expert in voice identification. However, in that case the witness was to speak to issues such as the dissimilarity in pitch between the accused's voice and the stand-ins who attended the parade, on which the jury were perhaps unlikely to have needed guidance.

Although Professor Clifford's report can be said to address aspects of a 'normal human process' (ie memory), the Commission does not consider that a jury would necessarily possess sufficient knowledge to assess the officers' evidence on the issues raised in the reports without specific testimony to this effect. Indeed, it is perhaps unlikely that a jury would address these issues at all without being focussed by such evidence. Some support for this conclusion may be found in the English Court of Appeal's decision in *R v Meads* [1996] Crim L R 519. *Meads* was convicted in 1985 of various offences which were investigated by the West Midlands Serious Crime Squad. The principal evidence against him consisted of admissions and confessions allegedly made by him while in police custody. At appeal, he sought to lead fresh evidence from two forensic experts which showed the speed at which the handwritten notes of the disputed interviews had been taken by the officers and questioned whether this could have been done within the time claimed by them. It was argued by the Crown that this evidence should not be admitted because the body of knowledge on which it was based was not sufficiently organised and relatively few tests had been carried out. The court held, however, that the evidence was admissible provided it was confined to the results of the tests performed. Significantly, the court observed that the fresh evidence was not opinion evidence any more than is the testimony of a police officer who times a journey in order to test an accused's alibi.

Although in terms of Professor Clifford's report, evidence of memory theory could conceivably have been led at Campbell's trial, the Commission has reached the view there is an explanation why this did not occur. The Commission considers that this explanation is capable of being regarded as 'reasonable' by the Court in terms of section 106 (3A) of the 1995 Act.

In the Commission's view, it is perhaps unlikely that such evidence as contained in the two reports would have been admissible at trial. It is also perhaps fair to say that the general attitude adopted by the courts to such evidence at that time would have been shared by many of those counsel and solicitors who appeared at trial. In general, those who appeared were possibly less likely to have been aware of the possibilities of leading such evidence than would be the case nowadays. This view is to some extent supported by Dr French's remarks that at the time of Campbell's trial no one, to his knowledge, was engaged in forensic linguistics. The development of these disciplines and the awareness of them as possible forms of evidence by court practitioners seem only to have occurred relatively recently.

In these circumstances, the Commission does not consider that those who represented Campbell can be criticised for not leading evidence of the kind which is now available. In terms of the instructions received from Campbell, it appears to the Commission that every possible means available to his counsel at that time was employed to challenge and test the evidence of the officers concerned. That this challenge was unsuccessful may in part be due to the inherent difficulties in overcoming evidence of this kind. The Commission also has no reason to believe that those who represented Campbell made a deliberate tactical or technical decision not to lead the evidence now presented.

Conclusion

The Commission considers that the terms of the reports of both experts are sufficiently strong to cast doubt upon the evidence of Campbell's arresting officers and, accordingly, the Commission is satisfied that the statutory criteria for referral of the case have been met. The Commission's decision is based upon its view that had the jury rejected the evidence of Campbell's arresting officers, it appears that there would have been insufficient evidence to convict him of murder.

The Commission is accordingly of the view that a miscarriage of justice may have occurred in Campbell's case. The Commission also considers that it is in the interests of justice that the case should be referred to the High Court of Justiciary for determination and accordingly does so.

A Day Out in Edinburgh

I was late, of course, I always am. A train from Glasgow was delayed and I stood there in the station wanting to scream at the tannoy,
'DO YOU NO KNOW WHIT AN IMPORTANT DAY THIS IS. A'VE GOT A PLACE TAE GO TAE.'
Sense prevailed – it would've been embarrassing to get lifted by the police that day of all days. I drank another coffee, smoked five more fags and waited.

The place was cold, freezing raw with the stone slabs outside the High Court in Edinburgh stuck to the soles of my boots. I was dressed as always – black suit, black T-shirt – just enough to cope with the warm drizzle of the west, of Glasgow. But my company were prepared. Old campaigners, used to hanging around for hours in the sub-zero. I stood among them – stranger in a pack of happy hounds – and clocked faces. They were all there – all the newspapers, TV crews, radio stations, press agencies. One or two had been in post in 1984, when the big TC was jailed. Most had to learn about him through reading the press cuttings. The press cuttings, I had them all and recalled what they had written back in 1984.

ICE CREAM WARS
MASS MURDERER
GANGSTER, TC CAMPBELL
Everything just short of HANGING'S TOO GOOD.

So what was on their minds today? I earywigged on their chat.
  'What you doing after this?'
  'Spell at the Scots parliament then the pub.'
  'You entertaining at Christmas.'
  'As usual.'
  'What's it to be this year?'
  'I've discovered this remarkable cheese . . .'
  Inside the court TC Campbell, Joe Steele and Thomas Gray awaited a judgment on their freedom, their innocence, their lives. Telling them if they had a life. But the Press chatted about Christmas dinner, holiday plans, what pub they would meet up in. They were happy as little Larry's, standing in the cold, knowing that today's big scoop was about to walk out of those heavy wooden doors right onto their lap. Fine, but what will they write now?
  Reg McKay
  11 December 2001

Myself, Tamby and Joe Steele appeared at Edinburgh High Court on Tuesday 11 December 2002. Joe and I were released on interim liberation. The Tamby fullah was returned to Barlinnie to finish off the remaining week of a short sentence which he was then serving. Having completed the fourteen-year sentence for the discharging of a gun at Andrew Doyle's van, convicted on the evidence of William Love and police verbal, he would be free to leave prison without bail by the following week.

  Then they were out. Big TC and the diminutive Joe Steele. Marching across the quadrangle straight to the press hounds.
  'TC! Joe! Over here.'

'Give us a wave, TC.'
'What does it feel like to be released?'
'Do you feel bitter?'
'What are your plans now?'
'TC, over here.'
'TC, give us a smile.'
'TC . . .'
'TC . . .'
Tommy looked calm. Happy but calm. The day he received the Commission's report deciding on an appeal, he had phoned me and quietly passed on the information. There were tears, of course, but at my end of the phone only. Not for Tommy Campbell. He belonged on the outside, a free man, why should he cry over something that was his right? Besides, years of incarceration and false start after false dawn had left him unmoved by the prospect of hope. Tommy Campbell would believe fuck all till he could breathe in the fresh outside air, feel the soft caress of his wife and reach out and touch his children's cheeks one by one.
'TC, are you bitter?'
'TC, what are your plans?'
'TC . . .'
'TC . . .'
'TC . . .'
Reg McKay
11 December 2001

Walking out that door again met with no sense of triumph, only that of relief. The fight was not over yet, the battle simply re-engaged, taking us back to the point where we had been almost four years earlier. Four more wasted years of trouble, hardship and heartache. The Press wanted to know how I felt. The reply was spontaneous, considering that this was the seventeenth year of a twenty-year recommendation, 'This is round seventeen of a twenty round bout, don't count us out just yet.' I then took my wife Karen and daughter Cheree Ann in my arms and headed for home, anxious to hold my baby daughter Shannon, only seven days old when I was returned to prison, in my arms once again and to let her see that I was in fact home as I promised I would be.

I watched him walk down the High Street. Just another big fella out for the day in Edinburgh with his wife and child. Nobody turned to stare. Nobody ran and hid. Nobody paid him any attention – just the way he wanted. All he had ever expected.

Tommy Campbell might be calm but I'm made of more high strung stuff. A rendezvous with a friend and a few drinks would fit the bill nicely. I was waiting for Kevin Williamson, the guy who had shown faith in the books to commission them for Canongate. Now a good friend and fellow traveller, I couldn't think of anyone I'd rather get drunk with that day. Kevin was busy as usual but I'd wait. The Café Royal was full of its usual lunch time cocktail of east coast trendies, businessmen in grey suits, tourists in waterproofs with street maps balanced next to their glasses. I couldn't stop smiling. My mobile phone rang time after time interrupting my efforts to order that extra large glass of cold, dry white wine. The young woman behind the bar smiled and waited as I fielded calls from the Press trying to get a bigger slice of Tommy and his family. An exclusive picture of the happy family. A visit to the Campbell household. Could you tell us where he is? Fuck knows, I told them, how should I know? Tommy Campbell's a free man at last and he can go where he wants. The barmaid served someone else and the phone went again. Paddy Joe Hill of the Birmingham Six and now the leading campaigner against unjust imprisonment. I could feel the wee hero do an Irish jig at the other end of the line. Karen Torley, the bonny fighter for Kevin Richey the Scot on America's Death Row. Hope was what she heard and her heart burned even stronger. John McManus up in Scotland to set up MOJO here to fight against miscarriages of justice. David Leslie, the newspaper writer who had serialised Indictment – Trial by Fire for News of the World. Aren't these guys meant to be cynical? David didn't sound cynical that day.

At last the phone stopped ringing and the young woman behind the bar slipped over. As she poured me the glass of wine she said, 'You look happy.' Silly grin still splitting my face.

'Aye, I am. Friend of mine was released from jail the day.' I watched her face closely – her looking at me, reappraising my appearance from dressed down arty-fart type to downright sinister. It is a thin line, after all.

'Eh, good,' she grimaced.

'Tommy Campbell,' I offered. Nothing. 'TC Campbell,' I persisted. Her face returned to its beamer of a smile,

'Really, did he get out! Wonderful. High time those guys were home where they belong.'

I drank my wine and made a little silent toast. To the good people of life who can see beyond the headlines. To the decent folk of the world who can spot an injustice for what it is. To the Press guys who were at that time writing celebratory headlines. To big TC – Tommy Campbell – who taught us all so much.

Reg McKay
11 December 2001

Lost Worlds

A prison gate has two sides to it, an inside and an
  outside.
When that gate closed behind me, a door slammed shut
  in my life.
Not only locking me in (containing my life in its
  confines)
but it also locked me out of the life I had once known,
isolating me from my home, children, family and
  friends.

When that gate opened up again, letting me out, setting
  me free . . .
Turning my life around once again.
I found that the door which had once slammed closed
  behind me,
remained firmly closed. Locking me out of the life I had
  once known,
only now it stands before me . . .

I have been let out, sure enough, but I have still to be
  let back into the life I had once known.

Reawakenings

Tuesday 2 April 2002 was the first of our procedural preliminary hearings before the High Court of Appeal in Edinburgh. Once again, like four years earlier, it was a pleasant enough drive through to the capital city. Despite the latest road diversions, myself, Tamby and another friend soon found parking space and on into the court in plenty of time for a chat and briefing with solicitors who still gave no clue as to what lay ahead. We had no copy of the formal, laid out grounds for appeal but were assured that they were, as expected, regarding the situation with Mr Love's confessed perjury as fresh evidence together with the Commission's points regarding the expert evidence attacking the credibility and reliability of the police verbal evidence.

Joe Steele's counsel spoke first, apologising that many of the points he would make would tend to overlap those areas more directly covered in my case. Which, I thought, could only be expected since we were, after all, convicted on an Art & Part basis and to the effective extent that one could not be convicted without the other.

He had, it transpired, seven points to make but the court would decide at a later date which, if any, of those points were valid and could go forward to the next stage. It transpired the court was yet to rule upon the issue of whether or not any points made outwith direct reference by the Commission could in fact be heard at all. If not, then this would entail that the real and main issues of Crown witness William Love's confessed perjury could not even be raised. The previous court, under Lord Cullen, had erred on the facts of the case that Love had 'not admitted' that he had fired the gun, therefore his sister's previously undisclosed statement to the police that she was a witness to the fact he had could not support his allegedly non-existent confession that he had admitted it. This would mean that this error of the facts had effectively barred this area of the enquiry from being reviewed at all. It also raised the question of whether or not a bench of three judges could overrule the opinions of a previous court – regardless of the fact that that court was in error of the essential facts – thus depriving the appellants of a fair hearing of all the facts and circumstances of the case.

It seemed to me that some attempt at a cover up was afoot here. I'm not a lawyer but you don't have to be to see when there are moves to gag you from airing the truth and the facts of the case in a court of law. I recalled that the old Act empowering the Scots Secretary to refer a case back to the court had been duly tested and interpreted to allow any point raised by the appellant to be heard before the court 'as if it were an appeal under this part of this Act'. I also recalled that the new Act empowering the Commission in the place of the Scots Secretary also retained this wording. In fact, it was the same Act merely replacing the words 'Secretary of State' with the word 'Commission' thereby allowing that any or all points could be raised before the court and not merely those referred to by the Commission.

This explained why we were now surrounded by prison officers. It appears that should we have proceeded with just the Commission's point of reference the court could have rejected that point at that stage as incompetent and invalid and sent us back to prison without further ado.

The thought of which had not even dawned upon me until then. However, both counsel for Joe and I had advocated extension of time on that issue to gather further detailed material and the like for extended expert reports and opinions. There was also some debate on the other points and some reference made to a higher constituted court, a sitting of five judges, though I couldn't quite follow this without the actual points of appeal before me. It appeared to regard the point of so called 'defective representation' on the part of the original defence at the trial, entailing the issue of why Mrs Agnes Love or Carlton was not called to give evidence at the original trial. This seemed to turn upon Lord Cullen's opinion that she could not be adduced as 'fresh evidence' because there appeared to be no reasonable explanation (as required by statute) as to why she was not called at the time of the original trial – the original defence must have been defective in that respect. However, this would have no bearing on whether it was, in fact and in law, competent to lead her as 'supporting evidence' (also required by statute) of the fresh evidence of her brother, William Love, who admits his confessions that the conversation in a bar, which convicted us of mass murder, never occurred. Love also confesses to the shooting of the van contrary to his evidence at court stating that it had been Tamby. Agnes Love confirmed the truth of that confession by her statement to the police at the time (not disclosed to the defence then) that her brother had, in fact, been the gunman.

The main thrust of the appeal, therefore, must be the issue of perjury on the part of the witness William Love and supported by the evidence of his sister. The Commission's material simply adds to this. Yet now it appeared that this main thrust of the appeal in proof of miscarriage of justice was to be suppressed, firstly upon the ground that, apparently, the law was being reinterpreted to restrict this appeal to within the limitations of those points referred by the Commission and because one appeal court cannot overturn the opinions of a previous similarly constituted court on the same issues. It appeared that Lord Cullen's crucial error of the essential facts of the case, allowing him to access the statutory technicalities preventing the appeal being heard, could not be challenged nor criticised by this court, burying the real issues and the controversy once and for all. But what use is a court that cannot address the fundamental issues of justice? This must surely raise issues of basic human rights like the right to a fair hearing of all the facts and circumstances of the case.

Possibly, strategy is the name of the game here. Should the point regarding defective representation at the original trial in respect of Agnes Love or Carlton be upheld then this would reopen the entire issue of the witness Love's confessed perjury at the trial. This seemed to me to be a very long route and a very long way around to stating the obvious. This miscarriage of justice occurred because the witness Love lied. Why then should it be so difficult to have that fact heard in a court of law? I felt that simply to restate that point and bring the proof of it in his confessions, supported by his sister, should be the obvious approach. Everything else – the police perjury and misdirections by the trial judge and so on – is merely by the way.

The hearing ended with a judgment that the defence had ten weeks to gather such fresh material as could be gleaned from the linguistics experts and a date would be set within a few weeks thereafter for a more lengthy and detailed preliminary hearing where the ruling on what can and cannot be heard before the court would be made.

We were prevented from leaving court by prison officers intent on returning us to jail. This was a rude
reawakening for me. Echoes of the last preliminary hearing four years earlier. Then too, we had been surrounded
by prison officers and the appeal had come to a sudden
and abrupt end, returning us to prison on the two to
one decision that the fresh evidence of Love's perjury
would not be allowed to be heard. Obviously then, the
prison staff had been warned in advance to come to the
court to collect us. It appears that this had been the
intention here also and we had narrowly escaped that
trap. The court must have intended to rule that only
those issues raised by the Commission may be heard and
that those said issues were to be dismissed by the court
as incompetent.

A prison officer took hold of Tamby by the arm, effectively arresting and detaining him but Tamby's sentence
was finished and he was not out on bail. He could
not have been arrested even should the appeal have
failed.

'Get your fuckin hands off me,' the big yin growled,
wrenching his arm from the screw's grasp. Trying to calm
the situation I explained that the appeal had merely been
postponed for another three months. The prison guards
wouldn't accept my word for it. They had been called
there to take us into custody and take us into custody
they would. However, a word with the prosecutor and
they stepped aside leaving us free to leave the court. With
the memory and the shock of what had occurred four
years earlier reawakened in our minds, wee Joe left the
court very abruptly.

To top the day off, we were fitted up with a parking
ticket. Pay £30 within two weeks or £60 thereafter for
allegedly illegal parking in Niddrie Street when in fact we
were legally parked in Baird Lane.

'Fuck this for a lark,' I thought. 'Come to sunny Edinburgh and be framed. Let's just get to fuck out of here,' I said, getting us lost and finding the scenic route home.

How Long?

TC Campbell and Joe Steele are not yet free. After seventeen years of hunger strikes, prison break outs, demonstrations, political pressure, solitary isolation, prison beatings, rights removed, prison video diaries, legal fight after legal fight they are free on a condition. On interim liberation pending appeal. An appeal that is unlikely to happen till late into the year 2003 almost twenty years after their wrongful conviction. An appeal whose outcome we should not prejudge. It is still conceivable that TC Campbell and Joe Steele lose their appeal and are sent back to prison. To do what? Continue the fight that's what.

The beat goes on . . .

Epilogue

The Iceman Cometh (April 2002)

I should have seen it coming. One minute life is tickety-boo with nothing much to worry about apart from a small matter of an appeal to prove my innocence. The next the media has written about an alleged fight between The Craw and Paul Ferris. Now wee Paul Ferris had no love for The Craw that's for sure and he'd revealed that in his own book, *The Ferris Conspiracy*, published the year before. But Paul was on best behaviour being, as he was, under supervision licence having just been released from seven years jail on gun running offences. A quick call to Paul confirmed that the press had got it all wrong. But the media wouldn't have it that way. One red-top in particular had Paul trying to kill The Craw – not alleged, you understand, but stating it as fact. And every day they claimed more, predicting gang warfare would set the streets of Glasgow on fire. Aye, right, like they would know. But I should've read it as a sign, seen something coming . . .

It was a sharp flashback to be introduced to the so-called Iceman in this way. 'Introduced' in the broader sense of course cos I actually knew this guy. Just didn't recognize him nor realize his new name though I knew his family well enough to realize that he'd plagiarized this title from his infamous uncle, Frank McPhee. A bank robber and major player from Maryhill, the original Iceman had been accorded the name on a number of fronts. Firstly, he was involved big time in the ice cream trade long before it caught on among the rest of us. Secondly, he had seen off a couple of rivals in the deadliest and most permanent of ways. Frank McPhee didn't boast about it, didn't swagger he just got on with it and took no shite from anyone. So, The Iceman cometh reckoned the population and that's what they called him – behind his back.

The original Iceman was assassinated by a sniper's bullet a few years earlier – a high powered .22 rifle cutting him down from a distance as he stood on his doorstep near his eleven-year old son. Even the hit man didn't want to get too close to the original Iceman. So, Billy McPhee then would be only too pleased to adopt the mantle of The Iceman in his uncle's stead. His ambition had always been to grow up to be a Gangster and, unfortunately, some people never do quite grow up.

He'd made all the right career moves over the many long years of my imprisonment. Teamed up with all the right crews as a debt enforcer on the smack scene. Gaining the reputation as a brutal killer to add some credibility to his growls is certainly the right step in the wrong direction towards his fantasy world come true. However, I was soon to discover that this wasn't his first delve into the darker regions.

The last I'd heard of him had been that murder in the Victoria Bar in the city centre years before. An innocent bystander had been stabbed to death in the toilets having intervened in The Iceman's enforcement of a dope debt, paid the ultimate price for his gallantry. However, it was two brothers from Queenslie, near Easterhouse, there with The Iceman, who had taken the fall. One brother bullied into confession, later retracted in court, had dragged the other down with him whilst The Iceman cooled his heels in hiding. Everyone knew who had done the damage and that the wrong man had been weighed-in on the debt. However, by the time The Iceman stood trial the two brothers had already been doled out life sentences by the court. The Iceman simply blamed them and was acquitted on a Not Proven verdict. Though openly boasting of his sins, The Iceman refused point blank to assist in the appeal against conviction lodged on behalf of those innocent convicted.

'No profit in that,' he'd proclaim. The subsequent seizure of their assets was more in his line . . .

I should've seen it coming right enough though. There was a time when I would've been better prepared. Only two days earlier my car had been written off from a stationary position at Parkhead Cross. The driver of the truck turned out to be an ex ice cream van operator in Easterhouse. The following day, on the way to the shops on foot, I'd been hailed and warned by a local lad.

'They're out in force, big yin. Three carloads and The Craw himself in his jeep. They're going tae try and nip you at the shops. Don't let on Ah told yeh . . .'

Sure enough! Once alerted, the manoeuvres were obvious. I should've seen it myself but just didn't have that para head on at the time and y'just don't see much of the dark side without it. My strategy then, alone, unarmed and on my feet was simply To Boldly Go directly at them rather than turn tail. Zeroing my focus directly in on the first car, zeroing in on the occupants, I walked rapidly and directly towards them from the side, watching them freak out and cringe as I approached. Peering in through the windshield and side windows, letting them see no fear but only that I was taking confident, close observations of just exactly who was taking any part in this cowardly conspiracy against me. As they turned away in an attempt to hide their faces, the second car came in behind me, screeching to a halt with dramatic effect. Its occupants, moving as if to exit all doors, hesitated, frozen in mid-movement as I turned facing them gesturing with both hands,

'Here I am. Come on. Take me.' The doors never did open, the cars screeched into reverse high speed, spinning and speeding away as the jeep and second back-up car cruised slowly by on the main highway, their occupants looking confused to see me still standing there.

This was a professionally laid plot. I don't believe I scared them off. It is more likely that they backed out on the first recognition of just exactly who their target was. Perhaps accounting for why the second ambush, next day, was such a bungling amateur pantomime.

I should've been prepared but once again I wasn't. My head just isn't into this gangster para crap and I had other things on my mind. My youngest daughter, Shannon, had just turned four. I should have been picking her up from nursery but, instead, we'd had the doctor out twice in two days. The wee soul was unwell and I was hurrying to the chemist for her medicine. My problem is that I have no fear of and am not impressed by these gangsters. They just do not come into my reckoning.

I'm shaken from my thoughts by the sudden presence of a big Jeep type vehicle imposing itself upon my conscious-ness. A bulky figure leaping from the moving vehicle as it screeches to a halt beside me. I look up to see the Craw sitting there on the high driver's seat grinning to himself at his own super shrewdness at catching me off guard like this. The hulking figure bearing down on me from the front. I hear the words,

'Y'calling him a grass?' as I parry an open left hand aimed at gripping me by the chest but pushing me back in the process.

'Whit? Y'trying to say th'y'don't know he's a grass?' I say, fending off the second left.

'You're the fuckin grass,' says the heavy as I turn to The

Craw saying, 'Tell this ejit, you're a fuckin grass are'nt yeh . . .'

Turning to the eejit, parrying a third attempt to take grip of me, I ask,

'Who the fuck are you anyway?'

'Whit? I'm The Iceman,' he proclaims, indignant at my lack of recognition and, I just had to smile.

'My! My! The Iceman himself,' I laughed outright and repeated, 'Like y'trying to say th'y'don't know he's a fuckin grass?' I gesture again to the Craw who glares furiously, gesturing with his head at his henchman who attacks.

It was a slow lumbering attempt at a flying header. Right arm straight out clutching a dagger coming in at me on an arc. Still with my head turned side on to him, looking at the Craw, I simply completed that motion by stepping one step back with my right foot, camouflaging the fact that I had just adopted a fighting stance, left foot side-on to my assailant. Turning to face him and tilting my head to the left, blocking his right with my left as his head missed its target to land on three rapid jabs to the jaw instead. Stepping back to prevent him stumbling into me. He's between me and the Craw now and tries the same discoordinated move again, countered in the same simple way. Parry and three more rapid to the chin should have been enough to let him see that his was not the best of tactics but it didn't dawn on him till the third lumbering effort while, in between times, I'm giving the Craw pelters to keep the pot boiling. Finally, The Iceman gets a grip with his left hand as I trip him with my right foot, he pulls me down on top of him.

The street is thronging with kids and mothers coming from the local school and nursery. The CCTV cameras are aimed right at us as we roll about the ground struggling for possession of the blade. Somehow it ended up in my hand with me on top. I wrapped it around his head and stuck it into his gut at least a half a dozen times but to no effect. It suddenly struck me why he was so bulky – he was wearing protective clothing. He was still holding onto my jacket as if he really fancied it. I stood up, slipping out of my jacket as I did so, leaving him clutching it there on the ground and made a move towards the jeep. It leaped forward. There was no way I was getting anywhere near this Crawbag. Not now while he was beginning to remember what it was I was good at – street fighting.

'Is that it then? Is that the best you can do then? Is that yer whack?' I said gesturing with open hands. 'Grass,' I added contemptuously over my shoulder as I walked away, continuing my journey to the chemist for the wean's medicine.

'Gies that other blade,' I hear The Iceman plead, as I wonder to myself,

'Where the fuck did that blade go anyway?' It seemed to have just appeared in my hand and disappeared again like magic. I strolled on till I hear the running feet behind me egged on by the Craw,

'Get'm! Get'm!' I turn round and The Iceman draws to a rapid halt, keeping his distance now. I'd picked up my jacket and it was on one arm, using it as a gladiator would use a net, as a shield and, attempting to snag the weapon. After a few more slight clashes without any effect, The Iceman backs away into the Jeep. I think the problem was that it was taking too long to put me down and he was getting jittery.

I turned away and walked on. Reaching the railings by the stairs at the community centre, I stopped there to take stock and catch my breath. Leaning, I noticed the Jeep hadn't moved. Both were inside. It looked like the Craw was giving The Iceman pelters, like he wasn't getting paid or something. Next thing I know is that the Jeep had turned round onto the main road and was heading up towards me, cutting me off from the shops. I walked back down the stairs into the car park of the community centre where the Jeep, having turned at the shops, was heading right for me. From where I stood then, I could see the CCTV camera follow its movements. They both got out now. It seemed to have been agreed that The Iceman needed some help and the Craw was it. One with a blade and the other with a golf club.

They circled me, as always, with one behind and the other in front. I could only keep them both side-on at either side for so long but once one made an attack and I had to turn and deal with that – parrying the golf club with my arm and jacket – the other would try an attack from behind with the blade. Each time I dealt with one, the other would strike but I was coping well and holding my own. Time was passing and I was aware that they had very little left to do the damage before they would be forced to split the scene. I stalled,

'You're going to the jail,' I reasoned, knowing it was the Craw's greatest fear. 'There are too many witnesses,' I pointed to the CCTV. The Craw looked scared.

'He's no a grass. You're the fuckin grass,' The Iceman argued as if trying to justify himself to me.

We all knew that this was not about calling anybody a grass. It was about the Doyle family fire murders and, who was responsible for that holocaust.

'You know he's a fuckin grass,' I said, 'but that's besides the point. This is about the Doyles. Are you trying to make out like you don't know it?'

'Whit do yeh expect me to do? Put my fuckin hands up to it or somethin?' the Craw interjected.

'You're the fuckin grass,' The Iceman shouted as he lunged forward, grappling with me and coming away with my jumper and jacket leaving me stripped down to the waist and empty handed. I couldn't get around in time to ward off the Craw's golf club. THUNK! I wasn't aware of it snapping on my forehead and spinning into the air but that's what the witnesses describe. I was only aware that I was sparkled on my feet, blinded and with only the one thought in my head,

'Don't go down or you're dead.' I didn't know why then. Not until the haze cleared and I saw the running feet and The Iceman scoop up my house keys from the ground and hand them to the Craw on the run. They jumped back into the jeep and drove off.

I started to walk back home. Realizing that I couldn't let the wean see me like this – my entire face and body were bright red with blood, I had a hole in my head and I'd been stabbed in the back of the neck and hip.

Remembering Shannon, the medicine, I turned to continue my journey to the chemist. Reaching the rail by the stairway, I noticed the crowds of teenagers and school kids and realized I couldn't walk the streets like this. A neighbour was taking me by the elbow, leading me.

'You have to sit down,' she kept repeating. 'The police have been called and there's an ambulance on its way. We all seen it, Mr Campbell. They'll not get away with it. They'll not get far.' I went into the community centre toilet and tried to wash. When I saw the hole in my head for the first time I wondered why I wasn't dead. Like my Ma used always to say,

'You're ok, you've got a heed like a chucky stane.' And, it seems that I've spent a lifetime confirming it.

The media went to town. By the next day they had fingered McGraw and Billy McPhee for the attack on me with no help from myself. There had been a score of witnesses, CCTV footage, the blood stained shaft of a broken golf club found at the scene as well as a knife. But instead of calling for arrests the media took another position.

ICE CREAM KILLER STABBED IN SECOND GANG-LAND ATTACK ran the most polite headline.

ICE CREAM KILLER'S HITMEN TERROR blasted the best selling red-top in the country.

GANGLAND ATTACKS REKINDLE NO MEAN CITY FEARS ran another in what was to be the theme of the next fortnight. Every day the head of steam built up with each newspaper claiming to know more than the others. One tabloid in particular seemed to have turned into some propoganda machine for Strathclyde Police and to what end? The focus of their attention was Paul Ferris and me. In Paul's case they stated blatantly that he HAD attacked McGraw and even produced the bloody knife they said he HAD used. It was an old police game, stirring up bloodshed on the streets and, while they were at it, reminding the people that I may be out on appeal but I was still legally THE ICE CREAM WAR KILLER. It felt like a return to the days of the trial back in 1984 when the press had me hung drawn and quartered even before the jury had decided what the verdict was. Now why should that be? The media had become supportive of the camapign of The Glasgow Two to prove our innocence – had been for years. So why should one red-top in particular change its tack now? What had changed? Well I had written a book, *Indictment*, and was out on appeal. In the book I slated the corridors of injustice, the corrupt practices of the police and a certain party who colluded with them – The Craw. So the polis and The Craw were annoyed and wanted me out of the way, that I knew already. So what else is new? But what had that newspaper to do with it? What were they getting out of acting as the unofficial department of disinformation? I must have criticised them too.

I told the police that there was no way that they would get charging these guys, McPhee and McGraw, in spite of the witnesses and the forensics.

'He's too valuable as a Crown agent.' I told them that their bosses' bosses would take the case off them and the Craw would be immune from prosecution.

By the weekend the police from another force were telling me that they were obliged to inform me that special intelligence sources had uncovered a plot to kill me that weekend. The same weekend that six Loyalist Orange Ulstermen were arrested for terrorist conspiracies in Glasgow. So much for the peace process then. Once again the police came back to confirm that the contract remained outstanding and that I remained in real danger. The Iceman drove past the house shouting something up at the window. Shannon, on the road to recovery, came in from the veranda saying,

'That bad man said you're getting it, Campbell.'

Karen, my wife, can't sleep at night. Noises at the window and at the door. I tell her not to worry,

'They'll no come to the door.'

'Aye? I bet the Doyle family could confirm that,' she'd say and she's right.

In the middle of all this Paul Ferris is told that his licence has been revoked. Strathclyde Police have written to the Home Office saying that he had breached his supervison licence, was a risk to the public and should be returned to jail forthwith. Do Not Pass Go, do not collect fuck all. They didn't tell Paul what he had done that was so bad. They never even interviewed the man. Just a 'phone call. What did they expect – for Paul to go on the run and allow them a high profile car chase and arrest? They were to be disappointed. Paul jumped in a car and drove

all right – straight into England where he handed himself
into Durham Police. With the hindsight of polis dirty
tricks on him for almost twenty years he was not about
to let the Strathclyde mob get their mitts on him now.
His trip to Durham was spur of the moment and top
secret. But, by the time he arrived at the police station
a posse of journalists were waiting for him from – yeah,
yer ahead of me – the same tabloid that had been acting
as the police propaganda machine. Now how could that
have happened?

After six weeks in the jail, Paul was called over by a
senior screw. It seems that Strathclyde Police's report to
the Home Office admitted that they had no grounds to
charge him with any alleged offence. However, the report
had also referrred to various reports in the media stating
that Paul had been involved in badness. Now what part of
the media was that? Oh my, it was that tabloid again. The
Home Office didn't give the same weighting to fanciful,
manufactured headlines in a paper renowned for keech.
They ordered Paul's immediate release. Like get on yer
civvies and leave this jail NOW. He didn't need a second
telling. Trouble is he had just lost six weeks of freedom
on the back of rumours and hearsay printed in one organ
of the press. Six weeks off the street that suited the police
and only the police. His partner and his young son had to
cope with the worry and the stress of him being whisked
away. All that work in them trying to settle down as a
family after years apart dented on a whim.

Back in Glasgow this attack hadn't phased me. Neither
did the threats of murder upon my life. But life wasn't
straightforward for me either. It's just another day in the
life to me but it was a new nightmare for Karen and the
wean. The attack on me had done the greatest damage
upon them. Before this, it was the Craw who had the nice
big house in which he couldn't sleep. The nice garden he

couldn't stroll in. This was his nightmare and a small dose of his nightmare had been inflicted on my wife and children. The Craw and McPhee on the other hand were going about their business – not charged, not warned, not anything – just as I had predicted to the police. No change there then.

'Don't go out, daddy, you'll get killed.' This advice from a four year old tends to give you pause for thought. I would rather that they killed me than have my children tainted by the poison of that world. I feel that I am responsible for bringing the nightmare home to their doorstep. Perhaps I should just split and let them live their lives in peace.

So, I left home. Moved out, found a safe refuge where I could live quietly, concentrate on the legal case and on my writing. However, after a short while Karen feels that things are no better at home without me and follows me to Sighthill. Sighthill, where they were dumping refugees as fast as they could. No problem there, I've been a refugee for the last 18 years of my life.

Up Among the Refugees (July 2002)

I guess it's inevitable that nothing could ever be quite the same for us after that kind of upheaval and trauma. I think it was more that Karen had grown to resent and perhaps lost some respect for me, both for the fact that I had made no move of striking back in kind for the attack and threats upon our lives and for the loss of her lifestyle and model home which she'd given up to follow me – seeking asylum in Sighthill.

Living as a refugee is a life of abject poverty and isolation which tends to deepen profound resentments. Added together with all the other pressures, like appeals before the high court and mass serial killers on your tail,

Karen's nervous disposition led to the bottle. Naturally, it didn't resolve anything. Only added fuel to the fire. She missed her way of life and she missed her model home. Who could blame her for that? I had just spent 17 years being Shanghai'd from one digger to another fighting a Miscarriage of Justice for a mass murder committed by those gangsters and the Crown agents now trying to murder me. There was nothing settled. It was I who had brought this nightmare to her door. Blown her sanctuary sky high.

I had left that little haven of our home for their sakes and steered for rougher shores. It was she who had followed, claiming that there was no life without me. Thank god in his grace, for I needed all the help I could get in the circumstances. I had no grounds to argue then when Karen decided enough is enough and left me again. The wean needs a school to get started in only a month and, after eight weeks, the Housing Department's only offer of homes are the worst of run down slums and deprivation. The Social Security had just refused us a resettlement grant but instead deducted £40 per week for repayment of loans and confiscated Karen's £15 family allowance saying, as we were married during those last years in prison, she had been fraudulently claiming Lone Parent allowance. Our appeal that we had married in prison and that she had remained alone was yet pending before the tribunal. Finally they had withdrawn their reclaim of about £900 and she was given her benefit book back but meantime we're skint, in debt up to our eyes and I'm just a barrel of trouble.

'Yeah I think you'd be better off without me,' I agree as she returns to the heart of Gangland, Barlanark, the Old Bar-L.

Yet I guess it's inevitable that nothing is ever the same again. This was no longer the living, warm and cosy sanctuary she had once known. It had become a cold, dead house of fear since the attack and, thus it remained with or without my presence there.

Within the blurry haze of her drunken outrage, the resentment of the intrusion of this living nightmare into their lives is somehow brought more sharply to the fore. It is I who am to blame for all this and, therefore, I against whom she should strike back with a vengeance. Hell hath no fury like a woman scorned, so they say.

I don't want her around me or the wean when she's drinking. Won't let her in the door. The call received from Karen's mobile was answered with slight trepidation.

'Look out the window,' was all she said.

'Wha . . .! What for . . .?' I stuttered stupidly stunned to see her jolting attempts to steal my car, listening to her devilish giggles as she dangerously reverses. Flying round the corner I catch up with her on the run. Leap inside the skidding vehicle to the sound of sirens wailing . . .

'BASTARD! I'm in fuckin control here,' she screamed. I guess I should've begged her to stay.

'Oh Shit!' I thought, this was no delinquent girly prank here. This was a fully-fledged demon and booze was in control.

'Sure! Sure! Absolutely,' I agree hastily catching my breath, clutching at my heart whilst clunking in the seat belt. I can't take the keys while the car is still moving because of the automatic steering lock. She's blitzed out of her skull and bombing up the motorway ramp with me a captive audience. I'm playing it cool as if everything was perfectly fine and normal. I cannot be seen to be in any way in opposition to her. Not distract her in argument. I must gain her trust otherwise she will resist my advice on driving. Like, 'You'll probably not be able to move out till that big truck passes ye.' For otherwise she'd expect the roaring Juggernaut to give way to her.

Hitting a curve astride lanes at 110 mph with a drunken driver not paying attention is a very real, hair raising, life threatening experience when you are just out of the jail after 17 years.

'I'm a better driver than you anyway ain't I,' she natters away to me not looking at either the speedo or the approaching bend.

'Yeah but! Yeah but! You're going too fast. Too Fast. TOO FUCKIN FAST for the bend, ya nut case yeh,' I blurted out in panic, jilting her into such conscious focus that she took the bend on the brakes. Without drive. The fact we came out of the bend straight as a die is more of a tribute to the car, an R reg Scorpio Ultima retained on insurance rebound. But I'd given the game away with my show of panic and she was on to me. I would now be classed as among the enemy and advice would have to be delivered with great caution. 'Which lane are you in anyway?' I ask diplomatically.

'The middle wan,' she sneers contemptuously, all the more determined now to show me once and for all just who the best driver is. Problem with that being that she had somehow concluded that speed was the determining factor and I have no say in those rules. You play the cards you're dealt and you deal with them.

Finally Karen pulls over to let me out near Easterhouse police station and I snatched the keys. Determined that I shouldn't win, however, she releases the handbrake causing the car in its lock to roll straight out blocking traffic on the main highway, one foot in the driving well, standing there shouting back at irate drivers, 'It's his fault, he's got the keys an he'll no gimme them.'

The polis soon arrive in force. 'He's drunk and a terrible driver,' she asserts angrily. 'He shouldn't even be driving in the first place. Ah'm no gettin in that motor weh him drivin. He's dangerous.' She could have taken the

words right out of my mind but I would never have
uttered them.

'Who was driving?' the polis ask.

'You're going to the jail,' she says aside to me. Turning
to polis, pointing at me she says simply, 'Him, an he's no
even got a licence.'

As I stood there gobsmacked on the pavement with
the keys I could only volunteer a breathaliser. It was the
irate drivers who pointed out exactly who was driving
and who was drunk. The bizzies just put it down to a
domestic dispute, pulled the car over to the side, gave
her back the keys and buzzed off. I'm left running with
the open door as she speeds off in hot pursuit.

'We're going to Bennigan's,' she laughs wickedly and
it seems that we were there as fast as it took to get my
seatbelt on. Right to the back car park where my dear
friend, the bold John Linton, a leading light of the Free
the Glasgow Two campaign, was cowardly assassinated
with multiple bullets from various guns in the back and
the back of his head. His assassins were never brought
to justice and still frequented this gang hut, a pub called
Bennigan's, more recently frequented by the Iceman and
the Craw.

Screeching to a halt, facing into the fields with the
back of our heads to the back door of the pub. Just
sitting there.

'So okay then, are we going in or what?' I ask casually,
intending for her to step out of the driving seat but she's
onto me. As a couple of John's Judas's approach, I step
out of the car circling to the driver's door. I get the door
open but she reverses beyond my reach, crunching into
the far wall. The car leaps forward again and again I
open the door. She won't give up control of the car,
even when I snatch the keys. Now I'm bodily removing
her from the driver's seat but she resists this by her feet

on the doorframe and her arms round the steering wheel
and gear stick. Kicking and screaming like a banshee as
I take hold of her feet pulling her straight out till she
is suspended in air between me and the steering wheel.
Finally she lets go and her back and the side of her head
thump to the concrete floor but she's up and attacking me
in a jiffy. I can't get the car door shut and when I get it
halfway she stands there and boots the door panels in with
her heels. I can't reverse safely because the swing of the
door would put her under the wheels. Meanwhile, John's
Judas's are now blocking my exit, holding the doors open,
trying to pick a fight.

'Get out the car and we'll talk.'

'There's nothin to say,' I reply.

'Whit! Yeh talkin tae me? Who'd yeh think ye'r talkin
tae eh?' The antagonism is apparent. That's enough.

'If you don't mind, Ah'm talkin to mah wife an, if you
don't mind, the doors eh!' I emphasised with a tug on
the door. 'If you don't mind, Ah've got places tae go and
business to attend tae.' I echoed the haunting cry of all
ghosts. No one, replied. The doors were closed and I left
her there still screaming blue murder as I rattled the car all
the way back home to the peace of the Asylum in Sighthill.
Hell indeed hath no fury like a woman scorned. I didn't
even say goodbye this time.

Shortly thereafter trouble came hammering at my door.

'Get this fuckin door open, y'fuckin bam. Ya big
shitebag, Ah'll kick ye'r bawz.' The door rattled under
a torrent of booting and abuse as Karen tore off the
letter box and posted it through the hole. Not listening
to reason and not going away. I had to open the door
to return her handbag which she'd left in the car. She
barges in punching and spitting abuse till I take her into
a bear hug and place her outside the door, locking her
out. The banging and abuse continues unabated until I

open the door again and again she tries to barge in but I'm ready this time and block her. Finally, I get her far enough away from the door to close it again but, as I sit there with my head in my hands, it dawns on me that I heard glass breaking. Unsure as to whether I had just heard it or if it had finally sunk in that I'd heard it, I go back to the door where it has all gone suddenly quiet. Imagining her tumbling out of the window of these high rise flats, I hurriedly open the door to find her sitting with her bum through the shattered glass of the low side window by the landing door. I took her out of it and checked that she was all right and, finding no damage, assumed that she was fine and returned into the house to run a bath while she resumed her screaming and hammering on the door. Stripped for the bath with bathrobe on, I hear her crying and saying something to someone about 'He done it'. I opened the door to find two uniformed polis standing there and invite them in. I hear Karen, thinking she's going to the nick for breach of the peace and malicious damage, telling the police that it was all my fault and adding,

'He threw me head first through the window.'

They were entitled to be cautious and on alert considering the broken plate glass window. I introduced myself explaining that I was the tenant of the household and although Karen was my wife, we were separated and she abided at her own house in Barlanark. That she was pissed out of her skull, kicking at my door and I refused to let her in. That I hadn't witnessed who, in fact, had smashed the window but, as she was the only one out there kicking up a fuss, then it would be my guess that she had put her boot through it, seeing as there was no injury.

Karen calls me a liar and that it was she who lived here and not me, producing our Social Security claim for the family resident at that address. The police separate us for further questioning. Nobody questioned me. After speaking to Karen, they came in and told me to get myself dressed, I was being taken into custody for questioning. I got a shirt and shoes on and made to leave but was stopped by the polis who told me that I should take a jacket or coat. I put on the nearest jacket and was promptly handcuffed.

At the station, I'm informed that I will be detained for up to six hours for questioning. I'm thereafter searched. Asked if I have anything sharp or open in my pockets I answer 'No' but in patting down my own pockets to prove the point,

'Oh shit!' I feel the hard bulk of steel. My first thought. was that it had been planted but then I remembered. 'Oh! it must be the tattie knife,' I said and, everybody became sharply alert. Somehow I didn't expect they would believe me when I put my hand into my pocket and pulled out a brammer of a wee lock back knuckle duster. 'Honest, it's the tattie knife,' I said realizing how feeble the truth can sound. 'Send it down to forensics and they'll come back with tattie peelings. Honest it's the tattie knife.' As I was led away to the cells I told the sergeant that I suspected that my wife might try to steal my car again and I would like my keys taken into custody with me and the house secured.

It seemed like days awaiting questioning. Back in those same cells, those exact same cells where we had been arrested nearly 18 years earlier to face interrogation on the Doyle murders. Nothing had changed. Except now prisoners weren't allowed to smoke. Echoes of ancient pasts. The waves of horror and, the power of that naive presumption which had withstood the psychic blast. But the spirit which rages was at a low peep this day. I shrouded myself in memory till my name was called.

I asked for a tape recorded interview but only notes

would be taken. Accused of pushing her head through a plate glass window I denied it. Asked how the window got smashed, I repeated my earlier account and asked for evidence of any injury to her. The small cut on my hand had stopped bleeding but how did I come across this injury? I referred to the earlier incident in the car park when Karen had stolen the car and smashed it. I'd noticed then that my thumbnail was cut as I drove away. Forensics should examine the steering wheel and driver's door handle for traces of blood since it is not alleged that I was in the car after the alleged assault . . .

'So you say that this happened when you battered your wife earlier?'

'Naw! Ah said that it may have occurred during an earlier incident when my wife stole my car and attacked me . . .'

'So, you're saying that it happened in an earlier fight?'

'No! Ah'm saying that it may have occurred during an earlier incident when my wife stole my car and attacked me.'

'During an earlier struggle then?'

'No, Ah'm saying that my wife attacked ME earlier . . .'

Waste of time. I was charged with putting Karen's head through a plate glass window and possession of an offensive weapon. I'd been taken to the doctor just before I was questioned. I thought it was to do with heart pills I needed to take regularly. Turns out that the cut on my finger was now to be used as evidence against me but somehow someone forgot to pick up my medication. I enquired about that again next day. The pain in my chest felt more like a dull bruise. My heart was simply aching. Nothing new, but the numbness in my arm wasn't normal. I was taken to hospital because . . .

'We don't want to take any chances weh you.' At least

I spent the last night in a hospital bed and managed a sandwich. It was only heart strain brought on by stress. So what else is new?

Court the next day was cold steel despair. Bars and Bars and Bars that is. I couldn't hear what was being said and it has always seemed designed that way. Though it later became apparent that the police and Crown had somehow managed to get the addresses confused thinking that it was Karen who lived in the refugee camp among the asylum seekers and not me. I was supposed to be living in Barlanark, inferring that it had been I who had gone to HER door. This was later leaked to the press where I was named not only as a serial wife beater but also of defrauding the Social Security by living in Barlanark while claiming to be living with her at the asylum. Of course it wasn't true. None of it ever is. So what else is new?

Refused bail and a six-week remand in custody. Do not pass Go . . .

Do Not Pass Go

(The Do-Lally Dine Ins Dine On, BarL Prison July 2002)

Back in Barlinnie Prison was a depressing flashback to ancient history. This place was over two hundred years old and it hadn't changed one thin slice from the prisoners' point of view. Right enough, they'd spent millions upon millions rebuilding, extending and refurbishing the new gate house, reception and external walls. It gave the impression of a modern, secure and efficient establishment whilst inside it remained rotten to the core and it stunk.

I'm two'd up on bunk beds in a cell with this poor guy

they call Fenian because he's Catholic. The stench of the hall itself is sickening enough but the poor Fenian fullah is a junky with seeping ulcers in his groin. As soon as the cell door opens for me to enter for the night I'm hit with the stench of putrid flesh and seeping pus. He constantly, unconsciously claws at his groin, wiping his pus smeared fingers on his shirt and down the leg of his pants. There is only a couple of piss pots and he needs one of them to vomit up bile every half hour or so. There is no water. The cell is filthy, uncleaned and uncared for over many years. Newspapers stuck up onto the window with toothpaste to block out the sparse sunlight. Smelly socks and under-wear litter the place mingling with broken up cigarette ends and cornflakes.

'Y'want somethin to eat'?' he'd say generously wiping his fingers on his shirt before halving his prison oatmeal biscuit ration, presenting the greater half to me.

'Thanks but no thanks, pal.' Even though I'd only had a sandwich at the hospital since my arrest four days earlier somehow nothing seemed very appetizing.

First priority in the morning when the door is open – water. Lots and lots of water. Two basins, two jugs, two towels, soap and more water. Second priority – snout, cig papers, tea bags, sugar and clothes that fit. Heaps of new undies and socks. Such things are easily obtained for me as soon as the door is open but the Fenian fullah stands back in awe at my meagre achievements.

'Fuck sake!' he'd proclaim, 'just goes to show what you can do when you're quoted eh!' Turned out that what I'd taken for granted as 'Entitled' he'd been unable to achieve nor acquire during the past fortnight. This guy was treated like trash. Dumped onto the scrap heap and abandoned. Locked up 24 hours a day, the door only opening for meals to be handed in and slammed shut again. But all that changed when I arrived. Now he had soap, water and a towel to wash his hands after a claw, crap or vomit. Now he had a smoke, fresh air, disinfectant arid the surgery dressing his wounds. 'Man!' he'd exclaim with a wide eyed cheerul grin, 'it's like being dubbed up weh the fuckin Pope.' In fact, he was a great guy, intelligent and widely read but I guess I wasn't much by way of good company in the circumstances.

Karen had rattled the wrecked car down to Baird Street Polis station, the turnkey had told me, 'Pissed and bitching', demanding my release. They had refused to accept my change of clothing nor my heart pills. Karen tells me that they'd said that I 'wasn't to be charged with anything'. Now she had written a long letter to the Crown Office telling the truth. The result being that after ten days imprisonment I was re-released on bail. The subsequent inquiry by CID instigated by the procurator fiscal ended with the indication that no further proceedings would be taken.

All that for what? For the uniforms at Baird Street not listening properly at the time. For them making assumptions. Living on clichés and using their power. It made me wonder, not for the first time, exactly why were our jails so full. Not what the polis said nor the courts decided but truly, truthfully, exactly why are our jails so full?

In the meantime, Wee Joe Steele, my co-defendant on the murder appeal, has taken a heart attack and undergone triple heart bypass surgery. The Housing Department can only offer us the heart of slumland, unacceptable accommodation for Karen and the wean. My wife and daughter have gone back to the heart of gangland instead back to Barlanark, the good old Bar-L which at least she knows with all its dangers.

I live alone now, back among the refugees seeking asylum until such times as we can be provided with safe and suitable accommodation to bring up a child. Dear little Shannon, I miss you so. God help you and shine a brighter light for your future.

As for my future? Well, the spirit lives and whilst it does . . .

The beat goes on . . .